A DRINKING COMPANION

A DRINKING COMPANION

ALCOHOL & THE LIVES OF WRITERS

by Kelly Boler

UNION SQUARE PUBLISHING

Union Square Publishing
857 Broadway, 3rd Floor
New York, NY 10003

FIRST EDITION
Copyright © 2004 by Kelly Boler
- All Rights Reserved -

ISBN: 1580421458
Library of Congress Card Catalog No.: 2004101406
Union Square Publishing is an imprint of Cardoza Publishing.

ABOUT THE AUTHOR

A Drinking Companion: Alcohol and the Lives of Writers is the first book by Kelly Boler. She has written feature articles for *The Boston Phoenix, Boston Magazine, SingleLife*, and *Mississippi Gulf Coast*, where she was art editor. She has a degree in writing from the University of Southern Mississippi. She specializes in popular history, vintage collecting, and the South. Currently, she covers the arts for *Rapid River Magazine* in Asheville, North Carolina where she lives with her husband and son.

"I have always loved biographies and history, not as an academic discipline, but as just the juiciest gossip possible. And as a voracious reader, I noted that in some books, liquor is so important to the story that it practically becomes a character: Calvados in *Arch of Triumph*; the gin gimlet in *The Long Goodbye;* the martini in *The Thin Man*.

"One day, at the bottom of a box in a library book sale, I found *On Drink* by Kingsley Amis. Nothing could have surprised me more than seeing this 'real' writer, this important contributor to literature, on a purple cover, offering the reader a glass of wine with a cocky look on his face. Inside were recipes and anecdotes, culled from his own prodigious experience with alcohol in its myriad forms; I paid my ten cents and took it home.

"I was struck by the difference in Amis's attitude and that of the prototypical drinking writer à la Ernest Hemingway or say, Dorothy Parker, and this was the beginning *A Drinking Companion*."

ACKNOWLEDGMENTS

Thanks first off to my husband Rob Morrison for being such a fabulous audience and a priceless editor who took over when I couldn't stand to look at another word. I am also grateful to his parents, Dr. Robert and Mrs. Wanda Morrison, who have made this possible with a hundred kinds of generous support.

Also: To Beth Godlin, the first reader for every chapter, and who never failed to respond with "You're kidding! He did what?!" To Alixandra Gould of Union Square Publishing, who brought a light but perfect touch with the pencil, and who never made a single suggestion that did not improve the quality of the read. To Gabriel Jacobs in Swansea, for his mean detective work. To Matthew Willard, who provided dinners and patience when they were sorely needed, and who rarely fails to laugh at my jokes. To Sally Conway, without whom I would doubt my sanity and worth. To publicist and best friend David Roberson, who offers more common sense in one minute than I have accumulated in my whole life. To Simon Morrison, who is my life and heart. And finally to Raymond Chandler, whose book *The Long Goodbye* introduced me to the storytelling possibilities in the form of a gin gimlet.

To June and James Boler, my favorite teetotalers.

CONTENTS

PART FOUR

PARTS SOUTH

PART FIVE

TAKE IT OR LEAVE IT

INTRODUCTION

"Writers are loners, and alcoholism is a loner's disease."
                              - Dr. Donald W. Goodwin, *Alcohol and the Writer*

"What is one to say? Some writers drink too much."
                                                            - Kingsley Amis

In an effort to cut back on his drinking, F. Scott Fitzgerald limited himself to beer—thirty glasses a day.

Dashiell Hammett drank himself into a writer's block that lasted thirty years. John Cheever conquered a decades-long addiction to create his greatest novel.

Malcolm Lowry would drink anything from gin to formaldehyde, and housewife/poet Anne Sexton always traveled with a thermos full of martinis.

There is no question that alcohol ran through the lives and works of great writers. Stories of the grand boozy excesses of twentieth century literature provide a substantial part of our cultural currency, and the question "Why?" returns again and again, decades after the phenomenon has played out. It is a question that may never be satisfactorily answered, because an explanation is not really what most readers want. Instead, we continue to ask because in doing so we are able to look at it again and marvel, to feel disgusted and impressed in equal measure. If we truly understood the cause, then it might ruin the story.

How does a writer who drinks become a drunk who writes? In what way does an artist go so wildly off track yet continue to create? There are hundreds of stories, many overshadowed by cliché, that hold the key to the many and varied ways that liquor worked its way through writing.

While we tend to think of alcoholic writers as a breed, there is no one kind, which deepens the mystery. A patrician poet isn't going to drink like a Welsh courtesan, and a gay playwright's addiction will be different from a hard-boiled mystery writer's. Of the fifteen artists in this collection, four committed suicide, while seven lived into their seventies or beyond. Three managed to quit drinking altogether. One is French, three are British, and the rest are American. Many enjoyed wealth and fame, others despaired in poverty and undeserved obscurity. Some were tragic, while others remained gleefully unrepentant.

Beyond words and booze, there are actually few common links. It is interesting, however, that there are some traits and that they shared, like perpetual drunkenness, that would stand little chance of being tolerated today. Almost every artist in this book had an incomprehensible capacity for helplessness. Most refused to learn how to drive a car. Several were incapable of simple, everyday survival skills, like buying food or using a telephone. There was also an inclination to an unimaginable selfishness, which was summed up perfectly by William Faulkner, who said: "The writer's only responsibility is to his art. He will be completely ruthless if he is a good one. He has a dream. It anguishes him so much that he must get rid of it. He has no peace until then. Everything goes by the board: honor, pride, decency, security, happiness. If a writer has to rob his mother, he will not hesitate."

A sometimes overlooked piece of the puzzle is the fact that they were allowed to do these things. Cintra Wilson wrote shrewdly about this in the online magazine *Salon*, when she described a drunken character in Eugene O'Neill's *Moon for the Misbegotten*. "Nowadays, a drunk…would be peer-pressured into AA, given intense, excoriating batches of psychotherapy, *tough love* and antidepressants, and not indulged in the boozy pity patch he keeps crawling into. He'd be kicked around and nobody would hang out with him anymore until he got sober, and he would clean up in a mildly shamefaced manner, and life would go on."

From our standpoint of improved treatment and increased social awareness, it is hard for us to accept that these amazing people were unable or unwilling to fight their way back. There is a common, contemporary lament about what was lost to art by the bottle. In a closer look at their stories, it becomes obvious that, under the circumstances, it is miraculous that so much beautiful work emerged at all. To think otherwise is greedy, grasping, and pointless. Liquor left us with a literary landscape both ravaged and brilliant, and it is what it is.

꽃 꽃 꽃

Having taken so much trouble to emphasize the differences between individual subjects' lives, I have gone on to shamelessly put them into categories that I hope will make them easier to compare. The first contains three writers from the middle class. "Gin in the Suburbs: Glass on the Living Room Floor" shows a picture of art and alcoholism lived out in the world of the two-car garage, mowing the lawn, the kids' piano lessons, and the PTA. Anne Sexton was the original mad housewife until her suicide at the age of forty-six; John Cheever was the archetypal buttoned-down Yankee who recovered from life-threatening guzzling to write his greatest novel; John Berryman negotiated the small-town, academic world he lived in for decades, waiting for his poetry to get the attention it deserved.

While all drinking lives contain despair one way or another, some are flat-out, epic disaster. In "Lost Souls: Wild Tales of Woe" are scenes like a train wreck in slow motion, impossible to turn away from. The novels of Jean Rhys sank without a trace in the 1930s, so she drank and brawled away the decades until her works were rediscovered, long after everyone assumed she was dead. Dashiell Hammett wrote five books in five years and invented a new genre, the hardboiled detective novel. He had to hurry; he was sure he was dying. His problem was that he lived, and in the remaining thirty years of his life, he never finished another book. Malcolm Lowry hid from the world in his beach shack for over fifteen years. He was so terrified of being published that he finished only two novels, one of them widely considered one of the greatest novels of the twentieth century.

"Myth Makers: Larger than Life, a Whole Lot Larger" are artists who were also performers, inventing and reinventing themselves for the limelight. The problem was that they had the talent to do it too well. Long before Hemingway, there was Jack London, the prototype of the two-fisted literary man who liked to fight, drink his whiskey straight, and eat raw meat dripping with blood. Robert Lowell was born to American aristocracy and never let anyone forget it, even when his bizarre episodes of heavy drinking and mental illness made him the subject of scandal in universities on two continents. F. Scott Fitzgerald forged himself out of jazz and champagne but never managed to write himself into the 1930s with a happy ending.

According to the *Encyclopedia of Southern Culture*, "Anthropologists who describe American drinking practices often use the word 'ambivalent' to describe conflicting attitudes toward alcohol. For the South, however, ambivalence is too mild a label; 'schizoid' comes closer to the mark." The chapters under "Points South: Cheers, Y'all!" give abundant evidence for this theory. Mississippi-born Tennessee Williams made a name for himself in the theater with plays that were part classical, part Southern Gothic weirdness, while off-stage he was notorious for his own promiscuous and mean-spirited performances. His friend Carson McCullers, of Georgia, published her first book at age twenty-three to international acclaim. Ten years later she was felled by the first of a series of strokes, although her paralysis did little to slow her ability to lift a glass. Poet James Dickey played at being a Georgia backwoodsman but was actually a college professor with a gift for the brilliant lie.

Finally, there is "Take It or Leave It: Love Me, Love My Bottle," a bunch of carousers with an almost compelling bravado. They are the ones who refused to make apologies for their persistent sodden state, who had no shame, remorse, or regard for consequences. For decades Marguerite Duras was a living legend, a national treasure of France, with a habit of referring to herself in the third person. No one wrote funnier novels about the drunken condition, and no one lived it with more cantankerous charm than Kingsley Amis; he even wrote three non-fiction books about alcohol. His second wife threatened to divorce him unless he gave up drinking, which meant that he was soon a single man. Novelist and short story writer Jean Stafford lived through an abusive marriage to Robert Lowell and emerged as a cult figure in her late-middle age, a status she lost no time in abusing with her wild behavior under the influence.

There may be readers who find me remiss in telling these stories without speaking directly against alcohol abuse. While this is certainly a perfect opportunity, the fact is that these tales are inherently cautionary, and if they are not an influence for moderation or abstinence, then nothing I could say would be.

PART ONE

GIN IN THE SUBURBS: BROKEN GLASS ON THE LIVING ROOM FLOOR

John Berryman
Jean Stafford
John Cheever

JOHN BERRYMAN

DRINK OF CHOICE

🕊 Just about anything, but later in life he usually traveled with bottles of Jack Daniels in his suitcase.

🕊 Martinis made with sherry instead of vermouth.

"As he became more inspired and famous and drunk, more and more John Berryman, he became less good company and more a happening—slashing eloquence in undertones, amber tumblers of bourbon, a stony pyramid talking down a rugful of admirers."

-Robert Lowell

"Something has been said for sobriety but very little."

-John Berryman

You didn't want to make poet John Berryman mad. If you wouldn't sleep with him he might tell all your friends that you had syphilis. If you were his host at a dinner party and were so bold as to disagree with his politics, he might leave the table screaming and walk into the ocean fully clothed. If he was drunk in the middle of the night and you wouldn't let him in, he might use your porch as a bathroom. And if you criticized him, at the very least he would faint—flutter his eyes and sink to the floor unconscious. It was a trick he learned in order to deal with his mother, with whom he had good reason to be angry: she probably killed his father.

Whether it was murder, as is suspected, or suicide, as was reported, the death of John Allyn Smith devastated his young son. No matter how many poems Berryman wrote about it, how many years he worked through it in therapy, it would not let him go until at last he took his own life at age of fifty-seven.

His parents met in a boarding house in Oklahoma. Smith attacked the young Martha, and the result was a forced and bitter marriage. In response to her own cold and unhappy childhood, she showered her children, especially Berryman, with obsessive affection, "an unspeakably powerful possessive adoring," he later wrote. In doing so, she planted within the boy the two overwhelming character traits that would dictate his life: raging ego and bottomless self-pity.

In 1928, his father lost his job, and the family moved to Florida where they opened a restaurant. There had already been affairs on both sides in the marriage, and now John Smith had a mistress, while Martha depended more and more on their landlord, John Berryman.

When Smith's mistress deserted him, she took all of the family's money with her. Distraught, Smith wandered the beach at all hours. Martha said she afraid for his state of mind, so she took his pistol and hid the bullets, five of them anyway; she could never explain why she left a sixth. The police said he shot himself but found no powder burns. Ten weeks after his death, Martha remarried and the eleven-year-old John Allyn Smith, Jr., was renamed John Berryman. The thin, awkward boy in glasses was the target of bullying at his school until he one day learned the value of the dramatic gesture. He was being chased by a group of boys who were going to beat him up. When it looked like they were going to catch him, he threw himself into the path of an on-coming train. The terrified gang pulled him off just in time and kept their distance in the future.

As Berryman grew older, his defense was storytelling, being a good talker. At seventeen, he was a would-be sophisticate: smoking, gambling, and taking friends to strip shows. He was and always would be an elegant dancer and fearless with women.

When he was eighteen, he got a scholarship to Columbia where he made an impressive beginning in the literature department. He was soon under the wing of poet and professor Mark Van Doren, but the nightclubs of Harlem beckoned, and all the drinking and partying took a toll on his work. The young scholar, whose goal was to be the campus rake and genius, was asked to take a semester off.

His mother was furious. His stepfather was out of work, and she was now the family breadwinner. As always, when unhappy with

Berryman, she would freeze him out with an aggressive silence that could last for weeks. He tried to placate her by writing her poems, and it worked so well that he decided to try a 330-line homage to Van Doren. He caught up on his coursework, and was readmitted to college. He would never again allow himself to fall behind and would go sleepless for days if it meant staying far ahead of the pack. In 1936, this grueling determination earned him a fellowship at Cambridge.

When he arrived in England via the *Britannic*, he was tall and thin. In later years he would be known for his substantial beard, but now he was clean-shaven and looked more like a banker than a poet. At Oxford he studied Shakespeare and shopped for old books, met T. S. Eliot, and drank whiskey with Dylan Thomas. He wrote poem after poem but was so dissatisfied with his work that one night he burned hundreds of poems in the fireplace.

In an interview with biographer John Haffenden, a friend said that in England, Berryman had three moods: hysterical joy, deep depression and obvious boredom. While at Columbia, he had suffered a breakdown. Now he felt another coming on that he described as "fits of terrific gloom and loneliness and artistic despair alternating with irresponsible exaltation." His diagnosis was a lack of alcohol and sex, which he remedied during the winter break.

Berryman almost missed his chance to have tea with his hero William Butler Yeats. Dylan Thomas was amused with Berryman's worship of the grand old man of letters, and tried to get him drunk on the afternoon of the appointment, but the woozy Berryman caught on, took a cold shower, and made the visit. For the rest of his life he would remember lighting the master's cigarette.

He returned to America in the summer of 1938 with tweeds, an English accent, and an attitude. Although his writing had won several cash prizes in Cambridge and *The Southern Review* had accepted five poems, he had little money and had to move in with his mother. She tyrannized her son with endless monologues, one-sided talks that would go on for hours. After three weeks, Berryman discovered that he could make her stop by fainting. So he did.

Finding a job was difficult for any academic during the Depression, but it was almost impossible if you insulted interviewers with obvious scorn, which was what Berryman did. By this time he was angry with everyone, and his response was still more fainting, as well as silent tantrums where he rocked back and forth for hours. He believed, again, that sex was the key, and again, he devoted himself to the cure.

In 1939, he was finally offered a teaching position at Wayne University in Michigan and at the same time was made poetry editor of *The Nation*. These were important moves in the right direction, and while teaching paid the bills, it took a lot of the energy that he needed for poetry. Added to this, he soon earned a reputation among the faculty for arrogance and heavy drinking, and he became increasingly isolated.

He shared an apartment with a married couple who were disturbed by his fainting fits. Years later, the wife told John Haffenden, "He would walk in the door without speaking, go rigid, and crash to the floor unconscious." He never ate and seldom slept, although he did spend lots of time in bed, hiding under his covers. His behavior frightened them so much they pushed a chair against their bedroom door at night until finally they just moved out. "I am more and more lonely and more and more tired," Berryman wrote.

His mood improved in 1940 when he got a job at Harvard. In November, his poems were featured in a collection of five American poets, though he was not happy with the book. "For two weeks I did nothing whatsoever except drink and wander from party to party." One night he met Eileen Mulligan. She was pleasant and good-natured, and being with her helped Berryman feel a little more normal.

The next summer he took Eileen to the movies and dancing and on all-night walks, and they soon became lovers. This gave him the energy he needed to move out of his mother's apartment. At Harvard that fall, however, his hatred of teaching spoiled everything. He felt sorry for himself, and believed that at twenty-seven he was still postponing his life. For comfort, he had taken to drink. He called scotch, ice, and water the New Trinity, as reassuring as the one in the Bible but more accessible.

In August 1941, a book of his poetry was published and his wedding approached. His feelings were decidedly mixed. After the ceremony he wrote his mother. "God was not there. I watched for him." Their first apartment was cold, and they drank hot chocolate to keep warm, but Eileen provided the stability and sanity that saved his life, and he adored her.

With so many young students fighting in World War II, Berryman's Harvard job dried up, so he did the housework while looking for a job. When he contacted fifty schools and got nothing, he sold encyclopedias door-to-door. Eileen was working at an insurance company, and she held Berryman together, but at a cost to herself. He still indulged in fainting and convulsions, which were doubly disturbing when she realized he could control them if he wanted to, an accusation he furiously denied. He imagined jumping to his death and wrote, "I believe one dies on the way down but I don't wish to hit anyone or be splattered on the pavement." At least he was drinking less—he couldn't afford liquor.

He was better the next spring. He met Robert Lowell, a rising star in the poetry world, and enjoyed a "lazy, agreeable, interesting & alcoholic" summer. (For a different version of that time, see the chapter on Lowell's wife Jean Stafford.) That fall Berryman had a job teaching at Princeton. His reputation as a character grew, typified by his English suits and accent, his lovely manners, and his nasty, backbiting remarks.

He fell in love with the wife of a student. What started as a casual affair turned into an obsession, as he projected his fantasies of longing, desire, and pain on a woman he hardly knew. It was a convenient way to feel the dramatic extremes of love, and he convinced himself that they had to be exorcised through poetry, so that when they made love he wrote passionate poems about lust, and when they were apart, he wrote passionate poems about loneliness.

He finished ninety sonnets in eighty days. "For weeks, for months, my will has been at the service of my passion and my imagination," he wrote. It soon became clear to his lover that this was not about mere adultery and that she was really just a stand-in. Soon, she realized, he would need to believe himself betrayed so that he could write about that, but it hurt him all the same when she went from being his luminescent figure to "SS woman" overnight with no change whatsoever on her part.

While he was busy at the service of his passion, Eileen was getting fed up. She was exhausted by his heavy drinking and his public cruelty toward her. When he felt guilty, which he often did, he attacked her and mocked her desire to have a career and be something besides his wife. At the same time he leaned on her for strength and support even more.

When Eileen hurt her back and was bedridden, he saw an excellent opportunity to pursue other women unencumbered. Since this made him feel guilty and he resented Eileen for his guilt, he rejected her when she needed him the most. He was depressed, and according to biographer Paul Mariani, living on a diet of "dexidrine [sic] morning & afternoon; martinis before dinner; nembutal & sherry after midnight." He hid under the covers.

A psychiatrist began to help him sort out his anger toward his mother and their mutual obsession. He talked about their correspondence and how when he was in boarding school she wrote him four hundred letters in five years. He felt he had been almost obscenely bound to her while in college. Now that he was an adult, she made him introduce her as his sister. With his doctor's encouragement, he wrote his mother complaining that she had never loved him. She wrote back saying it was the other way around, and on it went.

That fall Berryman learned that a colleague's wife was pregnant with his child. Forced with this moral dilemma, he fled to Seattle, where he taught, drank, and ran around with Dylan Thomas. His lover decided to raise the baby with her husband, and Berryman returned. He continued to sleep around. Sometimes he wondered if he was trying to punish his mother with his affairs.

In the spring of 1951, he gave a series of lectures on Shakespeare. At age thirty-six he was becoming a celebrated teacher. That summer was spent "loafing, swimming, eating & drinking, especially drinking." He took a job in 1952 at a school in Cincinnati. In this smallish city he was a celebrity, and he had his choice of women who didn't seem to mind that his wife was in tow. He took this as his due and did not hesitate to repeatedly act out a cycle of lust, guilt, abuse, and drink.

Soon he was working out his anger on a different kind of woman, one who had been dead for three hundred years. For five years he worked on a long, strange poem to Ann Bradstreet, the first published poet in America, and it possessed him. "She haunted his nights and days," wrote a friend. He believed that Bradstreet was arguing with him about religion and so persuasively that he considered converting. He worked on the poem with a pitcher of martinis in reach, and acted strange, laughing hysterically. When he finally wrote the death scene, it was a kind of terrible delivery. The finished *Homage to Mistress Bradstreet* ran 458 lines and was difficult to read, which did not keep it from becoming a big success in time.

Berryman and Eileen traveled to Europe that spring. He tried to cut back on his drinking which meant strictly limiting himself to beer, brandy, and vermouth. In Saint-Tropez, however, he got drunk and read the *Bradstreet* at five in the morning to the only person he could find, a baker on his way to work. When Eileen was forced to bed with more back pain, he left her alone in a strange town for three weeks while he slept with other women and regularly drank to the point of blacking out. When Eileen was able to move, they flew back to America, and she told him to move out. The sweet, complacent girl he married had finished her degree and was now a successful psychoanalyst, a professional about to open her own practice. There was no place in her life for a drunken, demanding poet.

He started off 1954 teaching in Iowa. On the night he arrived, he got so drunk that he fell down the stairs: "Hall dark, steep stair down travel blind, I crasht/& snapt a wrist, landing in glass." As a teacher of writing, he could be horrible or devoted depending on what he thought of your potential. Even with those he liked, he was sometimes tightly wound and rude. One night he pressured a student to be a good sport and leave his girlfriend with Berryman for the night. When the boy refused, Berryman hit him with an empty Scotch bottle and threatened to ruin his writing career.

One night he got drunk after a workshop. He staggered home but could not find his key. The landlord refused to let him in, whereupon Berryman cursed and crapped on his porch. The police came, and he spent the night in jail. When it hit the newspapers the next day, the university insisted that he leave. Fortunately, poet Allen Tate came to his rescue and found him a job in Minnesota. There he was chastened and drank less, but the job didn't start at once and he had too many weeks to sit around. Broke, aimless, and feeling sorry for himself, he went on a vicious bender. When he recovered, he began to plan his classes.

In 1955, as a kind of therapy, Berryman started to examine his dreams. He wrote them down and followed their various threads. Here he often found his continued obsession with his father's death. By the end of the summer he had 650 pages of dream analyses which would become *The Dream Songs*, works that were jazzy and sexual, using baby talk and black minstrel show riffs to illuminate the painfully confessional and outrageously funny. *The Dream Songs* would prove at last that Berryman was a poet of dazzling artistic and psychological talent.

First, however, he had another pregnancy to deal with. He got a quick divorce from Eileen and scrambled to marry girlfriend Ann Levine in a decent time. The *Bradstreet* was published and although it received little initial notice, it picked up speed and was nominated for both the Pulitzer Prize and the National Book Award. In November, he won a Rockefeller grant. In anticipation of the baby, he tried to quit smoking and drinking and went through a painful withdrawal.

In June of 1957, he was granted tenure, which meant security, but his behavior became increasingly erratic. While teaching a writing workshop in Chicago he twisted his ankle while drunk. He was paranoid and anxious around colleagues. He publicly condescended to Ann and often reminded her of his own importance. Once he hit her.

Despite the fact that he now had a new wife and son, he made plans to spend the summer teaching in Asia, India, and Europe. His first stop was Tokyo, where he immediately hired a geisha, then a prostitute. In Bombay the rain and the poverty overwhelmed his senses, as did his difficulty in getting enough to drink.

In September, Ann and baby Paul met him in Italy, and they traveled to Spain, where he turned forty-three and got drunk. One night he woke up in an alley minus his wallet and no idea how he got there. He took it out on Ann and struck her again on their way back to America.

The Dream Songs were coming together so well that he felt compelled to drink for inspiration. In "Dream Song 5" he wrote:

> Henry sats in de bar & was odd,
> off in the glass from the glass,
> at odds wif de world & its god,
> his wife is a complete nothing…

Unfortunately, he got so inspired that he had to be hospitalized for alcohol poisoning. Then he came to believe that the poems made him drink so he resolved to limit himself to one poem every two days. In September he was in the hospital again.

He was actually beginning to like it, being fussed over by doctors and nurses. It was an arrangement that allowed him to drink himself to the edge and know that he could go over it and have his every need attended to. He was almost always allowed to continue to teach, taking a taxi to and from his classroom, often hitting a few pubs along the way. In the next fifteen years he would be admitted to hospitals over a dozen times.

Although he had tenure and was known to be an inspired teacher, he was eventually shuffled into an ineffectual department position, and he wrote seething, self-pitying letters to his chairman. They had little effect. Berryman was the only one who did not realize that his brilliance was not worth the risks. At the same time his marriage was dying.

"Ann at first withdrew into herself when John complained about her in her presence, but came bit by bit to fight back," wrote John Haffenden. When Ann's mother died in 1959, Berryman did not notice that Ann was grieving. They were fighting all the time, and it clearly affected their young son. When she became pregnant again she had an abortion.

Ann left him, his job was in jeopardy, and his publisher was looking for overdue works. He thought none of this was his fault but felt sorry for himself and believed that he was being used by everybody. Days went by without sleep, and he had crying jags in bars. At last he drank himself into episodes of DTs and checked himself into the hospital, this time into an alcoholic ward and unexpected strictness. In April he missed the custody hearing for his son, then missed his first child support payment. He was furious with Ann for expecting the payment. Who did she think she was? He was important. She was nobody. He hid under the covers.

The next two years were repetitious: drunken teaching, scenes followed by hospitalizations, drinking alone in bars or his apartment, injuries while drunk, seduction of married women and pursuit of pretty students. "John was always infatuated with a number of the coeds," a student told Haffenden, "and generally tended, in my opinion, to exaggerate their intellectual capabilities."

In 1960 he took a teaching job at Berkeley where he got very drunk at a dinner party in his honor and proceeded to recite poetry for several hours. He continued to drink alone when he wasn't trying to seduce the wives of friends. Finally, he tried to reduce his alcohol intake to gin or bourbon only, with a quart a day as the absolute limit. He rarely ate and would not answer his phone, although he used it to make midnight calls to female students. One student remembered, "Mr. Berryman often called me, usually in a deeply agitated state, seeking reassurance that he had been 'outstanding' or 'brilliant' at his morning lecture."

When he returned to Minnesota in 1961, he checked into the hospital to dry out, checked himself out again to teach classes, and managed to arrive at lectures drunk. Once he gave a class the same lesson twice in one week, word for word; they didn't have the heart to stop him. He was released from the hospital but was back again in March. One night he signed himself out to take a young woman to dinner. Kate Donahue was beautiful, twenty-one, and in awe. When they married, he was so drunk that he couldn't sign the register without help.

There was critical excitement growing around *The Dream Songs* and interest in publishing them, but first he had to narrow them down to a volume of seventy-five out of hundreds. He worked without sleep and was troubled, surrounded by quarts of gin, his hands burned by cigarettes. One morning school employees found him sleeping off a drunk by the university pond. When he checked into the hospital again, he was kept sedated. Although he checked himself out for the birth of his daughter, he got drunk on the way home and snapped his ankle. While his wife was lying in one hospital, he was in another.

The Dream Songs came out in 1963, and Berryman's life would never be the same. Fame had eluded him for most of his life. From now on it would dog him until his death. He won the Pulitzer Prize and the National Book Award, received a substantial raise from the university, and was profiled in magazines and on television. Few twentieth-century poets before or since got the kind of attention and adulation that came to him now, and he accepted it with the same kind of grace he had shown in his anonymity—bad.

Now that some critics were calling him the greatest American poet, he believed more than ever that he deserved what he called special treatment, which meant more women, drugs, and booze. He acknowledged that he was "impatient with anything less than total prostration before the products of my genius."

Needless to say, a stay in the hospital was coming, but only on his terms. When he received his advance copy of the book *Dream Songs*, he checked himself out to celebrate with martinis. When it was published shortly thereafter, he checked himself out for a two-day bender and black-out.

> Why drink so, two days running?
> two months, O seasons, years, two decades running?
> I answer (smiles) my question on the cuff:
> Man, I been thirsty.
>
> (Berryman, "Dream Song 96")

He recovered enough to go back to teaching. He needed the money—the man that James Dickey called "the best living poet in English" was behind in his child support. In 1965 he went back to the hospital, and was soon well enough to travel to Harvard and read his poems. There he was inclined to make drunken phone calls to other poets to tell them how wonderful he was. His life had become a bizarre blend of literary high mindedness and abject drunkenness. He was so disastrously drunk at a reading in Wisconsin that even his drinking buddies were asking him to get help.

He returned to Minnesota where he was cruel to Kate who remained loyal even as he became progressively petulant and refused to speak to her. She sailed with him to Ireland in the fall of 1966, though the presence of his wife and daughter did nothing to stop him from being a regular at the ship bar where he tried to pick up women half his age. In Dublin he wrote seventy-five more "Dream Songs" and tried to edit a second volume. He was mad and sick and tried to write on Thorazine. In the early winter his wife had him committed to a Dublin hospital.

He was still abroad when the second volume of songs was published and he was asked to read at the Guggenheim. Although he was sick with DTs, his family tried to get back to America for the reading, a scene that Paul Mariani described as "muttering through his vomit while the steward tried to get into the darkened room to clean it."

The new poems brought awards, money, and a profile in *Life* called "Whiskey and Ink." He believed more than ever that the poems were keeping him drunk and sick, but that they had a life of their own. At the same time, they were an outlet for his sanity and he never left them alone for long. By August he was in the hospital again; when he was able to move, he was transferred to a Minneapolis hospital. Once again he was able to take a daily taxi to his classes—and pubs—before checking back in for the night.

When he gave readings now, he carried suitcases full of cigarette cartons and bottles of Jack Daniels. He was in demand, but colleges were careful to send someone to meet his plane and make sure he made it past the airport bars and to the readings reasonably upright. He lost thirty-five pounds that year, and what audiences saw was an increasingly frail and fragile poet. It made his performances that much more dramatic. Now money rolled in. He had five books in print, and they all sold unusually well for poetry. The university gave him a very hefty raise. His wife, however, was giving him an ultimatum—drinking or her. A week later he fell while drunk, ending up in the hospital and in the alcoholic ward.

After his release he was sober for twelve days. He wrote long letters to friends and made plans for a long-planned Shakespeare biography. When he began writing more poems he started drinking again to ease him through the excitement. When the poems drove him to the hospital again Kate held out her hand and said, "It's been nice to be married to you." He was released but returned two weeks later with DTs. Now the letters he wrote, including those to critics, were paranoid. He announced that he was "a wreck, but Sir a gorgeous wreck."

Kate got a job teaching school; it was a relief to be something besides the wife of a famous, tortured poet. She offered him a second ultimatum and received another excuse. Berryman continued to give readings at colleges and to teach and drink. He knew that the hospital was always waiting, as it was when he checked in during May of 1970. The ward secretary that night told biographer Haffenden that, "His beard at the time was untrimmed and shaggy, his eyes hollowed out, and there were large blisters on his hands from wayward cigarettes. He trembled a bit, and talked incessantly. He stood up and sang an old blues song, and he later offered some rather garbled philosophy."

During this stay he went through a religious conversion. He realized that God cared for him, and in May he began to write poems proclaiming that he was under new management—God's. He still insisted on making his own rules—or lack of same—for his treatment. When he was discharged in June, he was still sick and remained "hostile, arrogant & defiant."

He rewarded himself for completed poems with drinking binges. He tried to cut back, but it wasn't long before he was again up to a quart a day. When he could manage teaching he was still capable of brilliance. Other times he bullied students, or raved, or had students meet him in a bar for class. A breakdown was coming, earmarked by insomnia, nightmares, and lots of weepy, late-night phone calls. Finally one night he had to be strapped down and taken to the locked ward of the hospital where he wrote over one hundred poems in two months. In his biography, *Dream Song: The Life of John Berryman*, Paul Mariani quotes Berryman:

> I do, despite my self-doubts, day by day
> grow more & more but a little confident
> that I will never down a whiskey again
> or gin or rum or vodka, brandy or ale....
>
> It all is, after all, very simple.
>
> You just never drink again all each damned day...

A new book of poems, *Love & Fame*, came out and critics hated it, saying it was self-indulgent, bragging and vague. This actually humbled Berryman a little which helped him be more open about his treatment and therapy.

When he was released in December, he believed that he was sober for good, until a series of poetry readings took him through too many airports and their bars. He attended Alcoholics Anonymous, and would continue to on and off for the rest of his life. When he fell off the wagon now, he was sincere about climbing back on, and even tried to help other alcoholics in his group. More and more he relied on prayer. In May 1972 he was alone and sober in a hotel room with Jesus. He got up and wrote a poem about the presence of God, exploring the idea that a Savior died for sinner John Berryman. Strangely, this work of religious love and investigation is also a kind of prayer for death. *"Let this be it.* I've *had* it. I can't wait."

John Berryman resented being asked to do any of the work that Kate shouldered with their new baby. He was angry with her, furious that she would take him away from poetry. "I think you suffer from, among other things, the jealous hatred of the very weak for the decisively strong (yes, dear, that's me)," he wrote her. Too worn down to be the good soldier, Kate pulled farther and farther away. He felt guilty, then angry with her because of his guilt, and the old cycle continued.

He was sober at fifty-seven, but he wasn't aging well. His readings were still problematic, marked by frequent interruptions and rambling tangents. Even though he was practicing yoga, lifting weights, and reading the Bible, he continued to smoke four packs a day. He wrote in his journal of illness, religious doubts, old guilts, his fears about money, and his "pathetic penis" shrinking into the groin. Even prayer eventually deserted him.

Finally, after months of sobriety, he bought a bottle of whiskey and drank half of it in one sitting. Kate was just too sick at heart to care, and Berryman was left alone with his desire to die. He left the house, telling Kate, "You won't have to worry about me anymore." He took the campus shuttle to the school, but walked away from it and onto the Washington Avenue Bridge that spanned the frozen Mississippi River.

He climbed up on the railing and waved to onlooking students. He pitched forward and fell a hundred feet onto the icy river bank. Robert Lowell wrote, "I somehow smile when I think of John's whole life, and even of the icy leap from the bridge to the hard ground. He was springy to the end, and on his feet."

JEAN STAFFORD

DRINK OF CHOICE

🐦 Sherry or bourbon.

🐦 Often made Cuba Libres for friends: Add
one ounce of lime juice to two ounces of
rum, and fill the glass with Coke.

"From the first words I heard her utter it was clear that here was one of the funniest and most brilliant women I would ever meet. Also one of the drunkest."

-Dick Cavett

"She said I was selfish and no matter how hard I tried, I could not make her see...I hated to drink, that it made me unspeakably miserable but that I could not help it because I did not know why I was compelled to destroy myself."

- Jean Stafford

"For the millionth time what a prize jackass I am when I drink."

- Jean Stafford

Novelist Jean Stafford wrote, "Being a writer and being married to a writer is a back breaking-job, and my back is now broken." It was only a slight exaggeration. Her poet-husband Robert Lowell shattered Stafford's face in a (possibly deliberate) car wreck. Two years later he broke her nose in a New Orleans hotel room. Rumors of beatings ran throughout their marriage; friends said he made her sleep under the bed.

The mystery is why she allowed it to continue. Stafford was no helpless housewife; she was a popular writer whose work would win seven O. Henry Awards and a Pulitzer Prize. She was intelligent, well known, and feared for her withering wit, and she was tough. But she was a victim of this very toughness: Jean Stafford was proud of being able to take it.

She was proud of her ability to isolate herself in a secret, psychic room, a mental hiding place she discovered through her experiences with self-mutilation, self-mortification, and anorexia. A staggering capacity for alcohol didn't hurt but unfortunately, she didn't count on the anger that would build up over the years and how it would eventually move into the room with her. When she was seething inside and out, the only thing left was the booze.

Her gift for withdrawal began in southern California where she was born in 1915, on her father's walnut farm. Business was good, and John Stafford was able to dabble at being a gentleman farmer and writer. Stafford and her siblings grew up surrounded by her father's stories, but his career never really took off. There was a western novel, *When Cattle Kingdom Fell,* and a few short works, but little to show for the thousands of words he turned out each day; much of it was nonsense. His fecund output would intimidate Stafford as a writer, even as a grown woman.

In spite of his lack of literary works, his ranch was doing very well. Stafford received her first, terrible blow when her father sold the farm and lost the money—years before the Depression—on the stock market. It was hundreds of thousands of 1920s dollars and the young girl's life changed overnight. The well-to-do rancher's daughter was soon living in a world of embarrassing poverty.

When the family moved to Colorado, John did not attempt to work but let his wife support the family with a series of dreary jobs. She rented out rooms and turned their home into a boarding house where Stafford and her siblings did all the work. Her father spent his days typing in the basement, where his writing grew further and further away from reality.

One day Stafford would hate him. After a visit with him as an adult she wrote, "Seeing him again I am amazed that all of us did not commit suicide in our cradles." She lamented to her sister, "Obviously he was gifted but he was completely undisciplined and completely lazy and completely self-indulgent and I can't forgive him."

As a child, however, she saw her father as some kind of lost aristocrat. The girl who had been writing her own stories since she was eight was honored when he rented a summer cabin for the two of them, complete with father-and-daughter typewriters. As time went on, he became more delusional, a scraggly, unshaven figure wandering barefoot through the streets and talking to himself. Deeply embarrassed, she avoided him, then deeply guilty, she humored him, asking to hear his bizarre writing. In an autobiographical story she wrote, "This is always a terrible mistake for he turns the whole weight of his madness upon her." She learned to separate herself from both his insanity and the town's gossip about it.

In 1932, Stafford started attended the University of Colorado and majored in English literature. She was easy on the eyes, blonde and good looking, with a slow, husky voice, the voice of an undertaker, she called it. She posed nude for drawing classes to make money, scandalizing her fellow students, which no doubt was part of the point.

At college she began to drink concoctions like bathtub gin made by adding juniper spirits to grain alcohol, but she did not learn to sin from fellow students. In 1935, the twenty-year-old Stafford was taken under the wings of an unusual couple, Andrew and Lucy Cooke. They were only three years older than Stafford, but they might as well have been from another planet. They were rich and bright and Lucy studied law, an unusual ambition for a woman in Boulder. Husband and wife were both unapologetically promiscuous.

Lucy was the strong one and it was she who drew students into their circle and created a little commune. She paired up students for sex then encouraged them to cheat on each other. It was normal to wander around the apartment half—or completely—nude. One night they gave themselves wine enemas in hopes of finding a new way to get drunk.

She and Lucy grew very close and may have had an affair, although it is more likely their destructive intimacy was emotional. Late in 1935, Lucy, who had recently had surgery, became depressed. When she came home late one night, Stafford and Andrew were waiting for her. Andrew got angry and started questioning her about where she had been. Lucy threw a drink in his face, and with Andrew and Stafford close behind, she ran into the next room and shot herself in the head.

Stafford went inside her mind again to shield herself from grief and campus talk; it was the only way she could finish her coursework. That spring she applied for and received a grant to study in Heidelberg. One of her companions on the trip was fellow student Jim Hightower. He was a gentle guy, good company, and they drank and talked for days at a time. It was painful for Hightower that Stafford wanted nothing more than friendship, but she did not want someone gentle. She did cherish his friendship and probably the easy adoration, and with this she would wreak havoc on Hightower's emotional life for years.

In 1937 Stafford returned home in time for the University of Colorado's annual writers' conference. The conference chairman was also her writing mentor, and he gave her work to visiting luminaries like Ford Madox Ford and publisher Whit Burnett. They took notice and encouraged her to send them future work. "Know now for sure that I'm good—like hell," she wrote Hightower. During the conference she also came to the disastrous attention of Robert Lowell.

Lowell was an undergraduate at Kenyon College in Ohio, visiting Colorado with Ford. He was from a lesser branch of Boston's famous family and was on his way to fame as a poet. At the time he was gorgeous with an air of instability and danger. A friend said he looked like Heathcliff played by Boris Karloff. He was smitten with Stafford, her learning, good looks, and the unmistakable buzz surrounding her writing. When he returned to Ohio, he courted her by mail.

After the excitement of the conference, it was a letdown for Stafford to have to find a job. Despite heroic efforts, her only offer came from the English department of Stephens College in Missouri. In the 1930s, Stephens was basically a finishing school for girls, offering college classes like Scientific Eating and Posture. Stafford found it to be a training school for concubines. She was unpopular with students and faculty alike for trying to bring literature into a curriculum based on *Reader's Digest*, and for criticizing student essays with titles like "A Short History of Nail Polish." She was fired after a year.

She submitted her first finished novel to a publisher in December 1937 but it was not accepted. She moved to New York where she was sick with fevers, bleeding, painful stomach swelling, severe nausea, and aching. All of her life, Stafford would be prone to painful ailments and crippling accidents, she was well aware she brought much of it on herself. "My middle name is Psychosomatic," she wrote. This illness is of note, however, because some biographers believe it was not emotional, but rather gonorrhea, contracted in Germany. Biographer

David Roberts believes she also had syphilis. If so, it would account for why she never had children.

It would also explain why her relationships with men were so problematic. In the 1940s before the wide availability of penicillin, the cure for venereal disease was undependable, leaving a real and serious fear of intercourse. Before Heidelberg she had affairs, but afterward she seemed wary of sex. Except for one awkward night, she refused to sleep with her friend Jim Hightower, even though she wrote him many passionate letters. She sometimes claimed to never have had sex with her first husband Robert Lowell. "I have never been able to demonstrate love except when I have been drunk," she wrote, "and the love I have shown then has been trumped up out of the bottle."

She hated teaching, but she needed a job if she was going to keep eating and writing. "If only I could believe that I don't want velvet capes, champagne, fine editions, Coty's eau de cologne, a dubonnet candlewick bedspread," she wrote. She accepted a job offer at Iowa State only to flee in the night a few months into the job, leaving no forwarding address.

She was trying to get to Hightower who was studying at Harvard. After several intense letters from her, he thought they would become lovers at last. He did not know that on her way to Massachusetts she would spend one night in Cleveland with Robert Lowell, who came at her request. "I wrote him and said meet me and he did and we drank a good deal of beer and he said he was in love with me and wd. I marry him and to avoid argument I said sure, honey, drink your beer and get me another one."

In Cambridge she was distant with Hightower although she shared his apartment. At the same time she was being pursued by Lowell who sent a cryptic telegram to Stafford at Hightower's address: "Telegraphic restraint forbids objurgation." Hightower told biographer David Roberts that it meant, "I would tell you what kind of double crossing bitch you are, if I weren't writing a telegram."

Her love life was not the only source of excitement for Stafford that year. In December, a Boston publisher gave her an advance against an unfinished novel. She got a room nearby and began to write. Her routine was to drink coffee, read Proust for an hour, then type. She threw in morning shots of sherry and cigarettes. Hightower, a frequent visitor, wearily accepted the role of trusted friend. She told him she was afraid of Lowell, a fear that was well-founded. After all, when he was a child, Lowell nicknamed himself "Cal" after Caligula. However, Stafford's fear of Cal did not stop her from seeing him over the Christmas holiday.

On a December night, Lowell was drunk and driving her home. She told friends that she had refused his proposal so he plowed his father's car into a wall at the end of a dead-end road. Lowell walked away from the accident, but Stafford's face was shattered, and bones had to picked out of the back of her head. Five operations were needed to rebuild her face, but her looks were never the same. There was also substantial damage to her teeth.

Years later Stafford was diagnosed as masochistic. What else could explain her attraction to Lowell after this? She wrote Hightower, "He does what I have always needed to have done to me and that is that he dominates me." Other factors were in play: she was getting older, and she saw in Lowell an antidote to her own poverty-tainted childhood.

Lowell's family hated the idea of their only son marrying a nobody. Cal's mother, a cruel, troubled woman who traded hard on the Lowell mystique, called Stafford a hick, and belittled her at family gatherings. She was also behind the refusal to pay for Stafford's medical bills. The Lowell family stonewalled for years, even after Stafford received a judgment against their insurance company.

Cal's choice of Stafford was certainly a way of defying his family and their stifling expectations, but shortly before the wedding he showed his Lowell side when Stafford offered up a confession. She had led him to believe that she had learned German during her stay in Heidelberg, and now she admitted that she couldn't speak a word. He regarded her confession, as she knew he would, with disgust. It was the sort of thing that mattered.

There was also her drinking. Stafford wrote: "There is a bottle of rum in my room. He just came in and said you've got to stop drinking and I mean even 1 drink and I was panic-stricken for fear he wd take my rum away." They married anyway in April 1940. Poet Allen Tate gave the bride away, and there was no family from either side on hand.

Lowell returned to Kenyon to finish his degree while Stafford went to Colorado to wait for him.

Her second novel was rejected. Like the first, the rejection arrived with encouragement and guidance: "Verbally I think you are one of the most brilliant persons I have ever read, but I think all of these people are not merely lost, they are damned and I must say pretty repulsively damned at that." She started a third novel.

When Cal graduated in 1940, he told Stafford that he had a job, but she would soon find out that it was for her. Louisiana State University offered Lowell a fellowship on the condition that his wife learn shorthand and work as a secretary at their literary publication. In accepting, Stafford went from being Jean Stafford, instructor and writer, to being Mrs. Lowell, typist and faculty wife.

When she went to work every morning Lowell was still asleep. At noon she went home to make his lunch and often find him still in bed. "It has been dreadful arrangement here and I have not been good about it," she wrote to Hightower. "It enraged me during the winter to come home at noon and find both him and Peter Taylor [their housemate] still in their pajamas, having spent the morning reading or writing while I had been cutting stencil and wrestling with 'Accounts Receivable.'" When she came home at night, she typed Lowell's poems. "My life has become subordinate to all other lives to which I am related," she wrote.

This was a typical family dynamic in the literary families that they knew. In *Partisans*, his book about famous intellectual couples, David Laskin wrote, "The men and women were intellectual peers and companions, but socially, professionally, and emotionally, the men came first. The husbands wrote; the wives did everything else—the housekeeping, child rearing, entertaining, nursing, gardening—and then wrote. And it never struck any of them to arrange things differently."

At LSU, Stafford and Lowell drank Cuba Libres, white wine, and copious amounts of gin and tonics. Peter Taylor, the housemate who was to become one of Stafford's closest friends, told biographer David Roberts that one night the three of them had a very drunk discussion about English poets. "Stafford opened her purse, said, 'Well, I think

John Donne'—[and threw up into her purse]." Later he found her in the bathroom rinsing off dollar bills. Another night the friends drove to New Orleans where after a night of drinking and arguing, Lowell punched Stafford in the face and broke her newly repaired nose. Taylor was privately shocked at Lowell's lack of remorse and Stafford's passive acceptance.

It became more and more apparent that Lowell had a serious mental illness. It would eventually be diagnosed as manic depression, but early in their marriage it took the form of religious mania. He converted to Catholicism with an obsessive frenzy. He made the non-Catholic Stafford attend daily mass and say her rosary twice a day. He censored the most mundane aspects of her life. "The fact is that he has forbidden me 1) to drink ever again 2) to read the newspapers 3) to read any novels save those by Dostoevsky, Proust, James and Tolstoy 4) to get a paying job when he goes into the army," she wrote Taylor. "In making these prohibitions he is quite justified if tyrannical and I am not complaining."

All the same she was angry. "I fell in love with Caligula and am living with Calvin," she wrote a friend. "During Lent he starved himself. If he could get his hands on one, he'd be wearing a hair shirt." The penitential Cal got a job at a Catholic publisher in New York and the couple moved there in 1941.

Somehow, Stafford went forward with her own work, and more than one publisher was interested in her latest novel. She received an advance and in 1943 went to Yaddo Artists' Colony to rewrite her book. Lowell was preparing to enter the army to serve in World War II. He had applied for service before and been turned down. Now, upon receiving an official draft notice, he did an about-face and refused to go, declaring himself a conscientious objector. It was a strange, grandstanding gesture, one that he made sure the newspapers covered. Stafford knew what few others realized, that it was not so much conscience or ego that motivated it, but madness.

In 1944, Lowell was serving a jail sentence for draft evasion. Stafford turned to her husband's family for help while he was in prison and they responded with hostility. Cal's sole contribution to the household had long been a monthly check from his trust fund; his mother bitterly denounced Stafford when she continued to accept it. She also received public abuse from those who thought Lowell's act treasonous. Heavy drinking was her escape.

When he was released later that year, Cal was convinced he had a sacred duty to become a street corner preacher and that the two of them could live like the lilies of the field. Fortunately for Stafford, he was distracted from this notion when his first book of poems was published later that year. Stafford's first novel, *Boston Adventure*, was also published; she was secretly relieved that his book had been the first by a few days. There was nothing she could do, however, about the fact that his book languished while hers became a huge bestseller, bringing fame and money.

At twenty-nine, Stafford was a celebrity. She had written a spectacular first novel, a James-like story with shrewd observations on the manners of the Boston upper class, much to the consternation of her mother-in-law. She was interviewed on the radio and in *Life*, and was chosen by *Mademoiselle* as one of the ten outstanding women of the year. What should have been her time in the spotlight was marred by a sprained ankle and the death of her brother. She was soon on her way to Colorado to attend his funeral. There she endured a painful reunion with her family, and she medicated the pain, both physical and mental, with bottles of fortified wine from the local Piggly-Wiggly.

In 1945, the sales from her book allowed her to buy her first real home. She chose a beautiful old house in Damariscotta Mills, Maine. It would become the setting for important works by both Lowell and Stafford. Cal, who had married her to spite convention, was savagely scornful of her desire to decorate and be domestic; he became distant and mean. He was an incredibly spoiled and competitive man, and her success—she had just won a Guggenheim grant and an advance on her second novel—no doubt had a lot to do with his behavior toward her. Her acceptance of it is just as disturbing. She wrote in her journal, "I apologized for everything; I had no center and therefore I had no self and therefore I did not lead a real life. His vanity and passionate self-devotion fascinated me evilly."

He lived in a separate part of the house and would go for days without saying a word. When he did, he taunted her. "I did not know how to defend myself against his barbs, the cruelest of which was that I could not sin with style." In Stafford's account of those days, her fictional counterpart was told, "I learned to drink at home in the drawing room, so I know how. You don't drink well, dear. Not well at all."

In fact, Stafford was often drunk now, even though they had no car and the nearest liquor store was in the next town. She relied on the local sheriff to conduct her rum running. She kept a flask in her handbag and sherry behind the cookbooks. That summer they played host to a houseful of poets, wives, and lovers. The company initially kept some of the tension between the couple at bay but it also drove her crazy, the way the "Baby Bards" treated her as if she did not exist. The acclaimed writer was seen as someone simply to make meals, clean up, and type Lowell's poems.

Describing the atmosphere, David Laskin wrote, "So many of the women became alcoholics. So many were beaten, abused, deceived, betrayed, bested, and debased by the men they were involved with. So many dreamed of—or went ahead and took—revenge, both in word and in deed, and especially in word written for publication." Which is what Stafford did years later in her story *An Influx of Poets*: "At night, after supper, they'd read from their own works until four o'clock in the morning, drinking Cuba Libres. They never listened to one another; they were preoccupied with waiting for their turn. And I'd have to stay up and clear out the living room after they went suddenly to bed."

In August, a guest came whose visit would smash whatever was left of the marriage. Gertrude Buckman was the beautiful, doll-like ex-wife of Delmore Schwartz. She and Lowell were attracted to each other. Buckman gave him sympathy and understanding when Stafford drank alone night after night and into the next day. Buckman even tried to find and pour out Stafford's hidden stash while the drunken Stafford looked on and laughed.

That fall Stafford and Lowell left Maine and headed to New York by train. The marriage was over. He didn't want a wife, he told her, he wanted a playmate. In *An Influx of Poets* she wrote of the train and of the husband who promised to join her in the club car.

Liar, I thought. Swindler. Ten minutes before the North Station you'll come into the club car, where you'll find me drunk; the sight of you will drive me wild, for I will know what you have been doing, with your eyes so piously attentive to the Latin of your little book. You will have been dreaming, mooning, delighting yourself with thoughts of your reunion with your playmate, this very night.

They separated in New York, and she lived in a broken, twilight world of ever-cheaper hotels. She closed the hotel bars and went to her room where she guzzled applejack for the rest of the night. When she was at her lowest, Lowell asked for a divorce.

Her second novel, *The Mountain Lion*, was published in December 1947. The strange and beautiful coming-of-age story received great reviews, and *Life* proclaimed her the most brilliant of the new fiction writers. It was hard to enjoy the attention, however, because she was living behind bars at the Payne Whitney psychiatric hospital. She would be there for almost a year. She lived for visits from Lowell, but he rarely came. His only contact with his wife was to try to persuade her to give up all claims to alimony.

The Mountain Lion did not sell well, and when she was released from the hospital in 1948, she was broke. Biographer Ann Hulbert records a letter Stafford wrote: "I felt perpetually accused and guilt-ridden and it was partly the guilt itself that made me spend all the money and so madly, to get as quickly as possible back to the familiar state of poverty, of literally not knowing where the rent was coming from."

She got some relief from a second Guggenheim grant and an advance on her next novel. She also began publishing stories in *The New Yorker* in a partnership that would last for years. In April 1948, she flew to the Virgin Islands to establish residency for a divorce. When she returned, someone asked, "How was it?" She answered, "Where's the bourbon?"

In the fall of 1949 she met Oliver Jensen. The *Life* editor was handsome and self-confident, and he swept her off her feet. He lavished her with gifts, took her on dates to "21," and admired her as a writer. During their courtship she limited her drinking—Jensen drank lightly or not at all. In a few months they were married. Stafford should have been happy. Jensen was stable, adoring and could give her a comfortable life in a beautiful home in Westport, Connecticut. But Stafford would not allow herself happiness, and she proceeded to sabotage their relationship.

Jensen took a lot of verbal abuse, including attacks on his work. Stafford complained that *Life* magazine was middle class. She was drinking again, and she screamed at him when he hid her bottles. Even then he tried hard to hold her together. In a letter to Stafford's sister he wrote a painful description of an angry woman: "Her pessimism, catholic and profound, and her memory, which is photographic only, alas, in aspect of unhappy things, holds her in thrall. She believes in disease but not in cures." In a letter to Jensen she would admit that she was a liar, an alcoholic, and a hypochondriac, but she seemed to be unable, or unwilling to stop being any of these.

In 1952, her third and last novel, *The Catherine Wheel*, was published. It was a bestseller, but reviews were mixed. (In the 1980s it would be revived in James Wolcott's *Neglected Books of the Twentieth Century* series.) At its initial celebration, she and fellow *New Yorker* writer James Thurber got drunk and fell down the stairs.

She divorced Jensen but stayed in Westport, moving into a small apartment where she wrote short stories for *The New Yorker*. In 1953, a collection of her stories was published to excellent reviews but she continued to spiral downward. Her drinking was so severe that she began hearing things, voices calling her name, and she would see slimy things that weren't there climbing on her walls.

In 1956, she went to London. It was not the cure she had hoped for. She suffered from the "food (absence of) and drink (superabundance of) syndrome." All of that was about to change. A. J. Liebling, another *New Yorker* writer and the author of several wonderful books, was also in London. Stafford's editor fixed them up and they were soon companions.

Liebling was a large man who loved life, and he showered her with presents, such as flowers and a mink coat. He called for her in his Rolls Royce and took her on caviar picnics. He loved good food and drink, and his *joie de vivre* was like a bright light shining away her morbid thoughts. More importantly, he supported her as a writer. In 1959 they married. Ironically, she did little writing during their marriage. "Perhaps it's too simple an explanation, but I was happy for the first time in my life," Stafford said.

Eventually, even the fun-loving Liebling became concerned over Stafford's drinking. Like Jensen, he mistrusted her so-called intellectual friends and their effect on her. His own health worsened and in 1963 he died of heart failure. Stafford was left alone. She stopped eating, and soon malnutrition and alcohol put her in the hospital. A doctor's report, quoted in Robert's biography, said that she had "a benign gastric ulcer, chronic malnutrition, bronchitis, reactive depression with excessive alcohol intake, and fibrocystic disease in one breast."

She was, in short, a mess, and in April 1964, she had a heart attack. When she was released from the hospital, she resumed her life of cocktail parties, drinking and three packs a day. She was now living in the Hamptons where she was a popular guest at parties. Even when she was drunk she was a fabulous and funny storyteller. In her husky voice, she charmed the locals and college students with her wicked stories of famous poets and well-known society figures.

She kept two typewriters loaded with paper, one for journalism and one for fiction. Although she would never finish another novel, she maintained the illusion that a new novel was on its way for more than fifteen years. She survived for the rest of her life on money she made from articles—journalistic pieces noted for their shrewd insights and perfection of word and phrase. Like her anecdotes, they were often bitterly funny at the expense of their subject.

The late 1960s and the 1970s would mark a serious decline in her health, both mental and physical, although she would continue to win awards and sit on literary juries for the Pulitzer Prize and the National Book Award. In time, however, she went from being a well-loved character to being a pain, and her welcome wore thin. The storytelling, once cutting and clever, had turned into long, exhausting complaints and incoherent rants. She was barred from a hotel after setting the sheets on fire, and she developed a habit of calling friends at three in the morning. Finally, she began to abuse even her oldest and most loyal friends with hateful and paranoid raving.

"Anger alone keeps me alive," she wrote her agent. It was as if she trying to kill off any light places in her life. She fell down stairs a lot. The world she hated so much kept handing her awards. In 1970 she won the Pulitzer Prize for a collection of short stories and was nominated for the National Book Award. She was drunk when she was inducted into the National Institute of Arts and letters.

She wrote to Robert Lowell:

> I use booze as insulation against boredom and impatience, or to exalt my feeling of camaraderie to the point of mania. If I drink alone—and sometimes I do occasionally—I fall down and break something— either an irreplaceable piece of something breakable or one of my bones.

Her friend and neighbor Dick Cavett wrote:

> I asked her if she thought she *could* stop drinking. She stared out the side window for a long moment without speaking. Then she said in a tone that was neither offended nor melodramatic but chillingly matter-of-fact, 'I loathe alcohol. It is my enemy. And my seducer.' We rode in silence for a while and then changed the subject.

Near the end of 1976 she suffered a stroke that left her unable to write or talk. She continue to smoke and drink, while taking an arsenal of prescription drugs. With effort she managed to communicate in a language made up of monosyllables, long pauses and cuss words. "She continued her late-night calls to friends," wrote Cavett. "But since the stroke had affected her speech the conversation could be excruciating, especially when she was drunk. There was nothing to do but wait them out."

She died of cardiac arrest at the age of sixty-three, but for one friend, Stafford had "sort of stopped living her life" long ago. She made one last gesture to the world, one that may have guaranteed her withdrawal from literary posterity. In her will she named her cleaning lady, an elderly woman who could barely read, her literary executrix.

JOHN CHEEVER

DRINK OF CHOICE

❧ He wrote that Gilbey's gin was mother's milk to him.

❧ While traveling on a train once, he bought Rusty Nails for strangers: one ounce of Scotch to one ounce of Drambuie.

"The gin bottle, the gin bottle. This is painful to record. The gin bottle is empty."

- John Cheever

"Revolting, elderly, alcoholic novelist desires meaningful relationship with 24-year-old aristocratic North Carolinian with supple form and baroque biceps. Little gay experience but ready learner. Etc."

- John Cheever's imaginary personal ad
for The New York Review of Books

In spite of alcoholism and multiple affairs with partners of both sexes, John Cheever was a family man. He dyed Easter eggs with his kids, stuffed the Thanksgiving turkey, said grace, and took his daughter to church. This same daughter had occasion to refer to their dinner table and its sarcastic atmosphere as "the shark tank." It is also true that Cheever wrote, "When you find a good room to work in you will sure as hell be evicted by child-birth, a litter of puppies, visiting relations or if necessary fire. At least that's my experience."

His own childhood had been painful. Both parents were strict Yankees and distant when it came to affection. His father was a businessman who worked his way into the upper rungs of the middle class, whose "concern for sartorial preciseness was exhaustive," who loved to tell of his life on the road, of being wooed with champagne and oysters. When his business failed, however, he never worked again, and spent his days drinking and womanizing. So his wife opened a gift shop, allegedly selling family heirlooms as antiques, and neither he nor his son ever forgave her for succeeding.

Cheever was born in the Boston suburb of Quincy, Massachusetts, in 1912. His only brother was seven years older, and his parents made no effort to disguise the fact that he was unplanned and unwanted. His mother told him, "If I hadn't drunk two manhattans one afternoon you never would have been conceived." It was also part of family lore that his father invited an abortionist to dinner during the pregnancy. "My mother carried me reluctantly and my father must have been heard to say that he had no love in his heart for another child."

As an adult, Cheever wrote, "the greatest and the most bitter mystery in my life was my father." One morning Cheever found him wearing a necklace of seventeen champagne corks that he had acquired—one by one—the night before. Another time he found his missing father passed out in a nearby amusement park roller coaster.

By age eleven, Cheever already loved music and theater; they helped him make sense of life. He knew then that he wanted to be a writer. In grade school, his class would be rewarded for good behavior with a reading of one of his stories. Otherwise, school was challenging. When he was seventeen, he was asked to leave Thayer Academy. The reason for his expulsion remains unclear (like many writers, Cheever reinvented his life several times for public consumption), but possible reasons range from homosexuality to bad grades to garden variety not-fitting-in.

Cheever claimed he was caught smoking, a scenario he soon worked into his first published short story. The painfully funny "Expelled" was printed in *The New Republic* when he was eighteen. Seeing his work in print, Cheever knew his formal education was finished. Instead, he read everything; books became his university. He moved in with his brother Fred, who willingly supported him while he wrote.

Their parents' relationship grew more and more hateful, driving their sons together. In 1931, they spent a *wanderjahre* together in Germany, and they grew even closer. Too close. In 1979 Cheever wrote that he and Fred had been "morbidly close." Fearing for their emotional future, Cheever moved alone to New York, and Fred married. At age twenty-two, Cheever was on his own. He wrote stories that didn't sell, but in spite of hard times, he always dressed well and displayed old-fashioned manners. At his first cocktail party, he drank one too many Manhattans, but managed to thank his hostess before vomiting. He was only five feet tall, but thanks to his style and self-confidence, his diminutive frame never hampered him socially or romantically.

In the winter of 1934 he was cold and often hungry, living on stale bread and buttermilk. He befriended editor and critic Malcolm Cowley, who introduced him to the city's literary elite, like John Dos Passos, Walker Evans, James Agee, and Edmund Wilson. Cowley, who would become a lifelong friend, felt Cheever was stuck, so he gave him a challenge: to write as many short stories under one thousand words as possible over one weekend. It worked. Two of the resulting four stories were sold to *The New Yorker*, and established a recognizable John Cheever style.

In the early 1930s, he began a long relationship with the Yaddo Artist's Colony. At first he had to talk his way past manager Elizabeth Ames, but eventually they would become close friends. On his early visits, he worked on a novel based on his family. He also had many affairs, as he did in New York. Women were attracted to a sweet, gentle quality and a need to be mothered, as well his genuine capacity for deep friendships with them.

Simon & Schuster offered him an advance for his novel-in-progress, and he ran into a problem that would thwart his writing ambitions for most of his life. If he spent all of his time working on short stories to pay the rent, there was none left for work on longer, extended work. He was ultimately unhappy with the manuscript of the novel *The Holly Tree* and threw the only copy of it in a garbage can, accepting for now his lot as an author of short stories.

At age twenty-seven, his goals were, "a house a wife a bottle of whiskey and a chance to work." He found the wife in the form of his agent's assistant, Mary Winternitz. She was twenty-three, educated, smart, and pretty. Her family was cultured and ambitious, but Cheever impressed them as a gentleman and won their approval. They were married in March 1941 and settled happily into a small apartment in Greenwich Village. Mary continued to work while Cheever wrote constantly; he had traditional ideas about gender roles and intended to be the head of the house. While they didn't have much money, they were young and in love, and were both welcome additions to the frequent cocktail parties on the literary scene.

That December, Pearl Harbor was bombed, and a few months later, Cheever enlisted in the army. He joined willingly, but years later would compare military life to prison: the long, hard days, grueling physical training, practicing with bayonets and stuffed dummies, a sadistic Platoon Sergeant, who drank and was somewhat nuts. After basic training he was assigned to a base in Georgia, where he had time to create more short stories.

While there, Random House published his first book, a collection of short stories. *The Way Some People Live* received favorable reviews, and may have saved his life. An officer in the Army Signal Corps had read his book and requested Cheever for his unit. When Cheever's original company was shipped to Utah Beach, he was not with them, saving him from possible death. His new position allowed him to live with Mary and baby Susan in New York and commute to work, where he helped create war propaganda intended to raise morale. Military discipline rigor was relaxed, and with fellow soldiers William Saroyan and Irwin Shaw, he enjoyed lunches that began with double martinis and ended with chocolate *pots de crème*. Even among military men, he was noted for his heavy drinking. A colleague called Cheever the brightest person in the room until ten o'clock, when he fell over drunk.

At the end of the war, he was thirty-four and knew it was time to write a novel. As a respectable husband and father, not to mention Yankee, he rejected the eccentric artist façade. Every day he put on a suit and rode the elevator down with the other men in his apartment building. He got off in the basement, where he took off his suit and typed in his underwear. At lunchtime, he would put the suit back on, and ride the elevator up for lunch, then repeat the routine in the afternoon.

He continued to support his young family with his short stories. Son Ben was born in 1948, and Cheever reluctantly left the city for the suburb of Scarborough, an hour from New York by train. There, he and Mary joined a group of upwardly mobile couples for frequent cocktail parties and what Susan Cheever called post-marital dating. On Saturdays, the day's drinking started around eleven in the morning and went on into the night. Even in this world, John Cheever was noted for being unfailingly courteous and funny, as well as for his patrician image: tweeds, button-down shirts, and loafers.

In 1951, he won an O. Henry Award, one of ten in his career. Work on his novel dragged on for years, and it became a liability. Most critics felt that, as good as his stories were, he had to produce a novel to ensure his place in literature. More than a few of his contemporaries were scornful of his connection with *The New Yorker*, feeling—wrongly—that it put him in the literary second-class. He had faith in his work, though, and with encouragement from Malcolm Cowley, he kept at it.

His brother Fred moved nearby; their relationship was complicated and not always happy. Fred was an alcoholic, and he lived in a different social circle than his worldly brother. Their bond was strong, but now there was an element of hate between them. In an interview in the 1970s, Susan Cheever asked her father, "Did you ever want to kill Fred?" His answered, "Well, once I was planning to take him trout fishing miles away from everything in the wilderness, and I realized if I got him up there he would fall overboard, I would beat him with an oar until he stayed."

Cheever, himself a high school dropout, was offered a job teaching at Barnard in 1954. The money came in handy and he still had plenty of time for writing and drinking. In his journal he wrote, "These interminable cocktail hours leave me with a sprained sense of charity and love; leave me spiteful and mean." On his occasional visits to a psychiatrist, he admitted to concerns for both his alcohol abuse and his homosexual desires. He felt he was "an odd mixture of man and cockroach."

He was under constant pressure from Random House to finish his novel. To get out from under their watchful eye, Cheever approached Harper's, who bought out his contract with Random House and gave him the space he needed to finish his novel. When his mother died in 1956, *The Wapshot Chronicle* finally poured out of him. This story of an eccentric New England family mirrored his own family in many ways. Its patriarch is hapless and unemployed, wilting under his wife's determination to support the family. This dark, funny novel won the National Book Award in 1958, and in 1999 was selected as one of Modern Library's "100 Best Novels" of the twentieth century.

Before the book was even published, he had made forty thousand dollars on a movie deal, and used the money to take his family to Italy for a year. Mary was eight months pregnant, but she suffered in good humor, found schools for the children and the *palazzio* where they lived. In March their son Federico, called Fred, was born, followed shortly by the publication of *The Wapshot Chronicle*. When they returned to America, Cheever was a celebrity.

Fame did nothing to slow his drinking, and it affected his marriage. He wrote in his journal:

> I am a solitary drunkard. After half a glass of gin I decide that I must get a divorce—and, to tell the truth, Mary is depressed, although my addiction to gin may have something to do with her low spirits. So the gin flows, and after supper the whiskey. I am even a little sly, keeping my glass on the floor where it might not be seen.

One night, after a day-long binge, he looked up the number for Alcoholics Anonymous. Instead of dialing, however, he decided to drink whatever leftover whiskey, gin, and vermouth he could lay his shaking hands on. At age forty-seven he wrote:

> Year after year I read in here [his journal] that I am drinking too much, and there can be no doubt of the fact that this is progressive. I waste more days, I suffer deeper pangs of guilt, I wake at three in the morning with the feelings of a temperance worker. And yet each noon I reach for the whiskey bottle.

The alcohol was having an effect on the quality of his work, hindering his long relationship with *The New Yorker*. This career stumble made him even more reluctant to give in to Mary's wish to buy their own place in tiny Ossining, New York. There was no question of his turning back, however, after he overheard a lawyer at *The New Yorker* ask, "What makes John Cheever think a writer can live in a house like that?"

They moved in early 1961, into a new house and higher up the social ladder. (He told his dogs, "Now don't go playing with the Crotonville dogs, they're not the right sort.") His neighbors were the likes of actors Jose Ferrer and Howard de Silva, and it all meant lots of entertaining and social obligations. "Most people smoked, everyone drank hard liquor. Women didn't have jobs," wrote Susan Cheever. Soon her father was living out one of his short stories.

He was friends with many of the men in Ossining, and lovers with many of their wives, telling them Mary didn't love him enough. This was also an excuse to drink more, and these days when he was drunk, he was mean and unpleasant. For the first time in his life, his famous courtesy was prone to slip. This made for the shark tank, or as his sons called it, "the bear garden." The kids became clever and aggressive with words themselves to survive the sarcastic tongue of their father.

He did not hide the fact that he was disappointed in his daughter, both intellectually and socially. His son Ben wasn't masculine enough. But as time went on, he became aware that his children often played the role of caretaker to him. He asked Ben, "Don't you wish I was different? Don't you wish I didn't drink?" Ben always answered no.

Mary got a part-time job teaching at a nearby women's college. The work gave her more independence and self-esteem but it infuriated her husband, who accused her of selfishly sending their income into a higher tax bracket for no reason. As she bloomed and developed more interests outside of his drinking, he became more verbally abusive. One night he threw a drink in her boss's face. They both sought partners outside of their marriage.

Cheever sank deeper into depression. "The last twenty years of my father's life were spent in a struggle to escape the trappings and traps he had so carefully constructed for himself," wrote Susan Cheever. He considered suicide as he chain-smoked through sleepless nights. In a moment of self-preservation he threw away all of his shotgun shells.

In 1964, he published *The Wapshot Scandal*. This sequel was darker than its predecessor, riddled with death, adultery, and everyday moral despair, but it was also wickedly funny. During the same year, *The New Yorker* ran "The Swimmer," arguably Cheever's finest story. It is an account of soul-wrenching pain coiled in between the banal details of a suburban businessman's epic attempt to swim from the train station to his house via every pool—and cocktail—on the way.

"The Swimmer" was made into a movie starring Burt Lancaster. When Cheever arrived in Hollywood, his drinking surprised even the worldly locals. He fell in love with the beautiful actress Hope Lange, and would eventually begin an affair that lasted over a decade. On his return to New York, he was now a public figure, and as such, fair game for the press. When reporters arrived to ferret out juicy stories about his excesses for a cover story in *Time* magazine on the "Ovid in Ossining," he slyly avoided talking about himself by plying them with drink and turning the tables. His ploy was part protection, part old-Yankee code.

Alcohol continued to be part of his suburban life. As Susan Cheever wrote, "There were preprandial libations and postprandial libations, and soon there were libations all the time." He realized that "allied to my melancholy is my struggle with Demon Rum. There is a terrible sameness to the euphoria of alcohol and the euphoria of metaphor." He worked with a psychiatrist who told him he was subconsciously obsessed with his mother.

In a letter to his son he wrote, "The maid is cleaning the carpet. She stands directly between me and the gin bottle in the pantry but if I ask her to empty the ashtrays in the living room I will be able to sneak into the pantry. Will John Cheever hit the bottle or the Librium or both?" When he read at Susan's college, she held her breath, waiting to see if he got through it without incident.

After he won the Howell's Medal for best fiction in a five-year period, against such competition as Katherine Anne Porter and Saul Bellow, he again considered suicide. Mary pointed out that he was in the middle of a novel, and if he died, the kids would want to know what he had been doing for the past five years. He down-played the fact that he drunkenly swallowed a dental bridge.

Cheever wrote Frederick Exley:

> I keep telling myself that I am rich, beloved by many passionate and exceptionally beautiful women, the owner of an 18th century stone house and a brace of faithful Labrador retrievers, the father of three comely and brilliant children and a frequent guest at the White House. How could such a paragon be felled by a false tooth?

To his doctors, he blamed Mary. It was not drinking that caused problems in his marriage, but problems in his marriage that caused the drinking. One doctor said it was the old story: Cheever was dependent on his wife and resented it, so he acted out. He regularly used charm and evasion to get around his psychiatrists. They were educated, but he was good at words and playing with them, and at least one was impressed by his celebrity.

Mary didn't stand a chance. "I want a wife," he complained. When Susan married, he debated whether or not to warn her about the disappointments of marriage but decided against it. Not that he had to. She could see for herself that her mother "would leave the table in tears, or he would get up in a cold, self-righteous rage. Often after he left the table we would hear him stamp and stumble up the stairs and then there would be a series of crashes and thuds."

In 1968, he wrote in his journal, "Dear Lord—who else?—keep me away from the bottles in the pantry. Guide me past the gin and the bourbon. Nine in the morning. I suppose I will succumb at ten; I hope to hold off until eleven." He went further into his world of real and imagined dream girls, beautiful women who were easy to adore. He wanted love and affection, and while he craved stability, he felt trapped by it.

He met Hope Lange in New York for skating and drinking and afternoons in his hotel room. At the same time, he was not beyond visiting one of the city's bathhouses for homosexual encounters. In 1969, Cheever was interviewed for *New York* magazine in his hotel room at the St. Regis. He had room service bring up two bottles, one of Scotch, one of gin, and told the reporters, "I chain smoke, I chain drink. I chain everything else. I love to drink. I'm hooked on it."

In his journal he wrote:

> I am sitting naked in the yellow chair in the dining room. In my hand there is a large crystal glass filled to the brim with honey-colored whiskey. There are two ice cubes in the whiskey. I am smoking six or seven cigarettes and thinking contentedly. When the glass is empty I fill it again with ice and whiskey and light another cigarette although there are several burning in the ashtray. I am sitting naked in a yellow chair drinking whiskey and smoking six or seven cigarettes.

Now he showed up around Ossining slurring his words. His behavior made it hard for Mary to have friends over. She hid and finally poured out the liquor, which sent him to a neighbor's for a bottle at nine in the morning. She gave it to him reluctantly, and warned him that he was beginning to look like a bum. After a dinner party, he was arrested for DUI, but claimed to the police that his only crime was driving carefully.

At the same time, his relationship with the teenage Fred grew stronger. They hiked, cooked, and swam together, but Fred also had to care for his father, and would sometimes hit him when he had been drunk for too long. Once he poured a case of whiskey down the sink. According to Susan, her father kept "a bottle in his closet, a bottle in the desk where he worked, a bottle behind the New York Edition of Henry James in the library, and, in warm weather, a bottle outside in the hedge near the driveway."

In 1971, he heard that there were over two thousand prisoners in the Ossining Correctional Facility, known as Sing Sing, and only six teachers. This led him to offer a class in creative writing at the local prison for the next two years. "I get along wonderfully with murderers," he wrote. The small, tweedy man made quite an impression on the inmates in his care.

One was Donald Lang, who had been in jail for seventeen years. When he was released in December, Cheever was there to meet him. He lived with the Cheevers for a year and learned social survival skills, as well as lessons in writing. In exchange, Lang told Cheever story after story of prison life and survival, physical and emotional. This information would play an important role in one of his most important works.

If teaching gave him a chance to renew himself, he was worn through in another way: "I was tired of drinking scotch for breakfast, tired of worrying about money this late in life, tired of making love in motels to men and women I'll never see again." In 1973, he was felled by what looked and felt like a heart attack. He refused to go to the hospital until his family gave him a cigarette.

Once there, they found his attack was actually a pulmonary edema, a flooding of his lungs resulting from heart failure. He was unable to drink while in the hospital, and soon suffered painful withdrawal and DTs. Hallucinating heavily, he believed his room was a Russian prison camp and that he was being interrogated. When Susan showed him a review of his newest book, he waved it away, convinced it was a confession he was supposed to sign.

When he came to, the doctors made it clear that drinking would kill him. While he did quit for a short time, he rejected the idea of Alcoholics Anonymous. He soon visited the University of Iowa, appearing at its famous Writers' Workshop. There he met writers Frederick Exley and Raymond Carver, both known for their outrageous drinking habits. Soon he was hanging outside the liquor store in the morning, waiting for it to open.

He slept with students, both male and female. Some acted as his caretaker, making sure he got to class and ate from time to time. Even his platonic relationships were intense. He told them that his drinking was Mary's fault, that she didn't love him enough. It may be that he believed this, but he certainly didn't give much credit to cause and effect.

Back home in Ossining, he was supposedly at work on a new novel, but he mainly drank. Now there were glasses of whiskey before breakfast, and he passed out during the cocktail hour. He was increasingly sarcastic and mean-spirited with others. His son Fred was his lifeline, and now Fred threatened to move out unless he quit drinking. He tried, and went so far as to seek treatment at a hospital, but the cure was short lived. Instead, he headed for Boston and a job teaching at Boston University. It was a de facto separation from his marriage.

He arrived with three suits, two pairs of shoes, and little else. The school provided him with an apartment; he hinted that they should also throw in an intimate partner. Mainly, he turned to students for friendship, drinking companions, and handlers. Despite being estranged, Mary visited from time to time to clean his apartment and make sure there was food, although he rarely ate. One night local police found him on Boston Common sharing the bottle of a homeless man.

He was disturbed when he heard of the suicide of fellow BU faculty member Anne Sexton. "I shall miss Anne Sexton. We were really the only professionals on the scene and she always carried a bottle of vodka in her bag. When things got dim she would gracefully spike my drink." His teaching suffered more and more, and at last it became a challenge for him to walk to school at all.

His diet, when he ate, consisted of hamburgers and oranges, washed down with double vodkas. Writer John Updike came to his apartment one night and was met in the stairwell by a nude and unconcerned Cheever. He told his doctor that he was not a drunk, even though he could no longer light his own cigarettes, and sometimes he had to get to his apartment by crawling on all fours. There was a price for a life without restraints, and it was killing him.

Although he had plenty of money, actually paying his bills was too difficult, and his utilities were eventually shut off. He was found by his brother Fred. Several times in the past, Cheever had helped Fred when he was in the grips of alcohol. Now Fred was sober, and he checked his younger brother into the detox unit of a hospital. After withdrawal, and another inevitable bout with DTs, he entered Smithers Alcoholism Rehabilitation Unit in New York for a twenty-eight-day program.

It was housed in a mansion formerly owned by songwriter Billy Rose, but the inmates were far from pampered. Mary tried to find him a more relaxed institution, but he decided to stay on with the working and middle class drinkers. "Half the time I know why I'm here; half the time I don't," he wrote.

At first he continued to deny that liquor was a problem for him. He had no intention of dropping his "John Cheeverdom," and he high-hatted his fellow patients. One day he told his doctor that he could write just as good drunk as sober. His recovery began when she asked him if he could understand it the next day. He started to do the work, but with seemingly so little enthusiasm that his doctors had little faith in his future sobriety. They were wrong. When he checked out, he was twenty pounds lighter, and never had another drink in his life.

Adjustment was far from easy, but so was the alternative. In his journal he wrote that to go from continuous drunkenness to total sobriety was a violent wrench. He also gave up prescription drugs, although he continued to smoke. He didn't know where he fit in with his neighbors' heavy partying, but soon threw himself into hiking, swimming, gardening, and a new novel.

Regular meetings of AA were important to him. Although he would always keep a little distance—some Yankee reserve—he went on to devotedly help others stay on the wagon, both in his groups, and in the literary community; he talked Truman Capote into the program. Unfortunately, Capote relapsed shortly after, and became a tragic figure.

During the late 1970s, Cheever often toured college campuses as a visiting writer, and mentored young students. In looking for love, he turned more and more to gay encounters. He speculated to himself that while he wanted affection and sex, feminine complications were too cumbersome at this time of his life. He also acknowledged that he might be looking for the love of his brother Fred, who died in 1976. At the same time, he scorned the gay scene, and feared how ridiculous (he imagined) he would look if he came out at his age.

His last novel was published in 1976. *Falconer* was a strange, almost mystical book, about prison life. It was a beautiful saga of a man with an addiction, who goes to jail when he kills his brother, and finds redemption after learning kindness through an affair with another prisoner. It is hardly a biographical work, but his story runs through it.

Harvard University honored him with a degree in 1978, saying he was a "master chronicler of his times, he perceives in the American suburb a microcosm of the divisions, tensions, and incongruous ecstasies of twentieth-century life." The next year *The Stories of John Cheever* appeared, seven hundred pages of his collected stories. Nine hundred copies sold at a single book signing. It won him the Pulitzer Prize and National Book Critic's Circle Award, as well as a nomination for the National Book Award. It also made him wealthy.

Sex was just as important to Cheever as ever, probably more, and he was plagued with a sense of loneliness. In spite of his unhappiness with Mary, he decided to stay with her. Susan Cheever, who sometimes wished they would divorce, wrote, "Maybe it was habit that kept them together, maybe it was perversity, maybe it was love—a kind of love so different from what we mean by love these days that there should be another word." He beat his alcoholism, but the desire was still there, like an amputated limb. "When it grows dark I would like a drink," he confessed, but he continued on with AA and resisted. One night in 1980, he slumped over in a convulsion, which turned out to be a small but frightening stroke, which was followed by a second one six weeks later. Mary came to his side to care for him, and they found themselves friends again.

Early in 1981, he underwent surgery for his prostate and in July doctors removed his right kidney, but it was cancer and it had spread. He steadily lost weight, but his spirits were good. He wrote Fred, "Your mother's love, her thoughtfulness and her practical help have been quite indescribable."

"I got an intelligent nurse to see that my door was kept closed from six o'clock on so that I could do my vomiting in private." To Philip Roth he wrote, "I have been attacked by a nuisance of a cancer. My veins are filled, once a week with a Neapolitan carpet cleaner distilled from the Adriatic and I am as bald as an egg. However I still get around and am mean to cats."

Some days were better than others. He wrote Fred, "Towards dawn I felt that I was at long last John Cheever. For all I know I may be." He reminded his son that "[t]he only fatherly advice I have ever given you is not to eat your peas off a knife." He seemed determined to go out as a gentleman, always wore a suit to the hospital, and made jokes about his weakness and baldness. "I say this to the dogs while I drink my coffee and it is perhaps their imperturbability that leads me to ask," he wrote. "Whatever made me think that I would live forever?"

In April, his first grandchild was born. Soon after he was awarded the National Medal for Literature, and although he had to use a cane, he came onstage to accept the award. John Cheever died on June 9, 1982. He did not seem afraid. A flag draped his coffin, and flags in Ossining flew at half-mast.

On the verge of his own end, he had written that he was sure he was coming back as a dog. "I can't keep a journal when I return because I'll return as a labrador retriever. Didn't you know?" He dreamed that a canine council had decided to allow it. He wrote of seeing his favorite dog in the next world. "I expect we will renew our connection later."

PART TWO

LOST SOULS:
WILD TALES OF WOE

Jean Rhys

Anne Sexton

Malcolm Lowry

JEAN RHYS

DRINK OF CHOICE

❧ Whiskey

❧ Pernod

❧ Wine

"It is astonishing how significant, coherent and understandable it all became after a glass of wine on an empty stomach."

- Jean Rhys, *Quartet*

"Now the feeling of the room is different. They all know what I am. I'm a woman come in here to get drunk. That happens sometimes. They have a drink, these women, and then they have another and then they start crying silently. And then they go into the lavabo and then they come out—powdered, but with hollow eyes and, head down, slink into the street."

- Jean Rhys, *After Leaving Mr. Mackenzie*

"No place is a place to be sober in. That's what I think."

- Jean Rhys, *After Leaving Mr. Mackenzie*

In 1961, a parson in the rural English countryside of Devon was asked to look in on a troubled woman. He had heard of her, of course; she was the scourge of the neighborhood, known for her drunkenness and public brawling, but he was a kind man who did not judge. When he dropped in at her damp, mouse-haunted cottage, she told him she was writing a book but couldn't finish it, that she was stuck and miserable. He found it hard to believe that this boozy old soul was actually a writer but felt it was his duty to look for some evidence of it. Amazed, he found piles of papers all over the freezing room, tucked away in a dozen different spots. His daughter helped him gather them up, take them home, and tediously put them into some kind of order.

As the parson read on into the night, his surprise turned to astonishment. The work was good—better than that, it was great. He did not know then that it was written by one of the greatest but most completely forgotten writers of the 1930s, and that the manuscript he was looking at was destined to become one of the "100 great novels of the twentieth century." He did know that it was his duty to do what he could to help her finish the book. "She needs endless supplies of whisky, and endless praise, so that is what she must have," he said.

Jean Rhys was indeed a troubled soul. When she was drunk she was a harridan with a nasty habit of hitting other people that landed her in court time and again, and in prison more than once. She was unwilling or unable to work. Publisher Diana Athill wrote, "Her ability to cope with life's practicalities went beyond anything I ever saw in anyone generally taken to be sane." In her youth, Rhys had gone so far as to trade personal favors for money, and even in this she failed. She was too lazy to make a good courtesan.

But she wrote about her failure in such an extraordinary way. "How this hopelessly inept, seemingly incomplete woman could write with such clarity, power and grace remains a mystery," wrote Athill. Her five novels and various short stories are Rhys's accounts of her troubled world: of women who accept meals, money, and clothes from men they meet in cafes; of absinthe, Pernod, brandy and wine; of poverty and grueling disappointment. These writings, by one of the "greatest artists of self-pity in English fiction," according to biographer Carole Angier, are today considered classics, but no one in the 1930s wanted to read such sordid tales, and Rhys withdrew from the literary playing field to flounder in a nightmare life until the times caught up with her.

She was born Gwendolyn Rees Williams to a Welsh and Scottish family who settled on the island of Dominica. When she was a child, there were three hundred white people to almost thirty thousand blacks, and while slavery had been outlawed in 1834, there remained a kind of de facto slavery, a social order that made relations between whites and blacks painful and often violent.

She adored her father, a doctor who refused payment from his poorer patients. Rhys's mother was a somewhat cold Scottish woman caught in a hot tropical world she did not understand. She found her daughter to be a nuisance, and the girl grew to expect, even anticipate, her mother's criticism for being willful, moody, and absent-minded. She described herself as "a hell of a misfit."

Her black nurse, Meta, hated her white employers and took it out on the little girl. She taught her to believe in zombies, werewolves and other island monsters. "Meta had shown me a world of fear and distrust, and I am still in that world," Rhys wrote. In spite of this, Rhys wanted to be black. It was very simple: a world of mangos versus porridge, brightly colored cloths versus scratchy wool, fascinating superstitions versus a stiff, upper lip. She was attracted to the islanders and tried several times to befriend them, but her efforts were met with suspicion and rejection from the natives and mockery from her family.

Rhys loved to read and gained an early love for words and poetry. In 1904 she spent months in a local convent where she felt safe and good, but when she was fourteen, an elderly friend of the family ran his hands over her body and coaxed her with candy and flattery into a dark, mental seduction. "Mostly he talked about me, me, me. It was intoxicating." He also talked of sex and submission, and while he did not actually sleep with her, he violated her in an unmistakable way.

At seventeen, she was sent to school in England. She had heard endless stories of London and arrived with disastrously fairytale-like expectations of it. She wanted the fantasy of it so much that the reality of her maiden aunt's modest boardinghouse traumatized her. In her ignorance, she made a series of innocent blunders that were met with the kind of disapproval she had hoped to leave behind. Her pain and disappointment may have been at the heart of her lifelong anger and indifference.

School was boring and demanding, not at all to the liking of a girl from a slow and colorful world. There were so many rules that Rhys kept accidentally breaking, and her classmates taunted her, calling her "black." Her grades were poor, but she did receive compliments on a performance in a school play, which led her to try for a career on the stage.

There was one, small hitch—she wasn't any good. Acting and stagecraft were hard work and Rhys lacked the energy or discipline to make up for her lack of natural talent. Her father withdrew his financial support and attempted to bring her home. Instead, she showed the first and possibly only real initiative in her life, and found a job in a chorus line. It was the beginning of a pattern of lifelong stubbornness over situations that were patently self-destructive, of plunging into the inadvisable and refusing to budge.

This was not "The Theatre." It was a third-rate chorus but even here Rhys found her way quickly to the bottom. Like many young women she harbored the fantasy of marrying a rich or aristocratic fan. While this did happen, it was rare, and usually to women who were exceptional in the first place or who could see the rules of the game and play them like a master. Being neither, Rhys ended up touring around the rural North Country.

She roomed with other girls in a series of freezing boardinghouses, and they did their makeup in train station bathrooms. Sometimes her pay did not stretch even to these mean lodgings, and once she had to run out on a bill by leaving through the window. It was all horrible and demoralizing. One night a small-town audience walked out of the hall in the middle of the show, and Rhys, extremely upset, simply left the stage. "I haven't got what the English call 'guts,'" she wrote. It was clear even to her that she would never make a success of the theater.

In another show she met girls of a "better sort," who might actually meet and charm a gentleman, but Rhys preferred the tarts. Like her, they had been rejected by the world, and while she was startled by their coarse language and loose ways, she imitated them and made mental notes. When the beautiful Rhys finally met a man of means, they advised her to hold out for marriage, or at least an arrangement, which she refused to do.

She had been warned that Lancelot Smith, an older, well-born gentleman, went through a woman every few months, but she didn't care and became his mistress at once.

Smith wanted to help her, giving her dancing and music lessons, buying her the right kind of clothes. Mostly, however, Rhys just spent her days preparing for their evenings, dressing and doing her face for hours at a time. While Smith enjoyed Rhys's company, he could not marry her, and two years into the affair, he went on a long business trip and broke the affair off by letter. She never got over the fact that he made her accept a payoff allowance through a lawyer. "The whole earth had become inhospitable to her after the shock of that humdrum betrayal," wrote a friend.

She ran away in a heartbroken fury, and began her real decline into the seedy life that is synonymous with her writing. A friend got her a job as a "masseuse," where her work involved something less than sex, but where she was still encouraged to kiss and touch customers for money. She gave herself to the first man who wanted her, and then to a series of men, trying to exorcise Smith's memory. "I'm finding out what a useful thing drink is," she wrote.

In early 1913, she found herself pregnant and may not have known who the father was. In her despair, she turned to Smith for help. Genuinely grateful to find her safe, he sent her to the country to rest and wait for the baby's arrival. His cousin interfered, and at his instigation Rhys had an abortion. It was a dangerous and harrowing operation five months into the pregnancy. While Smith paid for her care and pampered her while she recovered, she knew a friendship between them was hopeless. Sick and thin, unable to work, she sat staring into space for hours, crying or sleeping for fifteen hours at a stretch. It hurt her deeply to take checks from Smith's lawyers, but she did it. On Christmas day, she decided to drink a bottle of gin and jump from her window but a friend convinced her that it wasn't high enough to do sufficient damage, so they got drunk instead.

One day Rhys saw some colored pens in a shop window. They were pretty and seemed to call to her, so she bought a bunch and some notebooks to go with them. That night something came over her and she wrote it all down: Lancelot Smith, the men, the failure, the humiliation. She worked for days, writing and crying, filling notebook after notebook, and when it was all down, she did not look at it again for ten years.

During World War I she was able to live off of an allowance from Smith, and volunteered her time at a local canteen. She had affairs with soldiers, more out of pity than need of finances. Most of her nights were spent at a bohemian nightclub called the Crabtree where she joined the demimonde of artists and writers and beautiful women on the make, talking and plotting over absinthe. Many men there were attracted to her, but she always chose the wrong ones.

In 1917, she was living in a cheap boardinghouse where she met Jean Lenglet, a fellow lodger. He took her to lunch and bought her perfume and cigarettes; when he did not try to kiss her in return, she was mystified. He was handsome, self-confident, and a good talker and they were comfortable together. They married, although unknown to Rhys, Lenglet already had a wife at home in Holland.

After the war, they found themselves in Paris with no money and a baby on the way. Lenglet set about finding a way to pay for a hotel; Rhys didn't really want to know where it came from. In her novel *Good Morning Midnight*, her account of this time, she wrote, "He brings out a mille note, a second mille note. I don't ask where he got them. Why ask? Money circulates; it circulates…"

She got a job teaching English to the children of a rich family. The Richelots were kind and pampered her, and Germaine Richelot, the children's aunt, became Rhys's friend and patron for years. When she had her baby, it was in a charity ward, after a long and painful labor. Never did the consequence of her "near-idiocy in practical matters" (again, Diana Athill) have a more tragic consequence than now. She placed her newborn son in a basket by a drafty, balcony window in the middle of winter. "This damned baby, poor thing, has gone a strange color and won't eat, and I don't know what to do, I'm no good at this," she wrote. In three weeks he had pneumonia.

They took the baby to a hospital for the poor, left him, and returned to their flat. Rhys was upset, and Lenglet tried to calm her down by going out for two bottles of champagne. They drank, and after the first bottle she felt better and was laughing. The next morning the couple discovered that their baby had died during the night. Her startling lack of remorse or responsibility is partially explained in *After Leaving Mr. Mackenzie*: "When you've had a baby, and it dies you're indifferent—because the whole damned thing is too stupid to be anything else but indifferent about."

The Richelots helped Lenglet get a job as a secretary for an international commission working in post-war Vienna. In 1920, it was a bright and glittering place, and for a year they lived in a huge, old-world apartment. Rhys, with her huge, dark eyes and mysterious air, was often the center of attention at the parties and functions they attended. In 1921 they moved into a grand hotel suite, and Rhys had a maid, a car, and beautiful clothes. "Good to have money, money. All the flowers I wanted. All the compliments I wanted. Everything,

everything." There was a cost, however, and it was Rhys's unwillingness to press Lenglet about where he got so much money.

One day he came home visibly nervous and begged her not to talk to any men that might drop by. He finally admitted that he had been working the black market with the Commission's money and had been discovered. He wanted to shoot himself, but Rhys talked him into running away, and they slipped from their hotel without notice.

They went to Brussels where in 1922, Rhys had a daughter, Maryvonne. Although her brother offered to adopt the girl, Rhys insisted that she raise her baby. Unfortunately, she had no money and Lenglet was in jail, so the baby lived in clinics paid for by Germaine Richelot, until she was old enough for boarding school.

Rhys tried, in her fashion, to get work. Employed as a dress model, she lived again in a twilight world of beautiful women and their male admirers, but even this did not suit her and she quit after a few months. Hoping to sell some of Lenglet's writing, she contacted Sheila Adam, a journalist she had known before the war. Instead, Adam, who knew something of Rhys's former life, wanted to see her journals. There she found the chronicles of Rhys's precarious existence living off men and their money, and Adam knew it was good. She helped Rhys fashion it into a novel, then gave it to her friend Ford Madox Ford.

When Rhys met Ford, he was an important editor and novelist with a weakness for damsels-in-distress. He found the pale and beautiful writer in the shabbiest of apartments, her husband in prison, with no food and only the cheapest of clothes. She grabbed his hands and kissed them while fervently begging him to help her. Ford took her home to be cared for by his wife, who recognized Rhys's genuine desperation, but also saw too clearly a complete absence of any desire for independence.

Soon Ford and Rhys were engaged in a messy affair under the nose of Ford's wife. It was a disaster. Rhys soon resented Ford's attempts at discretion that made her feel cheap, and soon enough, Ford's eye wandered to a frailer, wispier damsel. He still, however, believed in Rhys as a writer. He taught her how to edit, streamline, compose, and it was Ford who changed her name from Gwen Rees Williams to the more modern-sounding Jean Rhys. He also published her work in his review and wrote an introduction for her first collection of stories, *The Left Bank*, which he helped to get published in 1926.

Reviews were good, but sales were poor. Rhys was now drinking up to three bottles of wine a night, during the course of which she went from delicate to drunk, from quietness to cursing rage. When Lenglet got out of jail, she joined him in Amsterdam. One night Rhys flung her affair with Ford in her husband's face, and he walked out on her. She was soon starving, living on one croissant a day and any wine she could get on credit. She again considered suicide, but got drunk instead, walking up and down the street and taking a brandy and soda at every other café. Ford sent her some money, which she accepted but bitterly resented.

Her mother died in London in 1927. Rhys hustled up enough money to go to the funeral, then spent most of it on new clothes. On arrival she canvassed all of her family for money, which they simply couldn't spare. She almost missed the funeral, and when she did show up, she screamed unjust accusations at her sisters.

She again approached Smith for money. He had remained dependable through the years, but now he was wary of this woman who was forty, drunk, and destitute. He gave her twenty pounds with the clear understanding that it was to be the last. With nowhere to go, Rhys moved in with Leslie Tilden Smith, her literary agent, who she had met through Ford. Tilden Smith was impressed with her talent and work and wanted to help her while she was in London.

Despite his faith, her novel *Quartet*, published in 1928, received dismal reviews. Like *The Left Bank* it was recognized to be well-written, and critics admired her lean style, her gift for showing rather than telling, her brilliant nuance. But they rejected the story of an unapologetically amoral woman. How could they applaud a book by and about a woman who is honest about her willingness to live through near-prostitution, humiliation, and the degradation of poverty?

When Maryvonne was six, she joined her mother at Tilden Smith's. It was one of the few times the girl lived with her mother and it was a disaster. While Rhys wanted the love of a child, she had no intention of doing any of the work or accepting any of the responsibility. Maryvonne would never forget that Tilden Smith tried to be kind to her when her mother was too drunk or too busy to spend time with her. Soon she was back in Amsterdam, where she was shuttled between her father's friends and boarding school.

Rhys was working on *After Leaving Mr. Mackenzie*. Released in 1931, it is the story of her dismal return to London for her mother's funeral and her final parting from Lancelot Smith. It is a truly incredible, unflinching work, an account of what it's like to squeeze old flames for money and of the squalid rooms and cheap, pretty clothes it pays for.

> In her mind she was repeating over and over again, like a charm: "I'll have a black dress and hat and very dark grey stockings…I'll get a pair of new shoes from that place in the Avenue de l'Opera. The last ones I got there brought me luck. I'll spend the whole lot I had this morning. It seems a mad thing to do, but I don't care."
>
> (Rhys, *After Leaving Mr. Mackenzie*)

Still, it remains a story of a woman who insists on playing the role of victim and will not make even the smallest effort to redeem herself. Again, the literary world was not ready for such an unsympathetic woman, no matter how profound the writing was.

Tilden Smith's literary agency failed and in 1933 he went bankrupt; the only work he could get was as a freelance publisher's reader. The couple was destitute and through the years moved from one horrible room to another, always cheaper, always a step down. Rhys started beating Tilden Smith, who was too gentle to fight back. She loved him and leaned on him, but hated him for being nice and for disapproving of her.

His disapproval of her violence and alcoholism in no way diminished his devotion to her. He edited and typed her manuscripts and tried to sell them to publishers. He did the housework—shopping and cooking—and came up with whatever money they had. When she told him she couldn't write in London, he borrowed money from his family to send her on a succession of trips to Paris, the countryside, or the beach to work.

In 1933, she divorced Lenglet and married Tilden Smith. Her third novel, *Voyage in the Dark*, came out in 1934. It is an account of a teenage girl from the West Indies who becomes a chorus girl in London. It describes her life from her first love affair with a wealthy man to her descent into prostitution when he rejects her. More notably, it features an illegal abortion. While this meant the book had even less of a chance with nervous male critics, Rhys was beginning to have a few fans.

One was novelist Rosamond Lehmann, who had a telling series of encounters with Rhys. The two writers arranged to meet. Lehmann, having read Rhys's frank accounts of sex, compromise, and the often painful consequences of both, was a bit surprised to be met by a dignified, middle-aged Rhys in a suit and gloves. She hardly seemed like the fallen woman Lehmann had secretly hoped to meet. When they met again, however, Rhys had an unexplained black eye, and on their third, and final, meeting Lehmann came to tea and found her lying on the couch, drunk and incoherent.

In 1935, Tilden Smith's father died and left him a substantial legacy, one that would amount to over $300,000 in today's currency. The money could have bought the couple modest security for the rest of their lives, instead, Rhys insisted on a trip to Dominica, her first in thirty years. She blew everything on a momentary illusion, on beautiful clothes and passage on a fine ship. On the island she explored old haunts and acquaintances or sat in the sun and drank rum. They traveled on to New York, spending outrageously on first-class passage, more clothes, and expensive hotel suites. In a few months the money had run out and they made their way back to London, where Leslie's sister had to pay their rent on a cheap apartment.

In 1937, Rhys was writing again, feverishly and distressed. Tilden Smith had given her a copy of *Jane Eyre*, and it gave her an idea for a story. She wrote the first half of the book quickly but one night during an argument she burned the manuscript in the fireplace. She grew paranoid and angry and threw Tilden Smith's typewriter out the window during another drunken fight.

Her fourth novel, *Good Morning, Midnight*, was released in 1939. When it too was rejected by the critics, Rhys gave up. Maryvonne, now sixteen, joined the Resistance with her father, and Tilden Smith joined the RAF, but Rhys simply went to pieces. In a pub in 1940, she began yelling out her hatred of the English, becoming so hysterical that an onlooker threw water on her. It all ended up in the papers. In 1941 she made up her face and put on a favorite dress, then washed down a bottle of pills with a bottle of whiskey. She was found in time.

She stood up in English pubs shouting "Heil, Hitler!" when other patrons rubbed her the wrong way. These kinds of antics lost Tilden Smith his rank. He was demoted, forced to leave his post, and soon resigned. He tried to find work again as a publisher's reader, but in the days of paper rationing, those jobs were rarer than ever.

The couple moved to the lonely moors of Dartmoor, where they had loud fights. Rhys wrote that she was "ill and the strain smashed me up sometimes. Especially as I was trying to write." One day Tilden Smith had pains in his chest and arm. Rhys's accounts of what followed vary: she told his daughter that she was trying to find a telephone to call a doctor when he died. She told her own family that she had been sitting in the next room, having a drink and a cigarette.

Her brother made the arrangements for the funeral. He brought Rhys to his home to live but she made terrible scenes there, tying herself to the bed if anyone tried to get her up, and having screaming fits. When she was well enough, she moved to London and appealed to a cousin of Tilden Smith's for help. Max Hamer was soon under the spell of the helpless Rhys, so much so that in 1947 he divorced his wife of thirty-five years.

Trying to make money, Hamer fell in with the schemes of a slick criminal. Rhys knew that he was up to something, and she used this as an excuse to drink and fret. At fifty-six, she was paranoid and imagined—perhaps rightfully—that the neighbors were watching her. She threw a rock through someone's window and was forced to face a magistrate, though she showed no remorse. Near the end of 1948, the couple was forced to take in boarders. When Rhys slapped one of her tenants, the police were called, so she bit the officer and called him a dirty Gestapo.

Although she was taken into the station, she was soon released. Returning home without her key, she climbed in through the window and fell fifteen feet to the floor to find her boarders staring at her. She hit them again and barred the front door, so that they could not leave and call the police. This time the court ordered a psychiatric evaluation, which amazingly showed little except hysteria. She proved the diagnosis true by yelling and crying in the witness box during her next hearing. She was sentenced to Holloway Prison, but it was a short stay, and she was soon released on two years probation.

One day she saw an advertisement in the newspaper: "Jean Rhys (Mrs. Tilden Smith)…Will anyone knowing her whereabouts kindly communicate with Dr. H.W. Egli, 3 Chesterfield Gardens, N.W.3." Dr. Egli was the husband of Selma vaz Diaz, an actress who wanted to produce a version *Good Morning, Midnight*, but no one could find Rhys to gain the necessary permission. Her publishers were unaware of her whereabouts, and the BBC, looking into the matter, decided she was dead. Vaz Diaz checked death certificates to no avail; the newspaper ad was her last hope.

The attention was a balm to the weary Rhys. Her neighbors, however, thought the whole matter crazy and refused to believe that this horrible, contentious old woman could be a lost writer of any import. One neighbor wrote the BBC that Rhys was an old woman "impersonating a dead writer named Jean Rhys," prompting Rhys to observe that it was "a weird feeling being told you are impersonating yourself. You think: perhaps I am!"

Like Rosamund Lehmann, van Diaz initially found Rhys "so *gentle* and *quiet*—Not at all what I expected." Rhys wrote, "I gathered afterwards that she expected a raving and not too clean maniac with straws in gruesome unwashed hair. Maybe I should have played it that way." She would soon, when she was arrested a few days later, wandering around the road in her nightgown, stopping cars and waving a letter from the BBC. The laughter of locals enraged her, and she attacked one of them again. In January 1950, Rhys was involved with the police three separate times and was in court twice in the same month.

In May, the "smash" she had been expecting came. Hamer was caught and eventually jailed for stealing and cashing checks from his employer. Rhys waited for him in Maidstone, a dreary town where "Nobody wears red shoes." Living on her own in a room in a pub, she managed to quit drinking and started to write again. She may have given up on critical acceptance but she was convicted with the feeling that "If I stop writing my life will have been an abject failure. It is already to other people. But it will be an abject failure to myself. I will not have earned death."

When Hamer was released in March 1952, he was seventy and frail. They moved to London where they lived in terrible squalor. Life became a succession of dreary, uncomfortable rooms and just hanging on. Finally they moved to a small house in Cheriton Fitzpane, the heart of Devon, where Rhys was to live for the rest of her life.

In 1957, after a new radio presentation of *Good Morning, Midnight*, a little attention came her way again. This time she was offered a tiny advance on her new novel, *The First Mrs. Rochester*, which was to be her version of *Jane Eyre*. The book, eventually renamed *Wide Sargasso Sea*, would draw on Rhys's West Indian experiences and tell the story of the doomed, first wife of the Brontë novel.

It would still be years before the new work appeared. Drink, poverty, and caring for Hamer took all of her time and energy. She did not tell her young editors about her pathetic straits, or if she did, it was in letters that made it seem like a joke. What they didn't realize was that it was "One day drunk, two days hangover as regular as clockwork."

For the next eight years Rhys would try to sell some writing and work on her novel. The first draft was finished in 1959, and she continue to work with bottles at hand, putting it away to be revised carefully when she felt she was sober enough.

A few stories were sold, and she made money from a radio broadcast. Her new literary friends tried to help with small amounts of cash and wild amounts of praise and encouragement. It was about this time that Rhys and her manuscript were discovered and aided by Parson Woodard.

In 1961, Hamer went to live in the hospital. Rhys was able to write more but she was terribly lonely. She relied on the attention and letters of a few fans to keep her going. This partially explains why in 1963, she signed over extraordinary rights of her work over to Selma vaz Diaz: half of all of Rhys's past and future dramatizations, and all of the artistic control over them would now belong vaz Diaz. Rhys often tried to explain that she had been tipsy, calling her dilemma the "Adventure of the Drunken Signature," but this does not explain why she signed a formalized agreement drawn up by vaz Diaz' lawyer years later.

Rhys grew more bitter. She sought charity yet loathed it, hurling unimaginable ingratitude to those who tried to help her. In 1964, she was alone in the uncomfortable cottage, drinking steadily, writing and worrying. She had another breakdown and attacked one of her neighbors. This time her brother was forced to commit her to a hospital for a month. When she returned to the house it was freezing, and there were icicles in the bathroom. "So nothing but whisky to help and now it's time for another shot and another effort," she wrote.

That summer she was in London editing her novel when she had a heart attack. After she recovered, she insisted on going home where she spent the next few months alone. She hated intrusions on her privacy, yet constantly cursed the fact that no one visited her. In March 1966, she finished the book that had taken up so much of her life. To be done with it at last was a relief but also unnerving. She drank to fill the gap. "Whisky is now a must for me," she wrote.

A little more money was now coming in from grants and other literary sources. Help also came in the form of the "Rhys Committee," a retinue of literary agents, young publishers, interns, and various admirers who conspired to care for her in her last years. Sonia Orwell, literary philanthropist, widow of George, and herself no slouch in the anger and drinking department, took Rhys under her wing and spoiled her with winter vacations and other treats. She bought her pretty clothes, salon treatments, and champagne. It was wonderful but made returning to the old cottage that much harder.

Social mores had changed, and Rhys's early novels were reissued to acclaim. There were also new short stories. Prizes were coming in, as were money and respectability, attention, interviews, and filmmakers. *The London Times* called her a twentieth century master. But as her star rose, so did her anger. The fame had come too late, even if it was her own fault. The near constant attention that she had now was never enough, and only created a counterpoint where she perceived abandonment. The more her Committee gave, the more she demanded and damned them for letting her down.

She believed that Maryvonne was plotting against her somehow. More and more she treated her daughter with the anger she reserved for the people who disapproved of her. She hurled abuses at her during their visits but always wrote pathetically apologetic letters afterwards. The whole ordeal caused Maryvonne to call her mother "vicious and monstrous."

She pretended to be confused when she was faced with the slightest bit of responsibility, claiming that she did not know how to change the channel on her radio or use a telephone. Helplessness became a way to get attention, to manipulate, and to take life out on others. She had to believe that she couldn't do things, because if she could, then why had she been unable to save herself?

In the 1970s Rhys received a multitude of awards and grants. In 1973 *The New York Times Sunday Book Review* said she was the best living English novelist. She continued to publish short stories, selling five to *The New Yorker* in 1976. She was invited to Buckingham Palace, and in 1978 was awarded a Commander of the Order of the British Empire.

Her behavior became simply unacceptable. "The many years of fear and lies and drink and anger had twisted her," wrote David Plante, a member of the Rhys Committee. She spat, cursed, screamed, kept her caretakers up all night, while claiming that her friends were keeping her incarcerated in a hellhole. She alternately cringed from and begged for attention and saw plots in the most innocent and well-meant care, her litany of self-pity and complaints issued through smeared mascara and lipstick.

In 1977, the Committee arranged for a last trip to Vienna. She was wined, dined, and cared for with clothes and make-up. Early in 1979, she was so ill that she at last went to a nursing home, and soon she had to be admitted to a hospital. One of her young friends who had endured so much at her hands came by to visit, and softly sang "Je ne regrette rien." She died a few hours later.

ANNE SEXTON

DRINK OF CHOICE

🐦 Traveled with a thermos of martinis.

🐦 Her daughter wrote that the stinger
was "one of Mother's favorite lethal
postprandial libations." A stinger is two
parts brandy to one part crème de menthe,
served up.

"This August I began to dream of drowning. The dying / went on and on in water as white and clear / as the gin I drink each day at half-past-five."

- Anne Sexton, "Imitations of Drowning"

"Where others saw roses Anne saw clots of blood."

- Sexton's niece in a letter

Nice people didn't talk about things like masturbation in the 1950s, especially if the masturbator was a woman. They certainly didn't write about anything as shameful as their stay in a mental hospital:

> the kingdom of the crazy and the sleeper.
> There is blood here
> and I have eaten it.
> (Sexton, "For the Year of the Insane")

Topics like menstruation, adultery, and abortion were simply not fit topics for something as fine as poetry. For Anne Sexton, that was just too bad. She would say to an audience, "I'm going to read a poem that tells you what kind of a poet I am, what kind of a woman I am, so if you don't like it you can leave." They never did.

Sexton was born in 1928, squarely into the upper, middle class of Newton, Massachusetts. Her parents loved a good party. They were young and gorgeous, and they clearly preferred their own company to that of their three daughters. Fortunately there was a large extended family that provided Sunday dinners and family vacations for the girls, and it wasn't bad.

Her mother, Mary Gray, attended Wellesley in an era when few women went to college. She quit in her junior year to marry Ralph Harvey, a charming, handsome self-made man. He was strict about clothes and appearances and expected his children "to stay on the *qui vive* girls," meaning they should always be prepared to be on. Anne, his youngest, was untidy and did not always meet his expectations.

She competed with her sisters for her parents' limited attention and felt she never got enough. Her aunt Nana, who had once been a writer, lived with the family and spoiled her with games and trips to the movies. As Nana got older her health declined and somehow Sexton blamed herself for the rest of her life, with the kind of guilt that hallmarked her later mental illness. Being sick was a way of being loyal to Nana's memory.

In the 1940s, her father began drinking heavily and when drunk, his buoyant wit was replaced with mean-spirited criticism. He mocked Sexton and said he couldn't stand the sight of her when her skin was broken out. She was sent from the table for the pettiest of reasons. Her mother also drank. In later years Sexton would joke that, like her mother, she preferred to be called "drunk" rather than "alcoholic."

In her teens, Sexton was popular and the captain of the high school cheerleading squad. She drank Singapore Slings, smoked, and danced with boys in her country club set. She also began to write poetry but her mother who was intensely competitive and possibly jealous, claimed Sexton's poems were too good to be her own work. She sent them to an expert for examination hoping to prove they had been plagiarized. The gesture wounded her daughter and she stopped writing, but soon Sexton had another thing on her mind: getting a boy to talk diamonds.

She was already engaged to one boy when she met Kayo Sexton in 1948. His father was a successful businessman who drank too much, and by his teens Kayo had considerable experience in keeping up appearances. Anne and Kayo were writing letters to each other before they actually met. When they did, it was love at first sight. They began an affair, and a month later Sexton wrongly believed she was pregnant. On their way to get married she got her period. They were, however, in love and they had a license, so they carried on with the ceremony.

At first Kayo returned to college, but he didn't want his parents to support him so he quit school and got a job. The young Sextons lived with his family while they saved for a house. Sexton worked occasionally as a model, but mainly she did as little as possible and spent many of her days in bed, to the dismay of her mother-in-law. She had been married little over a year, when Sexton fell desperately in love with another man. Her mother made her break it off and Sexton took her first overdose of sleeping pills. She was found and threw them up before much harm was done.

After their daughter Linda was born in July 1953, Kayo went to work for Sexton's father. Working for Ralph Harvey was problematic. The older man was subject to fits of temper, and he played mental games. While Kayo was a good salesman, that part of his job kept him on the road for weeks at a time which was hard on Sexton, especially after their second daughter Joy was born. She did, however, have lots of help from Kayo's parents, who doted on their grandchildren.

At twenty-seven, Sexton wasn't doing very well. She had a two-year-old, and a newborn and she simply couldn't cope. When Kayo was away she had anxiety attacks and endless crying jags, and she was terrified of leaving the house. She continued to degenerate, even after taking medication for postpartum depression, and was often oblivious to her daughters' most basic needs, like food. Sometimes she would slap, and even choke, Linda to stop her crying.

Soon she was afraid to be alone with the girls. Ralph Harvey felt that his daughter's breakdown was a sign of weakness, but he supplied a part-time housekeeper, while the Sextons paid for a psychiatrist. Baby Joy was raised by both sets of grandparents for months at a time while three-year-old Linda lived with a series of relatives, ending up with Sexton's sister, whose alcoholic uncle abused her. In an interview with biographer Diane Wood Middlebrook, Linda Sexton said, "I was exiled from my childhood home to make room for someone else: Mother's mental illness, which lived among us like a fifth person."

Linda lived in a vague terror that it was she who made her mother sick and that it was her fault Sexton might die, a prediction that almost came true when Sexton took an overdose of Nembutal in 1956. Joy still lived with her grandmother Billie, who also did much of her daughter-in-law's housekeeping, which Sexton resented even while refusing to do the most simple things for her baby. "I just pretended Joy wasn't mine," she said. She wept and depended on a variety of tranquilizers for sleep; she spent hours every day masturbating.

While Anne Sexton was a woman of extraordinary selfishness, it cannot be overemphasized how limited and primitive the treatments for depression and mental illness were in the 1950s. Thorazine, one of the few medications available, was the equivalent of a chemical lobotomy, and caused an indifference to surroundings and emotions. Little wonder that it contributed to Sexton's ambivalence, and little wonder she often went off the medication, against her doctor's advice.

In 1956, she told her psychiatrist that she had no talent, except for maybe one. She believed she would make a good prostitute, and for practice she picked up man after man in a parking lot and performed oral sex in her car.

Dr. Orne suggested another idea. She was clearly creative: had she ever written anything? He recommended a class, but the prospect was too terrifying, besides, her father had refused to help with the tuition, saying that Sexton could never do the work.

In an unlikely compromise, Sexton bought a new antennae for her television so that she could pick up the local educational channel. One night a TV professor was coaching viewers in the art of the sonnet. Sexton sat up and thought, "I could do that." She took notes and that night wrote her first sonnet, then another. Dr. Orne praised her work and after another suicide attempt told her she had an obligation to live and write. By the end of the year she had written sixty poems.

Dr. Orne had a colleague at Harvard look at her poems. They suggested Sexton continue with her writing and go to college. He helped her find a poetry class at the Boston Center for Adult Education, and she enrolled with trepidation. The night of the first class she brought a friend along to hold her hand, but she went, in high heels, perfect make-up, clutching a sheaf of her work. Many of her classmates were academics with published works, but she knew right away that these were her people.

There is an almost mathematical component to poetry, one of counting syllables and rhythms, then applying the images to them. Sexton quickly found that she could do this, that she was a natural. Teacher John Holmes helped her train her already impressive poetic "muscles," while providing discipline and an education in the more formal aspects of the craft. In a few months, she won a New England Poetry Club prize for best lyric. Now Sexton had a vocation, and for the rest of her life it would come before everything else. "I'm going to aim high," she told her mother. "And why not."

She became close friends with classmate Maxine Kumin. While Kumin had the education that Sexton would always envy, Maxine was in awe of Sexton's glamour, and was impressed by her innate gift for imagery in her writing. They were both mothers of young children and understood the demands that domesticity made against art. "I'm always willing to cuddle," Sexton wrote, "but I won't bother to prepare food: there I sit. I want her to go away, and she knows it."

She needed space and commandeered the dining room, now strewn with books and papers. Poems were submitted aggressively, as many as sixty at a time and when one was finally accepted by the *Christian Science Monitor*, her family sat up and took notice. This is a good place to look at a prevailing Anne Sexton myth, the one that holds that her problems originated in her family's lack of support.

Certainly she was not helped by society's lack of expectations for women, but it was also true that she was not forced to be a mother, this responsibility landed on her relatives. She was not forced to be a housewife, as her husband did the shopping and cooking, and everyone paid for the therapists. It was more to the point that she pretended it was true. When asked to help in even the smallest way, she went to pieces. One day in a fight with Kayo, she tore up a batch of poems and threw her typewriter across the room.

They would often fight when drunk. Martini after martini held up dinner while the two of them argued. When Sexton's nastiness went too far, it was not unusual for Kayo to hit her, then the girls would have to physically push them apart and beg Daddy not to hurt Mommy.

Then Sexton would start again because in a way it's what she wanted, to be punished for her neglect. She also craved the high that came with Kayo's regret and ardent reassurances of his love, which followed his abuse.

One of Sexton's classmates was Sylvia Plath. After their workshop Sexton and Plath, with poet George Starbuck in tow, would head to the Ritz for martinis and stingers. Sexton wrote, "I would park illegally in a LOADING ONLY ZONE telling them gaily, 'It's okay, because we are only going to get loaded!'" Starbuck told biographer Wood Middlebrook, "They had these hilarious conversations comparing their suicides."

Sexton's poems were being published in important magazines. She had arrived, although secretly she feared that she was another Edna St. Vincent Millay, clever but lacking the skills that make a great poet. At the same time, she saw that being a sexy young woman in a red sweater wasn't going to hurt her career any. She wanted recognition and fame, and she was about to get it. With the publication of her first book, *To Bedlam and Part Way Back*, Sexton attracted the interest of established literary figures like Robert Lowell and Elizabeth Hardwick who gave a party in her honor.

In March 1959, her mother died of cancer, taking with her the love and approval that Sexton had pursued for so long. Her father died a few months later. In his will he reneged on a business promise made to Kayo. When she heard the news, Sexton smashed her foot through his portrait.

In one world she was a devoted wife to Kayo. Among poets, however, George Starbuck was accepted as her lover and companion. "My friend, my friend, I was born/doing reference work in sin, and/ born confessing it," she wrote. In 1960, she was pregnant. Kayo badly wanted the baby, but Sexton, secretly uncertain of its paternity, had her doctor terminate the pregnancy due to her "ill health." In the wrenching poem "Abortion" she mourns, "Somebody who should have been born is gone."

When *Bedlam* was published in 1960, it was the heyday of the confessional poet, but no one had read anything quite like these raw accounts of mental illness. It was nominated for a National Book

Award, which was unusual for a debut work. Suddenly she was in demand for readings and interviews, even though these frightened her so much that she carried a thermos of martinis to get her started.

She felt she could not be a first-rate poet without an education. "As a poet, it may be better to be crazy than educated. But I doubt it," she said. She took summer classes in modern literature and studied great books, while a lover coached her in great poetry. The crazy part got a workout too, in her readings. Her performance of poems like "Her Kind" was just that, a performance, one that traditionalists scorned and that audiences loved.

By the time her daughters were five and seven, they lived together as a family. Sexton used their childhoods to trigger feelings about her own, then turned them into poetry. She loved her daughters, but on her terms. "My feeling for my children does not surpass my desire to be free of their demands upon my emotions," she later wrote her doctor. Billie still did most of the babysitting, which Sexton accepted with bad grace. The devoted grandmother gave the girls the only security they knew in their lives.

In 1961, Sexton's mental illness continued to take its toll. She found it impossible to leave the house or cross the street without having a panic attack. She rallied when she won a prestigious Radcliff grant to study at Harvard's sister school. She was featured in *Newsweek*, and offered a first reading option with *The New Yorker*, a coveted contract that paid for the opportunity to be the first to publish any new work. Later that year she turned thirty-three and finishing her second book, *All the Pretty Things*. Unfortunately there was also another breakdown when Kayo and her psychiatrist were out of town at the same time. After dropping the girls off with a friend, she took an overdose of pills and threw them up.

The reviews for *All the Pretty Things* were powerful and positive, but Sexton floundered emotionally. That summer, she was pushing Dr. Orne too far. During their sessions she regularly went into trances called fugue states that made therapy impossible. She visited his office when she didn't have an appointment and passed out on his couch. Finally he slapped her out of one-too-many trances and told her that her neediness took him away his family and other patients. She walked out, only to call him at midnight and asked to be committed. He obliged.

All this did nothing to slow her celebrity. Her fans wrote her letters while her books sold unusually well for poetry. Her songs had a frightening way of tapping into the well of horror that resides in some psyches, the loneliness and spiritual need that are taboo in conversation. Readers were moved to find that they were not the only ones who felt this way. Demand increased for readings and television broadcasts, she won a Ford Foundation Grant, had another nomination for the National Book Award, and was offered a fellowship from the American Academy of Arts and Letters.

Sexton wrote:

> But suicides have a special language.
> Like carpenters they want to know *which tools*.
> They never ask *why build*.
>
> (Sexton, "Wanting to Die")

In 1963, Sylvia Plath, who shared what Sexton called a lust for suicide, killed herself. She told Dr. Orne, "Sylvia Plath's death disturbs me. Makes me want it too. She took something that was mine, *that* death was mine!"

At age eight, Linda was mixing and delivering her mother's martinis. When she turned nine, her mother wanted to be nine, too. Linda said that "Playing nine means that I—the real nine-year-old—slide up in the bed and she slides down, puts her head on my chest while I pat her head. 'Now you be the Mommy,' she says. 'And I'm your little girl.'" After an hour the pressure made it hard for Linda to breathe. When she asked, "Could you be thirty-four now?" Sexton began weeping and accusing the mommy-Linda of not wanting the little-girl Sexton. Sometimes she cuddled with Linda whether Linda wanted to or not, masturbating in the girl's arms. Sexton told her doctor, "Her body wants my body."

"I would lie there like a stone, pretending to be asleep, waiting for something to be over," Linda says. "I don't think I wanted to know what it was."

Sexton planned a trip to Europe with money from a fellowship. Travel terrified her and in preparation she spent an hour on the floor of Dr. Orne's office, praying in a trance. Once she was abroad with a friend to hold her hand, she loved it. She wrote Kayo passionate love letters while having an affair with a barber in Rome, reporting everything to Dr. Orne. By October, increasing panic sent her home months ahead of schedule.

On her return, she visited Dr. Orne with a stash of "kill me pills" and a razor. When she went into a trance he made arrangements for her commitment at a hospital called Westwood Lodge. There he hoped to wean her off of her addiction to pills, but she didn't want to because, "It's not that I'm killing myself but that I'm controlling myself. Also when I drink. I'd really be a mess if I quit."

After her release, Sexton became close friends with Anne Wilder. Wilder was a psychiatrist with an affinity for writers, which made her perfect for Sexton. While she lived in California, the two wrote long and enthusiastic letters and talked often on the phone. In July, Sexton had a breakdown and spent a few weeks at Massachusetts General. She was given Thorazine to control her manic excitability, but she resisted it because it made the rhymer go away. It also produced an incredible sensitivity to the sun, and this was a woman who believed that being in the sun was like "having intercourse with God." She would sometimes go off of her medication so that she could work on her tan.

Although it made her anxious, she went on another reading tour, stocked with a cache of vodka for before readings, and milk and pills for after. Traveling alone was unthinkable, so she asked Wilder to accompany her. Like anyone who went on the road with Sexton, Wilder was assigned endless duties as caretaker. The couple also began a tempestuous affair, but they drifted back to friendship on their return.

In 1966, a crew from National Educational Television spent two days with Sexton and fashioned a documentary about her life. After editing, they had a thirty-minute feature about a lady poet in the suburbs, co-starring the loving husband, doting kids, dog, swimming pool, and literary success. After her death, the remaining footage was reworked into a more realistic ninety-minute version that included drinking and ramblings about music and orgasm and their influence on her work.

Early that year she conducted an intense, but unconsummated affair with poet James Dickey. He had repeatedly criticized her work in high-profile reviews and she was determined to change his mind so she worked what she called the female con on him. They drank and talked, and she confided in him. When he asked her, "Do you sleep around?" she convinced him they were crazy enough without that. Even so, they wrote intimate letters and had drunken phone conversations where Kayo could hear. It only added to her husband's opinion that all poets were jerks.

In April she participated in a series of readings in the South. Anticipating a potential problem, she wrote the organizers that, "If Virginia is a 'dry' state [this is] to prepare you for my need of a semi-wet state before dinner and a reading." She took thirteen-year-old Linda with her on the trip, ostensibly to broaden her horizons. The girl, in reality, was forced to act as her mother's handler. She was responsible for every detail of Sexton's life on tour including the painful fallout from pills, drinking, and acting out. Linda Sexton wrote, "Later I would look back on this trip and realize that I had been there for one purpose: keeping things straight and cleaning up the mess."

A local high school teacher, Robert Clawson, invited her to teach one of his classes. It was a success, and when she attended a conference in Long Island, she asked him to accompany her. As they pulled away from the Sexton home, Kayo and the girls called out and told him to take care of Sexton, which made him wonder, "Why does she need taking care of?"

He began to find out when she made him stop a few minutes later for a six-pack. The road trip was one of trance states, a short but passionate affair, and Sexton's repeated efforts to throw herself from a ferry. Somewhere in between, she proposed. When he pointed out that they were both married, she set fire to a twenty dollar bill and hurled a bunch of poems that she claimed she had written for him.

In fact, these intensely erotic pieces had been written some time before for her new therapist. When Dr. Orne transferred to a new job, she chose a Dr. Ollie Zweizung for a replacement. Their sessions soon turned sexual and to add ethical insult to professional injury, he charged her for these sessions. No one reported him, even though several of Sexton's friends knew about the affair. Maxine Kumin, for one, was disgusted. "Imagine paying to get laid twice a week!" she said.

What was it like for Kayo, writing a check for his wife's lover twice a week? Listening to her protestations of love over the telephone? He loved her, and he believed their marriage would outlast the affairs. She made a little of it up to him by taking him on an African safari. On their return, her book *Live or Die* was released. While it was a huge success, some began to feel, legitimately, that she was limiting herself in subject matter, and of course there were others who simply had no intention of accepting a poem entitled "Menstruation at Forty."

In the fall of 1966, her therapist resolved to break off their sexual affair after his wife—and his accountant—found some of their romantic writings. Sexton was losing a lover and a therapist, and in November she punished herself by breaking her hip, an injury that involved months of excruciating recovery and resulted in a lifelong limp. On the other hand, it also allowed her to reward herself with a secretary and housekeeper and by bringing her family's responsibility for her to a new level.

In 1967, she won the Pulitzer Prize. The Poetry Society of America gave her an award for her body of work, an impressive prize for three books. Sexton was now a full-fledged celebrity and like many artists, this was the death knoll for her best work. From now on, she would rely more on her amazing imagery and less on the demanding work of formal poetry, and it would show.

For the time being, however, she was invited to read at the Poetry International Festival in London where she shared the program with living legends W.H. Auden and Pablo Neruda. Primed with vodka, she provoked Auden by deliberately ignoring her time limit. When she finished reciting, she opened her arms wide and threw her audience a kiss, a diva-like gesture that fell flat.

In English radio interviews, she tried to rewrite her past, erasing her mentors and inventing a new, improved version of her bootstrap beginnings. At her hotel, she drank and slept with fellow poet George MacBeth and toured the countryside, enjoying a handful of smaller flings with other young admirers.

In 1968, she was made an honorary Phi Beta Kappa at Harvard, a moving honor for a woman with a high school education. That fall one of her students suggested putting her poems to music. He and four other budding musicians formed the group "Anne Sexton and Her Kind" to accompany her while she read her poems.

Like all aspects of Sexton's art, you either loved it or hated it. Many, including some friends, felt that it went too far and sacrificed poetry to please a larger audience; for others that was part of the point, Sexton's willingness to reach out to another crowd. She took another chance in 1969 by writing an off-Broadway play called *Mercy Street*, a strange, supposedly autobiographical work about incest, insanity, and suicide. During the months she wrote the play, the only food she could keep down was caviar, and lots of it. When the play opened in October, the reviews were good but not great. It made the biggest impression on her family, who were devastated by so-called revelations of family crimes that had only occurred in Sexton's imagination.

The affair with Dr. Zweilung was on again and now he manipulated her, threatening her with his wife when things got too weird. She was terrified of losing him—she was in the middle of the play, had a heavy schedule of readings, and performances with Her Kind, and she needed help. Somehow she managed to make a break and began work with a new psychiatrist, Dr. Constance Chase.

Sexton, who should have been on top of the world, was rapidly sliding downhill. She did not bother with martinis anymore, instead she drank "Jack Daniels, Canadian Club or rot-gut bourbon." Chain-smoking led to a violent cough, and she usually threw up what she ate. Family dinners, such as they were, became an agonizingly protracted cocktail hour. "One night she fell straight forward and her face landed in the mashed potatoes!" Linda said. "My father would say, 'Anne, stop it, you're frightening the children.'"

Despite the outward, suburban normalness of barbeques and a swimming pool, Linda and Joy didn't dare invite friends to their house. One night Linda woke up to find her mother lying over her, kissing her on the mouth. The girl threw up and while she was terrified to reject her mother who needed so much, she made the decision to push back and make some distance.

In 1970, she won the Pulitzer Prize. She was a celebrity, a household name, and would play by her own rules now, ones that would guarantee her a bigger readership and even bigger money. From here on out, her poems would rarely be published in literary publications, while demand would grow with popular ones like *Playboy* and *Cosmopolitan*.

When Kayo lost his job in 1970, Sexton gave him the money to start his own business. They needed each other now as she took on the pressure of added touring and teaching, and he grew a new business. A teaching job at Boston University added to her fear. She enjoyed the job, but she knew that many of her colleagues resented her because she did not have a college education.

That August, she had a frightening fit of verbal and visual hallucinations and treated them with an overdose of barbiturates. When she called Maxine Kumin she was incoherent, but Maxine managed to get Joy on the phone. The girl then called Billie, who called Kayo, and they all rushed Sexton to the hospital in time to have her stomach pumped, again. Linda was not amused. "I thought Mother took a certain pride in this kind of behavior," she said. "I was getting very tired of it all. Very tired."

Sexton was at odds with her maturing daughters. For years, she had been involved in their yet-to-happen sex lives. When Linda was age nine, she fondled the girl's genitals to show her where she would feel "mating," and when the girl was thirteen she demanded to know all about her (nonexistent) masturbation habits while sharing all about her own. Linda was upset, not the least because she had been forced to witness it often enough. She pressured Linda to have sex so she could hear all the details. Not surprisingly, Linda was in no hurry. "Unlike my friends at fifteen, I didn't worry about kissing and dating—I worried about whether or not I had to sleep with someone to live up to Mother's expectations."

In her compassionate and courageous book, *Searching for Mercy Street*, Linda remembered good times as well. When she began writing her own poetry, her mother was generous and taught her everything she could. They loved to shop for books together. "There's always money for books, Linda," she said. She was proud of her daughter when she was accepted to Harvard. Sexton also openly acknowledged Linda's contribution to the popular *Transformations*; the 1971 collection of poems was based on fairy tales that Linda loved. It garnered strong sales and public acclaim, more awards, another honorary degree, and an offer to teach at Colgate College for a semester. She accepted, and chose for her course topic, "Anne on Anne."

Her latest therapist was not quite the pushover her first two had been. When Sexton wrote a cruel poem about Linda and showed it to her, Dr. Chase criticized her. When she reminded Sexton that "people come first," Sexton raged back, "the writing comes first." Maxine Kumin was worried about her: "She was writing like a fugitive one length ahead of the posse," she said.

In 1973, she asked for a divorce. The couple had grown apart. They had few interests in common, but it was also true that Sexton's fans gave her a false sense of stability. Kayo's anger didn't help. For years, he had put up with the interference of analysts and with Sexton's other men. He was the one who had written the checks so she could sleep with Dr. Zweilung twice a week for years. He admitted that he was a heavy drinker and egged on Sexton's alcoholism, but he told Wood Middlebrook, "Somebody was always paying the price of living with her. Always, it was me."

Sexton expected—and probably wanted—an explosion. This time she didn't get one. Instead Kato said only one thing before leaving, and that was, "You are crazy. You don't know what you're doing." With that the last person who could have helped her left her life. When Sexton, often drunk, started falling into trances again, Joy made an effort to stay away from home as much as possible.

A few months later, Sexton was having a frustrating affair with a married man. When he refused to leave his marriage, she took an overdose of barbiturates and vodka. She was found, treated, and released. The next night she repeated the process.

This time she was hospitalized for a month, although she was allowed to leave the hospital on Thursdays to teach her class at Boston University. For once she was less than forthcoming about herself, and told no one at school about her situation. She called both daughters several times a day, saying "Oh, God, I'm so lonely. Won't you come and see me?" She felt deserted by Linda, who refused to visit her at the hospital. "I resolved that I would not allow her to draw me down into the quicksand of her disintegration," she wrote.

Sexton was touchy, argumentative, and acted out. She was drunk from breakfast on, and it became unbearable, even to her most loyal friends, who were worn out by her tendency to drink and dial in the middle of the night, carrying on a one-way conversation in a slurred voice of self-pity. She imagined herself abandoned, but the truth was that those who cared about her did not know how to help her. At last she even alienated Dr. Chase, who abruptly terminated their treatment by saying that dealing with Sexton's demands were like a "straightjacket."

When *The Death Notebooks* was published in 1974, she gave more readings, usually preceded by five double vodkas. A new therapist tried to help her get on track and keep teaching, but every time she attempted suicide she missed a lecture. When she did make it, her teaching was increasingly wild. "It was as if she would take you down into hell with her," said one student. He also remembered a conversation they had about suicide. "She told me that the best way to kill yourself would be in the garage with the car engine running. I asked, 'Why is that they best way?' And she said, 'It's painless, it's quick, it's sure.'"

The very things that disturbed some fans and students continued to attract others. She was a cult figure who had no intention of behaving. She had started out believing that the highest compliment she could receive was "you write like a man." Now she made it abundantly clear that this was no compliment at all, and her refusal to accept society's limitations made her a totem for the women's movement.

Anne Sexton's late career is often compared to that of Judy Garland: the arsenal of pharmaceuticals tossed back with vodka; the necessity for an entourage; a vulnerability that was part of the show. It was part of what drew fans to her. "She took that audience into her heart with her frankness, humor, and spontaneity. I realized that the audience had become her family now—they were the ones who loved her without reservation," Linda wrote. Her final reading at Harvard was promoted as heavily as a rock concert. The Sanders Theatre was packed, standing room only. Sexton was fashionably and dramatically late. Although she started off a little woozy, she managed to visibly pull herself together and give her all to the audience. While it was an undeniable tour de force, Linda saw it differently and felt that "In her desire to make the audience love her she would drink so much that she would humiliate herself."

Writer David Trinidad was another witness to that final performance, and in his essay "Searching for Anne's Grave," he records, "She was a mess: drunk and on drugs. She slurred her words, wandered all over the stage. The audience was whistling and shouting, 'Anne! Anne! We love you, Anne!' Egging her on. They wanted her to act outlandishly."

She was the last woman in the world who should have lived alone, but now that Kayo was gone and her daughters were at school, that's what happened. Her friends despaired of her addictions and now when she took an overdose, she wasn't found until the next day. One night, she put on a red dress and went wading in the Charles River. A stranger found her washing down handfuls of pills with a thermos of milk, and he took her to the hospital.

Joy was lured home with a false promise of good behavior. Instead, when Sexton had an overnight guest visiting what Linda called "the obscenely revolving door into my mother's bedroom," she kicked Joy out of the house. She had increasingly volatile, childlike fits, complete with screaming. When Joy returned to school, Sexton placed personal ads in the paper, and drank with strangers in bars.

In her poem "Suicide Note" she wrote:

> So I will go now
> without old age or disease,
> wildly but accurately,
> knowing my best route,...

One October day she met with her therapist, but gave no clue of what was coming, except for one seemingly trivial gesture—she left her omnipresent cigarettes and lighter behind after the session. After meeting Maxine for lunch, she went home, put on her mother's fur coat, and took a tumbler of vodka to the garage. Anne Sexton switched on her red Cougar, turned on the radio, and waited.

MALCOLM LOWRY

DRINK OF CHOICE

🕊 Gin

🕊 Mescal

🕊 Anything he could get his hands on,
including shaving lotion, mouthwash, and
formaldehyde.

🕊 There is a cocktail named after Lowry: one
ounce tequila, one-quarter ounce white
rum, one-half ounce triple sec, and three-
quarters of an ounce lemon juice. Serve in
glass with salted rim.

"What right had she, when he had sat suffering the tortures of the damned and the madhouse on her behalf for fully twenty-five minutes on end without having a decent drink, even to him that he was anything but, to her eyes, sober? Ah, a woman could not know the perils, the complications, yes, the importance *of a drunkard's life!"*

- Malcolm Lowry, *Under the Volcano*

"Where would I be without my misery?"

- Malcolm Lowry

Malcolm Lowry was afraid. He was afraid of authority, no matter how small; of sexual inadequacy, with good reason; of certain combinations of numbers; and of his father. Most, and saddest of all, he was afraid of writing.

The publication of his first novel subjected him to charges of plagiarism. He lived in such absolute terror that it would happen again, that the popularity of his next novel, *Under the Volcano*, generally considered to be one of the great books of the twentieth century, was a torture to him. He never published another work in his lifetime, although he wrote without ceasing.

Lowry told anyone who would listen that his childhood had been one of perpetual suffering. He spoke of his mother with hatred, and his father with fear. Arthur Lowry was a successful cotton broker in Liverpool, the head of a firm that bought and sold goods in many different countries. Evelyn was an old-fashioned wife and mother in an era when it was considered normal to leave her children in the care of servants for months at a time while she traveled with her husband.

His parents' long absences were hard on the boy. He felt abandoned and often helpless in the hands of a series of nannies. At age seven he was sent to a boarding school, and between the ages of nine and thirteen, his face was disfigured by an eye infection. He would always claim that his mother couldn't stand to look at him, and would not allow him to come home at the holidays.

As a teenager, he gained a reputation as a discreet drinker and became known for an eccentric hobby—playing the ukulele, on which he composed jazz songs. One tune, entitled "Three Little Dog-Gone Mice: Just the Latest Charleston Fox-Trot Ever," was actually recorded by a band and played on the radio. When it came time for college, he surprised his family with an unlikely ultimatum.

He would enroll in Cambridge only if he could first spend a year as a sailor. For years he had loved the stories of Jack London and Joseph Conrad; now he wanted to discover life on the high seas for himself. He was delivered to the ship in a chauffeur-driven Rolls Royce, and feted on the boat by local reporters. His working class shipmates were not amused.

It took all of two days to destroy a lifetime of romantic illusions. After six months of painting coal bunkers, chipping paint, swabbing the deck, and serving meals to officers, he was only too happy to go to school. This did not, however, stop the eighteen-year-old Lowry from beginning university life with an impressive sea-swagger and a world-weary air. "When he spoke, he bellowed; when silent, he contrived to glower," wrote biographer Douglas Day.

A classmate remembered him as "fat, witty, bibulous, charming, bawdy, with a vast warehouse of a mind." His grades were poor and he barely scraped by in exams, but he was well-known for his literary pretensions and for being a character. "[H]e presented the world with a persona of a drunken sailor in a dirty sweater playing a ukulele," wrote John Davenport. Davenport, a future literary critic, was a fellow student and the editor of a campus publication that published Lowry's early stories and poems. Like many others, he was already convinced of his friend's genius.

Lowry's role in the death of a fellow student would scar him for life, and become a set-piece in his infinite theater of guilt and damnation. Paul Fitte was a friend who harbored a secret shame, probably that he was homosexual, for which he was being blackmailed. Lowry was uncomfortable with homosexuality, as well as resentful of the fact that Fitte had recently criticized his literary heroes, Conrad Aiken and Nordahl Grieg. "He hated them both," Lowry wrote, "and taking this as a spiritual affront upon myself led me to be hardhearted when I should have been compassionate."

One night, they shared two bottles of gin, and Fitte grew increasingly depressed, and announced that he was going to kill himself. Lowry's response was to help him stuff the windows of his room with rags and newspaper, and leave saying, "Now do it!" He did. At the coroner's inquest, Lowry was upbraided for his role in the death, but not charged. For the rest of his life, the anniversary of that November 15 would almost always result in a maudlin binge.

Conrad Aiken, the writer whose books played a small part in this mess, was popular with the public and critics alike; he had recently won the Pulitzer Prize. Lowry wrote to Aiken in America, introducing himself and asking if he could visit. In spite of the older writer's celebrity, he had lost everything in the crash of 1929, so that when Arthur Lowry offered him five pounds a week to care for his son, he accepted, both the visit and the fee. From the first time they met, Lowry knew that he had found a surrogate father.

Aiken was a character after Lowry's heart. Born in the American South, he also suffered a painful childhood. When he was ten years old, he discovered his parents' bodies after a murder-suicide initiated by his father. He was then raised in New England by a distant relative and grew up to be an accomplished but dark-hearted and misogynistic writer. Aiken and Lowry were delighted with each other: they drank, wrestled, and exchanged dirty jokes. To others their behavior was alternately disturbing and boring.

Aiken gave his protégé writing exercises and advice on the novel he was writing. He was disturbed, however, by the younger man's tendency to crib phrases and allusions from others, including Aiken himself. Lowry had a lifelong tendency to hysterically identify himself with another person, and so it was now. He stole passages and ideas in order to absorb Aiken, to become him. For Aiken's part, he said that he wanted to invent Lowry. They were both playing a dangerous game.

"I associated Malcolm with catastrophe," wrote Clarissa Aiken. "He might set fire to his mattress, break a leg, or damage my husband still further. Just meeting him was a calamity…" One night the two men got drunk and had a "javelin" throwing contest, using beached wood near the water's edge.

Aiken failed to release his homemade spear and followed it into eight feet of mud. When Lowry tried to rescue him, he too fell in. When two, drunken, mud covered-authors showed up for dinner three hours late, Clarissa was not amused. She wrote in her journal, "How much longer will Conrad put up with this madman?"

In the spring of 1931, Lowry was back at school, drinking and writing. He did not, however, concern himself with academics. Aware that Aiken was preparing a report for Arthur, Lowry warned, "Don't tell him that all I know of the Life and Thought of any period is that people once wore tights." That fall Arthur hired John Davenport to be his son's new caretaker. Davenport promptly put out the word that "Bar opens at 10 a.m., drinks all day to residents. Lowry *pere* pays the bill."

That fall he moved in with his parents and worked on his novel, poems, and stories. He also drank, and when drunk, turned abusive. His hours were erratic, and his behavior inconsiderate; the housekeeper was less than thrilled about cleaning up the vomit. Several times he had to be bailed out of jail.

Small wonder his father was willing to pay for him to live in London. From now on he would do whatever it took to keep his son out of Liverpool. He supported him there on the condition that Lowry collect his weekly allowance from Arthur's London firm. Lowry's fear of authority, however, and his staggering capacity for helplessness, meant that he would do anything to avoid this. Instead, he would go for weeks without funds, making an ideal situation for an endless cycle of self-pity and subsequent heavy drinking. He would allow others to clean him up or retrieve the money for him, but he refused to do either of these things for himself.

Remarkably, considering his standard level of chaos, he had finished a novel. *Ultramarine* was a story about a well-to-do young man who wants to become a sailor, only to find that the reality of sea life has a high moral and spiritual cost. He submitted his only copy to a publisher, who put it in his briefcase, which was stolen from his car. Five year's of Lowry's work was gone.

It was another good reason for an extended binge. When he came out of the haze, he found that he had once again been rescued. The year before he had stayed with a friend, who had found a rough draft of *Ultramarine* in the trash. Uneasy at Lowry's lack of caution, he fished it out and made a copy, which he now forwarded to Lowry. The book was quickly rewritten, but with a bit of carelessness that would cost him dearly. At the time, however, he simply found an agent who sold the story and got him a small advance.

In April, Arthur paid Conrad Aiken to take Lowry to Spain for a vacation. In Grenada, Lowry was out of control—rude, sly, and constantly drunk. Aiken was under a lot of strain—he had tried to commit suicide the year before—but he needed the money in order to complete his next book. He wrote his brother, "My trip to Spain wasn't a holiday by a damned sight—I was in charge of a dipsomaniac, and was paid for it."

One night Aiken spotted a young American woman in a local café. Jan Gabrial was intelligent, literate, and very pretty; she was destined to become the love of Malcolm Lowry's life. She and Lowry spent several days together, and while she initially refused a physical relationship, she was taken by his garrulous talk, his magnetism and energy. Only later did she realize that he had been drunk the whole time. As the relationship between Lowry and Gabrial grew, so did Aiken's anger. While he hated women, Aiken had fully expected to share Gabrial with Lowry. His lasting anger at being cut out would wreak havoc throughout his relationship with Lowry.

Gabrial enjoyed Lowry's company, but was far from sure about their future together. "I do adore the writer," she wrote in her journal. "Can I? feel equal devotion to the man?"

When she left Spain alone, he encouraged that devotion by letter. Gabrial did not want for suitors or proposals, but Lowry's letters were unnervingly romantic and persuasive. What she didn't know was that he was in jail again for drunkenness, and that during an argument he had threatened to kill Aiken.

Lowry was sexually inexperienced. He had a fear of syphilis that amounted to a phobia, and was painfully aware that physically he was somewhat under-endowed. When he wrote to Gabrial, he poured out a passion and desire that he was unable to show in real life, but when they met again in London, he did not even meet her at the station. After weeks of begging her to come, he was nowhere to be found. Four days later she ran into him by accident, and was unmoved by his threadbare and self-pitying excuses. On their first day in England together, he took her on an unromantic pub crawl. She bitterly came to the conclusion that he was only a "paper lover."

Given another chance, he attempted a drunken seduction, which she rejected. In the following days he stood her up time after time; when he did show up, he was drunk. She had other misgivings: "His is a strong and dominating nature, egotistical as Cain, and while he claims to love me, he wills always to be the *master*." So why did she agree to marry him? "Sober, Malcolm is funny, gentle, appealing, vulnerable, and dazzling by turns. At times he is a spellbinder...sober or drunk, his exuberance is unflagging." Common sense didn't stand a chance.

Their first intimate experience did not bode well. "Not much of a much," Gabrial confided in her diary. There, she recorded his physical shortcomings and the details of their failed lovemaking. One afternoon when she was out, he read her journals, which also included accounts of her experiences with another lover, long before they met. The journals gave him an excuse to go on an epic bender and hurl cruel accusations at his soon-to-be wife. His jealousy would be a problem throughout their relationship. On New Year's Eve they went to a party and Gabrial accepted a dance from another man. Lowry pulled them apart and knocked the man to the ground. When another guest tried to stop him, Lowry held the guest's arm over an open flame before others could get him off. Six days later, Lowry and Gabrial married.

Gabrial loved to dance and go to parties while Lowry liked to drink and talk, mainly about himself. He did not want to compete for her attention. He wanted to control her, and she had no intention of being controlled. On the other hand, they were truly in love. "Though I tried hard not to show it, I was absolutely delighted to see him…Neither of us wants to let the other go and we are miserable apart," she wrote.

Gabrial loved France, and Lowry's father paid him to enroll at the Sorbonne, which he never did. They moved to Paris, where Gabrial discovered she was pregnant.

Sadly, neither was ready for this responsibility—in both of his marriages Lowry insisted on being the child—and Gabrial agreed to his suggestion that she have an abortion. Later, he would claim that she did it without his consent, one of the many shocking lies he would spin around their life.

Gabrial went to America to visit her mother. Alone in Paris, Lowry was drunk for weeks at a time, and trashed their rooms so badly that they were evicted and sued by the landlord. His father took care of the mess, and brought his son back to England. As the weeks went by, Gabrial waited for Lowry to send her the money for her return, but received instead a series of incoherent excuses.

Lowry's parents did not know he was married. He told them now, and while Arthur was angry, he was resigned, as usual, to fixing things. Rather than bring Gabrial to Liverpool, he decided to send Lowry to her in the United States; his son's place was with his wife, and as far as possible from his parents. He met Gabrial in New York, they traveled to Provincetown, where they were very happy, swimming and talking, in love again. In spite of the fact that he was drinking, often to the point of unconsciousness, it was to remain one of the happiest interludes of their marriage.

They settled down in New York, where Lowry was hard at work on a new novel, *In Ballast of the White Sea*. Gabrial was writing stories of her own. When *Ultramarine* was published his joy was overshadowed by charges of plagiarism. He himself was aware that some of the direction and ideas for the book came from Aiken and Grieg. There was also distinct uncertainty over the haste and confusion in which he recreated the final story from the rescued rough draft. Now a third writer, Burton Rascoe, appeared and claimed that the published book contained some of his work. In a humiliating scene, he demanded that Lowry sign a confession in front of his agent. Convulsed with fear and guilt, he did.

It was part of his make-up to absorb his literary heroes; he did it consciously and unconsciously. What he actually took from others, in fact, was little more than an isolated turn-of-phrase, an unusual word, or a provocative idea that he then took and made his own. It was hardly wholesale copying, but from now on, the fear of the accusation traumatized him to the point he could not bear to publish; his very success was torture. The split desire of ambition and the desire for anonymity would tear him up.

In 1936, his drinking was out of control, and the marriage was in trouble. Gabrial was beginning to realize that, while her husband loved her, what he really wanted was "a mother who was a good lay." When drunk, he was capable of being nasty and infantile; more and more she was put in the position of apologizing to friends he insulted, and of trying to explain his behavior to others. He often verbally abused her in public.

Trying to ease the strain, they moved into separate apartments in the same building. One day while she was out, Lowry and another man came for his things and moved him out, leaving no word or letter. She searched all over the city until she found him, drunk in the other man's bedroom. Although he claimed he could remember nothing of what happened, he believed he had contracted syphilis from his host.

They both hoped that a trip to Mexico would revive their relationship. Instead, "Malcolm fell fatally in love," Gabrial wrote. "Introduced to tequila, mescal, and habanera, he embraced all three with such abandon that when it came time to leave [Acapulco], he'd disappeared." Police found him the next morning in the gutter; he told her the incident made "an interesting statement."

He looked for, and found, the darker side of Mexico: mysterious rituals, primitive beliefs, and corruption. On the pretext of collecting local color, he disappeared for days into cantinas and bars. Gabrial would search for him, always one bar behind.

Some biographers have wrongfully accused her of coldly abandoning him. In fact, even during this dangerous time, she wrote in her journal, "Nothing in life means anything to me beside my husband. He is my heart's blood...." She wanted more than anything to save him, and his genius.

This effort became almost impossible when Conrad Aiken and his fiancée arrived on their doorstep in May, 1937. It was hard enough to work and control Lowry under the best of circumstances; now the couple had permanent houseguests and were turned out of their own rooms. Aiken drank and undid all of Gabriel's efforts to keep her husband sober. Aiken did not bother to disguise his hate for her, and at every turn accused her (wrongfully) of infidelity and then poured his suspicions into her already insecure husband.

Now Lowry had the shakes so bad that he could not control his hands, so he rigged a pulley from a handkerchief tied to his hands and slung over his neck, to lift a drink to his mouth. One too many nights Gabrial watched these two literary geniuses drink themselves into oblivion, so she got on a bus headed for Mexico City. It was a matter of survival. At first, Aiken was delighted, but the first night she was gone, Lowry fell into an open sewer. Alone, with no restraints, the toxic friendship took a nasty turn. "He pretends to the deepest friendship for me," Lowry wrote, "but secretly…the only real depth in our relationship is the extraordinary malicious extent of his hatred."

Gabrial still loved her husband. In *Under the Volcano*, Lowry bases a character on her, who plaintively asks her alcoholic spouse, "Must you go on and on forever into this stupid darkness, seeking it, even now, where I cannot reach you, ever on into the darkness of the sundering, of the severance!" When Aiken returned to America, Gabrial asked Lowry to try again. They reunited and lived together in a beautiful cabana. When he was sober, he worked on the story that would become *Under the Volcano*.

Over and over, Lowry insisted that there was nothing wrong with his drinking, that it was not destructive, and that it was not a problem in their marriage. Now he wanted to visit Oaxaca, where they made the world's best mescal. At twenty-three, Gabrial realized that her life and sanity were at stake. She wrote in secret to a friend in Los Angeles and asked for a job, then begged Lowry to come with her.

When she told him, he insisted that he had to go to Oaxaca and that she had to go with him. He flew into a rage and threw her, dressed only in her underclothes, out of their hotel room. When she actually left, he cursed her as she drove away. In the weeks to come, she wrote him often: "I send you all my love and my whole heart and all my thoughts and prayers." His answers, when they came, were conglomerations of bizarre and hateful accusations, and futile excuses for his behavior.

He went to Oaxaca, and spent weeks tripping on mescal. His hallucinations were often terrifying. In local cantinas and brothels, he raved at the top of his voice about local politics, which landed him in jail and under interrogation. Soon he imagined the police were spying on him, and his paranoid behavior landed him in jail. Upon release, he got drunk and refused to pay for a bottle of mescal, which sent him right back to jail.

Painful and disoriented telegrams reached Gabrial, begging her to come to Oaxaca, but her sense of survival made this impossible. The more she refused to rescue him, the more he drank. He told anyone who would listen that his drunkenness and desperate state were her fault, and inevitably, people Gabrial had never heard of wrote her and chastised her for neglecting this great genius. Then a pair of con artists took the little money he had. When another couple tried to help him, he repaid their care by attempting to rape the wife. By now, he was notorious, and immigration also wanted to have a talk with him.

Gabrial now contacted Arthur Lowry, who dispatched private detectives to straighten out the mess and deliver Lowry to his wife whether she wanted him or not. Without warning, he showed up in California, rumpled and bruised. She took him in, and tried to get him into psychoanalysis. She even offered to reconcile, if he would give up liquor for two years. He refused. His father was forced to hire a lawyer to keep him sober, or to try. This handler allowed Lowry a strict, twenty-five-cents a day allowance. On this, he could still afford fortified wine, at fifty cents a gallon, which led directly to the night he nearly killed a woman in a drunken rage. She was badly beaten, with cracked ribs and her eyes swollen shut. He showed no remorse but refused to let the lawyer pay for her medical bills. Informed of the situation, his father wrote, "My heart you have pretty well broken."

It was at this low point he met Margerie Bonner through a friend. It was love at first sight. "Stars were floating. We were immediately in love," she wrote. Margerie was a pretty and savvy veteran of silent movies who now worked as an assistant to a popular actress. She and Lowry were soon inseparable. Gabrial filed for divorce sending Lowry on a four-day bender. He trashed his room, and burned his furniture and blankets.

In order to avoid visa complications, he went to Canada, where Margerie joined him. She was about to find out what caring for a genius was like. With the war on, his father was having trouble getting money out of the country, and their funds were dwindling. They were rescued when a friend sent a check for fifty dollars, which Lowry bet, and lost, on a horse before he got home from the bank. When he returned empty-handed to the drafty attic he and Margerie shared, she took him for a long walk to clear his head. He started screaming and ran away from her. She searched for him through the night, and finally found him in a dirty brothel. He had traded his clothes for a bottle, and was dressed only in his underwear.

She demanded, and received, a shabby suit and shoes, then tried to get him home. He refused to go without a drink, and as they had no money, he stood in the street and panhandled until he had enough for a beer. In the coming weeks, he managed to eke a little out of writing newspaper pieces, which allowed them to live on two dollars a week. They had hope in an early version of *Under the Volcano* that was making the rounds, but eventually most publishers pronounced it too "cerebral," and lacking in action. He continued to write, while Margerie typed his manuscripts and worked on a novel of her own.

When a little money came through, they decided on a small vacation. Lowry saw an ad for a cabin on a beach in Dollarton, near Vancouver. Several primitive cottages littered the seaside there, and they rented one for ten dollars a month. What was meant to be a month turned into fourteen years; it was the happiest home Lowry would ever have.

There was a table, a bed, and a wood-burning stove, and that was about it, but he could dive from the back porch into a cove and swim, and they were surrounded by beautiful, unspoiled forests. If there were few conveniences, there were also few complications; no rent or bills to pay, and his meager allowance was enough.

A new draft of the novel was not doing well, but the good news was that his divorce became final and he and Margerie could marry. They were happy and safe and away from watchful eyes, he rarely drank. In fact, they toasted their marriage with a cup of tea. When they did drink, it was light gin and orange juice, but there was no drunkenness.

In April, they bought their own cottage for one hundred dollars, and got down to painting and repairs. "We have now bought a supershack on the sea—all paid for, no rent, no tax, but lovely, surrounded with dogwood and cherry and pines, isolated, and a swell place for work," he wrote Aiken.

At night they watched the skies, and Margerie taught him about astronomy. He reworked his novels *In Ballast From the White Sea* and *Under the Volcano*. Even in paradise he was suffering. He worked compulsively on several projects at the same time, but finished nothing. On some primal level he was afraid of finishing another novel, and this sabotaged his career just as much as alcohol.

His literary ambition envisioned a trilogy of novels, a travel guide exploring the dark geography of the physical and the psychic, "an honest Baedeker, I believe, for he who would travel in hell." While reworking *Under the Volcano*, he met Charles Stansfield-Jones, student of the occult. For years, Lowry had been interested in hidden knowledge and entertained morbid superstitions, looking for signs in all things. "Stan" brought Lowry books on the occult, and these ideas soon entered his book, giving it an even stranger, doomed mystery.

In June, Lowry's cabin caught fire and his idyllic beach life came to a horrible end. While Lowry tried to get help, Margerie ran into the flames and rescued as many manuscripts as she could. His only copy of *In Ballast* was not one of them. He ran into the cabin himself, and was seriously burned by a falling beam. All he could retrieve were a few charred pages before on-lookers dragged him out. He was hysterical, and the loss would haunt him for the rest of his life, not the least because he truly believed that his forays into black magic had opened a dark door that let in the fire.

After the fire, they stayed with friends. Lowry went back to drinking, and his penchant to turn his life into relentless melodrama wore on their hosts. An advance for one of Margerie's novels and her occasional work for the Canadian Broadcast Company brought in money. He continued to work; he scribbled prayers at the top of his manuscript pages. After the first of the year, they returned to the beach, determined to rebuild. In early 1945, his father died, which left them with a substantial amount of money, although it would be tied up for years. They decided to visit Mexico. He returned nervously and with good reason; a man who read signs into everything was too easily spooked by the prospect of reliving a dark place in his life, and he was convicted of the sense of rushing to unavoidable doom. He believed he was helpless to avoid becoming the Consul, the damaged hero of *Volcano*, and started to have a seriously neurotic transference.

Lowry had been asked again to revise *Volcano*, and he was in despair. He sobered up long enough to write a careful letter, asking the editor to read it again. "There are a thousand writers who can draw adequate characters till all is blue for one who can tell you anything new about hell fire. And I am telling you something new about hell fire." He wrote that his earlier problems could be blamed on "Youth plus booze plus hysterical identifications plus vanity plus self-deception plus no work plus more booze."

The letter was an impressive account, honest and imploring, and it worked. After nine years, *Under the Volcano* was scheduled for publication. This story of an English alcoholic going to pieces in Oaxaca is today considered to be one of the greatest novels of the twentieth century, a true masterpiece. Both grim and funny, it intertwines the mystical with the sensual as the Consul hurtles headlong to his destiny. On the eve of the book's public birth, however, the Lowrys were in trouble.

Local authorities showed up and told him that he had no right to be in the country, due to an outstanding fine of fifty pesos from his former stay. It is likely there was no such fine, but an attempt at *la mordida*, or bribe, which Lowry refused to pay. They were forbidden to leave town and bullied for weeks by various sadistic officials. He wept with a bottle of mescal at hand, and tried to pray but could only curse.

While Margerie went to Mexico City to try to straighten out their paperwork, he got drunk. She returned with a check for the fines, but he couldn't hold a pen to sign it. This small disaster led her to insist on a joint account, a perfectly practical act that Lowry would later use to damage her reputation. Even after he paid the fine, they were not allowed to leave. After ten days, which Lowry spent drunk, they were allowed to travel to Mexico City. In the capital there were more demands for money to insure their papers were "approved." They were detained, jailed, then driven to the border by a crazy guy with pistols, but they made it out of the country.

Lowry was on the brink of great fame, but his terror of exposure as a plagiarist made him ambivalent to the book's success. On the one hand, he had worked on this manuscript for nine years, but on the other, attention meant that his signed confession regarding his first novel might surface, and with that a closer examination of the sources of inspiration for *Volcano*. That's all it was, inspiration: an unusual word first encountered while reading Faulkner, an image he admired from Virginia Woolf, a section prompted by the letters of D. H. Lawrence, but he lived in terror. Final publication was delayed by months due to Lowry's extensive re-editing, which really meant re-writing. While he did this, the couple worked on the shack, and enjoyed their beach. In the fall of 1947 they headed for New Orleans and from there on to Haiti, where Lowry disappeared for days at a time into the world of voodoo, drums, and rum. Shortly after his return, he walked into the hotel swimming pool holding a glass aloft, and would have drowned had he not been pulled out by on-lookers.

They were staying with friends when he had a fit in the bathroom and banged his head into the wall. The convulsions left him on the floor behind the toilet. Although he was taken to a hospital and sedated, Margerie and his editor Albert Erskine were understandably worried. Prepublication buzz was intense around the new book, and opening day already promised to be hectic. Reviews, press, interviews, and requests for photographs were very unnerving to Lowry.

In New York, he attended interviews toting and sipping a gallon jug of wine. By the time he got to a dinner party in his honor, he was silent and uncommunicative, until his host started to quote from *Moby Dick*. "That's not right," Lowry said, and proceeded to recite the first two pages of the book word-perfect. He then stood up and said he had to leave or something terrible would happen.

When he met his publisher for the first time, he referred to him as an office boy and walked out. This drunken rebuff would cost him dearly in the future, but he could get away with it, for now. Reviews from critics and fellow writers were extraordinary. John Woodburn of the *Saturday Review* wrote, "I have never before used the word in a review…but I am of the opinion, carefully considered, that *Under the Volcano* is a work of genius."

He continued to startle hosts with his utter silence, borne of part fear, part contrariness. At one party, he smeared his blood on the bathroom mirrors, which led to a short hospitalization. On his discharge, Lowry wanted to return to his shack on the beach. After years as a squatter with few conveniences, Margerie was enjoying the parties and the attention, so she sent Lowry on ahead. When she arrived a few weeks later he was too drunk to pick her up, and was living with a roguish couple who did not bother to conceal their interest in his money.

In April, there was a radio broadcast of *Volcano*, starring Everett Sloane of Orson Welles' Mercury Theater. With no electricity and dead batteries, they had no way to hear the show at their own shack, so they imposed on a reluctant neighbor, bringing with them two bottles of whisky. She went out for the evening and returned to find Lowry on the bathroom floor "flat on his drunken back in a pool of his own leakage…britches half-off—mother of God! What price genius?" When he came to, he ate nine raw eggs and nearly squeezed her dog to death.

At the cabin, he was working on a new piece. The problem is, he was working on several new pieces. For the rest of his life, he would add and add to existing novels, refusing to finish one—that was too dangerous. He offered to send his publisher a novel in installments, "unless my multiple schizophrenia gets the better of me and I decide I ought to revise *Ultramarine*…first." From now on he would make the mistake of treating his publisher as an active collaborator, therapist and cheerleader rolled into one, and he sent him thousands of unedited pages.

In the meantime, Margerie wanted to travel. Lowry hated to leave the beach, but he realized he owed his wife a great deal. He took her to Paris, but he needed to punish her for taking him away from the safety of his cabin. Soon he was in a French jail for drinking. On his release, they traveled to the south of France, where one night he tried to strangle Margerie. Her cries brought the hotel staff. When he was admitted to a hospital in Paris, the doctor advised Margerie to run away while she still could. "He's either going to kill you or himself," he said.

Often Lowry drank in front of mirrors, seeing who knows what. His excess, tricks, and the lengths he would go for a drink strained the marriage. "Although he makes a great pretense of working (nothing has been written) & of exercising & tries his best to fool me it is too obvious he is drinking all afternoon," Margerie wrote in her journal. It did not help that she was drinking, too.

When they traveled to Italy, he disappeared and she found him in jail. He sobered up long enough to move on to Rome where he worked on some stories. One day Margerie left the hotel to change money, and when she returned, he was screaming in the bar where he had assaulted a guest. It took several men to drag him to his room and lock him in, where he continued to scream and pound his head against the wall.

He was sedated and taken to a sanitarium. Margerie had a connecting room, and during the night he burst in and tried to kill her. Her screams brought the guard. A few days later they were back at a hotel and he was "sweet but sweet & strange...I have never seen him so subdued." More and more she had to control him, and she did this with drugs, feeding him barbiturates and what she insisted were vitamins that she shoveled into his mouth when he was on the point of passing out.

Near Giverny, they stayed with a friend, who patiently watered his wine. When she gave a party, one of her guests, a man, had his eye on Lowry; Lowry had his eye on the bottle of gin the guest was carrying. They found a bedroom but "We were finally discovered," wrote the guest, "& a disagreeable scene followed." The gin was taken away, but they sneaked out and got another bottle.

> We stripped and went to bed with the cognac. By noon Nancy [his fiancée] & Malcolm's wife...were at the door & we refused to open. I said, 'Can't you understand when two men want to be alone together?'

Margerie was desperate to get him to Switzerland, where she hoped he would submit to psychotherapy. She wanted to get a job and put an end to some of the madness. She asked his family to pay for the treatment, but while they sympathized, they would throw no more good money after bad. By this time, in fact, his brother kept suitcases by the door at all times, so that if Lowry visited they could be out the door with, "What a pity, we're just off on our holidays."

On their return to Dollarton, he drank six whiskies before the plane left the ground, followed by several more bottles and topped it off with pills. Once at the beach he was a little better, but then Margerie left to visit her family, and he got so drunk that he fell off the pier onto the rocks below.

He was discovered hours later. A doctor was sent for, but Lowry was so abusive to the man that he refused to treat him. Instead, he was sent to a hospital where he was so rude that the nuns locked him in a room with bars. He roared for hours until he was ejected, and sent to another hospital with a padded room.

When Margerie returned, she was able to get him discharged. For six months he had to wear a special brace for his back. The winter was brutally cold, but he was drinking less and writing more. His short stories were not selling, and his long work kept getting longer. Short stories turned into novellas that turned into novels that in turn wanted to be a trilogy. He was working on nine novels and a short story collection, and a volume of poems, all at the same time.

In 1951, he received some of the money from his father's estate, and they could relax financially. He began the year with an encouraging advance and monthly retainer from Harcourt Brace. His editor, Albert Erskine, was more accustomed to a professional relationship than the twenty-page letters he regularly received from Lowry, full of self-pity and justification that clearly took days to draft. Lowry went into despair when Erskine sent a telegram that did not include the salutation "love" at the end.

Over and over, Erskine asked for finished manuscripts, while Lowry continued to only send him long, disjointed "bits" of hundreds of pages, expecting creative direction. While he was an admirer of Lowry, Erskine expected a novel with a plot and narrative, not the imponderable cycle of ever-deepening mystery inherent in a writer's effort to write about a writer writing about a writer writing a book. Part of the problem was that Lowry and Margerie both believed he was a genius, and she honestly believed that he was incapable of imperfect work. What he needed was someone to tell him to cut, trim, discard, and rework, He only had Margerie, who told him that every word was sacred.

In the summer of 1953, he tripped over a tree root while drunk and broke his leg. While going for help, Margerie was mauled by a neighbor's dog, which meant that Erskine received another letter, this one explaining that neither one of them was in shape to do any work. Lowry—again—described, at incredible length, his unfinished manuscript, saying it contained "the magic of Dr Lowry's dialectical-Hegelian-spiritualism-cabalistic-Swedenborgian-conservative-Christian-anarchism."

In his childlike expectance of reassurance, he was hurt when Erskine replied that he was having trouble with "the Keeper of the Contracts." Lowry felt betrayed by this business-like attitude, and demanded his deadline be extended. Editing was out of the question: "Where it insists on growing, I must give it its head," he wrote. When he submitted an impossibly long excerpt, his monthly stipend was suspended. This led to more drinking. He was unable to feed himself, and Margerie had to do it for him, spooning food into his mouth, to the disgust of their friends who witnessed it. She oversaw his medication for hangovers. "She used to literally jam the pills down his throat, nights, once he was half-way under," wrote a friend. They screamed at each other, and matched hysterical scene for hysterical scene.

Margerie wanted a break, and he wanted to stay at the shack. By now, however, he was so terrified of being alone that he accompanied her to New York. He made her pay with increased drinking and bad behavior. Critic and friend Malcolm Cowley thought it was his way of telling Margerie, "See, it's the suicide of my talent and it's all your fault." Even the woman-hating Aiken wrote, "…Malc is revenging himself by as it were drinking the Great Genius to Death. You see how it works? A fine drama, with Random House putting up the dibs."

They stayed with friends, who found him in the middle of the night sitting in a tree with a bottle of gin. Another time Margerie had to leave him at the house of friend David Markson who wrote:

> The man could not shave himself…Mornings, he needed two or three ounces of gin in his orange juice if he was to steady his hand to eat the breakfast that would very likely be his only meal of the day. Thereafter a diminishing yellow tint in the glass might belie the fact that now he was drinking the gin neat, which he did for as many hours as it took him to.

When Markson had to leave him alone, he carefully hid all his liquor, but he underestimated the wiles of Malcolm Lowry, who found, and drank, a bottle of shaving lotion laced with alcohol.

That night was his last meeting with Conrad Aiken, who traveled all the way from Massachusetts to see him. Throughout the evening, Lowry sat in complete silence. After an hour, oblivious to everyone, he put his hands to his mouth and began to make beeping noises, in an approximate impersonation of jazz cornetist Bix Beiderbecke. Aiken listened for half an hour before he left saying, "Goodnight, Disgrace." Lowry then jumped up and tried to force himself into the old man's taxi, knocking Aiken to the floor of the cab in the process.

Lowry and Margerie sailed for Italy. He was drunk during the entire trip, forcing the captain to threaten to lock him in the ship's jail. In Sicily, he fled their hotel. Margerie found him only when the police told her to come and get him from the prison they were holding him in. In all the weeks they were there, he drank, swam, and wrote endless letters he would never send. The locals were not amused by his antics, and he wrote bitterly that "…endless are the hypocrite lectures I receive about drinking their bloody wine even at the moment I am being overcharged for it & cheated everywhere."

In Italy, they had a visit from a former Dollarton neighbor who observed, "He wouldn't get up till noon, and he couldn't get up until he had a drink, and then we'd sit for two hours watching him try to get through a piece of bread and a piece of cheese. It was just…agony." In two months he lost over forty pounds.

In July 1955, they went to England, where Margerie hoped to get psychiatric help. The doctors recommended a lobotomy, which she considered but ultimately rejected. At the hospital he was able to dry out and rest, and he became more lucid. After a few weeks, he was able to start writing for the first time in over a year, although this came to an abrupt halt when he fell off the wagon and checked himself out of the hospital.

One night he joined friends at their house for dinner, and finished off a bottle of cooking sherry in one swig. At the end of the night, they took him to the train and had to roll his body from the platform onto the car. He checked into another hospital, one with an alcoholism program. "The patient arrived very drunk and was with difficulty persuaded to go to bed in a side-room," read a report. Even when sober, he was uncooperative, and said outright he didn't want to be cured. He did not want to be re-socialized, deprogrammed, normal.

His stay this time was marked by electric shock treatment, alternating with escapes and binges. Finally the doctors suggested aversion therapy. First he was given drugs that reacted with liquor to cause violent vomiting, then placed in a tiny room with all the alcohol he could drink. After ten days of this, he still wanted a drink, but at least now he wanted to be cured. Margerie brought him his manuscripts and he made an effort to work.

On doctor's orders, she looked for a quiet place in England to settle down. She chose a cottage in a village called Ripe that was close to London by train. It had a garden, room to work, and a kindly landlady. There Lowry managed to stay sober, in spite of the fact that Margerie still drank heavily, which led him to complain to her, "This is more than Alcoholics Anonymous, this is Alcoholics Synonymous."

In May he went on a small binge with big consequences. While drinking, he became so abusive to Margerie that they were thrown out of the only pub in Ripe and forbidden to return. A subsequent bender was so violent that Margerie had him confined to a London hospital. She told him if he didn't recover this time, she would commit him permanently to a mental hospital. He tried aversion therapy again, and though he made some progress, he continued to sneak out to the nearest pub.

He was discharged and returned to his wife. Now it was her turn to break down and spend some time recuperating in a nearby hospital. Usually her absence meant a blind jag, but this time Lowry remained sober. When she returned home she weighed seventy pounds and was frail. As he worked hard to take care of her for a change, they grew closer. In a few weeks, he was drunk again.

In May, the couple got drunk together in a nearby village, as they were not welcome at the pub in Ripe. They were fighting and Margerie was crying. Lowry bought a bottle of gin at the bar to comfort her but it only made her cry harder. They went home and listened to the radio, drinking gin and orange squash. The fighting continued when he turned up the volume on the radio, despite the nearness of their neighbor, whom Margerie hoped not to disturb. In anger, she smashed the gin bottle. Permanently expelled from their local tavern, there was no way he could get another drink that night. He took the broken bottleneck and tried to attack her. Margerie ran to the neighbor's and stayed. When she returned in the morning, she found her husband on the floor, surrounded by scattered food and the broken bottle. He had swallowed fifty sleeping pills. It may have been deliberate or he may simply have thought he was taking his "vitamins." There were even a few people who suspected the pills had been shoveled into him by an exhausted Margerie.

Malcolm Lowry's sole important contribution to literature was an excruciating, exhaustive, and achingly beautiful account of the moral, spiritual, and mortal cost of the desire for oblivion. Now at last he could stop pretending he wanted to live. But there was a piece of writing from his hands that shows perfectly the humor he found in all of the horror, an epitaph he composed for his gravestone, sadly unused:

> Malcolm Lowry
> Late of the Bowery
> His prose was flowery
> And often glowery
> He lived, nightly, and drank, daily,
> And died playing the ukulele.

PART THREE

MYTH MAKERS: BIGGER THAN LIFE— A WHOLE LOT BIGGER

F. Scott Fitzgerald

Jack London

Robert Lowell

F. SCOTT FITZGERALD

DRINK OF CHOICE

🕊 Champagne by the case.

🕊 Gin by the tumbler.

🕊 Amory Blaine, the hero of *This Side of Paradise* got drunk on a cocktail called the Bronx: Mix two ounces of gin with one ounce orange juice, a dash each of dry and sweet vermouth. Shake with ice, strain, and serve in a martini glass.

"That young man must be mad—I'm afraid he'll do himself some injury."

- James Joyce

"How could he know people except on the surface when he never fucked anybody, nobody told him anything except as an answer to a question and he was always too drunk late at night to remember what anybody really said."

- Ernest Hemingway

Francis Scott Fitzgerald died young, but not young enough. At twenty-three, he invented a literary persona of reckless, madcap youth then strained to live up to it the rest of his life. He succeeded so well that by age forty-four he was dead. *The Great Gatsby* sold fewer than twenty-five thousand copies in Fitzgerald's lifetime but today sales have topped ten million, and in 1999, the Modern Library chose it as the second-greatest novel of the twentieth century, after James Joyce's *Ulysses*.

His life began with a mostly idyllic childhood—a blonde-haired, blue-eyed boy in a sailor suit, rolling a hoop down the sidewalk of a nice St. Paul, Minnesota, neighborhood. Two of Fitzgerald's sisters died as babies, and his mother was sometimes overly protective and always over-indulgent of her son. His father was an ineffectual man of business, but also a dandy, always dressed to the nines, with an air of elegance that his son emulated. They lived on money his grandparents had earned in a family grocery store. As Fitzgerald's social pretensions grew, he would hate his mother for coming from "trade."

His popularity in school, with which he was already obsessed, lagged somewhat due to his unmistakably supercilious attitude towards his classmates. In 1913, he applied to Princeton. The fact that his grades were below average and that he failed the admissions test twice did not discourage him. He believed in his destiny as a Princeton man, a personage he believed to be lazy, good-looking and aristocratic. In spite of his poor academic performance, he convinced the admissions board to give him a chance.

He cut classes, perfected a new dance called the Turkey Trot, and drank a cocktail called the Bronx. This combination of activities meant that he was perpetually on probation, which officially barred him from many campus activities. On the productive side, he wrote plays for the campus Triangle Club, including one musical with the rather amazing title *Fie! Fie! Fi-Fi!* In college theater, he collaborated with fellow student Edmund Wilson, who had already begun his career as writer and editor for the college magazine.

During World War I, he served as an officer in the infantry where he was, in his own words, "the worst lieutenant in the whole American army." This was more than comic exaggeration. He no more wanted to be a real soldier than he had wanted to be a real scholar. What he did want was to cast himself in the role of dashing military man, and he saw no reason to go any farther than adopting a convincing facade. To that end he had his uniforms tailored by Brooks Brothers. He already had a gift that allowed him to turn his military experiences, real and imagined, into several very good short stories. He also plugged away at a novel.

While stationed at Camp Sheridan near Montgomery, Alabama, he met Zelda Sayres, the youngest daughter of a judge and a society matron. She was dark-blonde and sublimely lovely, and wielded a beautiful pout. Although self-consciously belle-like and feminine, she also smoked, did not always say no to a snort of liquor, and was considered fast with local boys. Fitzgerald courted her on the front porch and told her he was going to be famous. In his uniform he looked like a prince, and years later she wrote:

There seemed to be some heavenly support beneath his shoulder blades that lifted his feet from the ground in ecstatic suspension, as if he secretly enjoyed the ability to fly but was walking as a compromise to convention.

They began a sexual relationship, which for Fitzgerald implied a de facto marriage. He wrote, "in my heart I can't stand this casual business. With a woman, I have to be emotionally in it up to my eyebrows, or it's nothing." While Zelda was in love and she longed to be free of Alabama, she refused to marry him. Spoiled and indulged, she could see no reason why this should not continue to be the case and would not even consider a future unless he could provide this to her. She began to keep him at arm's length. After one visit, his insistence and self-pity were so much that Zelda sent him away. He spent the next three weeks "roaring weeping drunk on my last penny," then moved in with his parents in St. Paul.

After Princeton and the army, he hated his parents' middle class affectations, and this goaded him into finishing his novel. He pinned scenes and chapters on the curtains and furniture around his room; he worked through the summer, refusing to see anyone or be interrupted. The book was completed in September. Two weeks after being submitted, *This Side of Paradise* was accepted.

When *This Side of Paradise* was published in 1920, it was a huge hit. The semi-autobiographical story and its hero Amory Blaine touched a nerve with a generation coming of age after World War I. They applauded Blaine's suggestion for a new method of suicide: "They should each order a Bronx, mix broken glass in it, and drink it off."

Fitzgerald sent for Zelda and they were married in New York. The reviews of his novel were astounding and he was compared to a young Dreiser. He shamelessly loitered in bookstores, hoping to hear someone mention his book. He loved to make entrances: "Let's go down to the Plaza for lunch. They'll swoon when they see me come in." Not everyone swooned. A friend visiting the couple in these early days wrote, "Called on Scott Fitz and his bride. Latter temperamental small town Southern Belle. Chews gum—shows knees. I do not think marriage can succeed. Both drinking heavily."

For all of his bravado, Fitzgerald realized that Zelda sometimes needed explaining. Biographer Andrew Turnbull quotes a Fitzgerald letter:

> Any girl who gets stewed in public, who frankly enjoys and tells shocking stories, who smokes constantly and makes the remark that she has 'kissed thousands of men and intends to kiss thousands more' cannot be considered beyond reproach. But I fell in love with her courage, her sincerity and her flaming self-respect. Zelda's the only God I have left now.

He was hardly more conventional. During a play, he stood up in the theater and started taking off his clothes. When he was down to his undershirt, ushers took him away. Together they were incorrigible. They ran hand in hand down Fifty-seventh Street and jumped fully clothed into public fountains. They commandeered a taxi and one rode on the roof while the other took the hood. They slid down the banisters of the Biltmore Hotel lobby.

The couple decided to retire to the country where Fitzgerald could write in peace. Unfortunately, Connecticut was too peaceful, necessitating regular trips to New York for additional noise. They could also be counted on to create lots of it themselves locally. Fitzgerald egged Zelda on to further and further extremes of drinking and outrageous behavior which he would sit back and enjoy, copying down her actions and remarks on any scrap of paper at hand.

During a weekend party, a publisher found and read Zelda's diaries. He begged for permission to publish them, but Fitzgerald refused, saying that the material in Zelda's journals belonged to him. She was a commodity that he owned and part of its value lay in her ability to attract other men and hold them out with just the right tension. It made for drama, which made for copy. He loved her the way she was, but she made a dangerous muse. Her love for him was childish and grasping; she demanded to come first before all other parts of his life, including writing. He could not do this and work on the first-rate novel that he had in mind, so he turned to magazines like *The Saturday Evening Post*, writing short stories for quick money.

In an effort to make a new start on the novel, they went to Europe in April 1921. The night before their scheduled departure, Fitzgerald was so drunk that he was asked to leave the bar. When he refused, he got into a fight with the bouncer. In Paris their behavior was so bad that they were again asked to vacate their hotel. At age twenty-five, Fitzgerald wrote, "I should like to sit down with 1/2 dozen chosen companions & drink myself to death but I am sick alike of life, liquor and literature." They returned to America to await the birth of their daughter. Scotty, born in October, would suffer a troubled childhood of money and neglect, raised by a succession of nannies, governesses, and boarding schools.

The next spring, Fitzgerald's second novel *The Beautiful and the Damned* was published. The story, while not factual, had clear autobiographical sources: the rise and fall of a beautiful, young married couple; their painful confrontations with reality; the husband's growing abuse of alcohol. Fitzgerald hauntingly uncovered insights about his life and marriage that he had yet to admit to himself, a vision of decay and desperation.

Reviews were good but not great. One particularly telling piece of criticism came from Zelda. Commissioned to cover the book for the *New York Tribune*, she delivered an amusing swat at their old argument about who owned the family stories. She wrote:

> It seems to me that on one page I recognized a portion of an old diary of mine which mysteriously disappeared shortly after my marriage, and also scraps of letters which, though considerably edited, sound to me vaguely familiar. In fact, Mr. Fitzgerald seems to believe that plagiarism begins at home.

They went to New York to celebrate the book's publication. Fitzgerald hoped that he would have a chance to work with friend and writer Edmund Wilson, but apparently things didn't go this way, as he later sent an apology to Wilson that read:

> I'm sorry our meetings in New York were so fragmentary. My original plan was to contrive to have long discourses with you but that interminable party

began and I couldn't seem to get sober enough to be able to tolerate being sober.

The Fitzgeralds counted on the fact that their bad behavior could be apologized away. "I'm running wild in sackcloth and ashes because Scott and I acted like two such drunks the other night," Zelda wrote a host. For many, their charm and winsome remorse made them easy to forgive. Writer John Dos Passos, who bore a few scars from his pass through their orbit, wrote, "I couldn't get mad at him and particularly not at Zelda; there was a golden innocence about them and they both were so hopelessly good looking."

That fall they moved to Long Island and made a short-lived resolution to stay on the wagon. Zelda wrote friends in St. Paul that, "We behaved so long that eventually we looked up [a friend] which, needless to say, started us on a week's festivity, equaled only by ancient Rome!" When she found herself pregnant shortly after the birth of Scotty, it was too much too soon, and she procured an illegal abortion.

Wild parties with their celebrity neighbors like Gloria Swanson were the order of the day. Rules were made and posted: "visitors are requested not to break down doors in search of liquor, even when authorized to do so by the host and hostess." And "week-end guests are respectfully notified that invitations to stay over Monday, issued by the host and hostess during the small hours of Sunday morning, must not be taken seriously."

Their escapades were by no means confined to home. During a trip to New York, Fitzgerald staggered around the Plaza tearoom with a bottle of champagne. When they kicked him out, he drove himself home, sipping from a case of warm champagne stashed in the car. Anita Loos was with him, and they joined Zelda for a candlelit dinner, which ended when he pulled the tablecloth out from the table, dishes, champagne and all. In response, Zelda stood and asked Loos, "Shall we have our coffee in the next room?"

No matter how much money he made, Fitzgerald was always in debt, borrowing from his agent, publishers, and magazine advances. In 1923, he pulled himself together enough to write a series of stories.

He considered this kind of work trash because it sold easily to popular periodicals. It was very hard on his morale but actually, many of the stories he wrote for quick cash were good, and showed his talent and craft.

With financial disaster postponed, there was time for more three-day benders, more passing out on the lawn at daybreak to the dismay of nearby neighbors. His actions at dinner parties—cutting off his tie with a table knife or eating his soup with a fork—made people increasingly uncomfortable, as did the time he drove a Rolls Royce into a pond because it looked like fun. Basically he was acting, playing the role of zany, irrepressible youngster, and he often watched his audience out of the corner of his eye to see how the performance was going over. On the other hand, Zelda's behavior was becoming more and more erratic, and she was not acting.

They traveled to the Riviera, where Fitzgerald hoped to finish *The Great Gatsby*. Cutting back on the excessive lifestyle was easier for him; he had real work to lean on, but at twenty-four, Zelda was at odds with life, ambition, and herself. She spent a lot of time on the beach working on her tan. There she met a young French flyer who was soon escorting her to dances and casinos. For his part, Fitzgerald was only too happy to have someone entertain her while he was trying to work. Biographers are divided on whether it was an affair or a flirtation, but whatever it was, Fitzgerald was shattered when he realized that something was happening. Years later he hinted that he encouraged it, and why not? Some of the benefits he reaped from Zelda's *folie a deux* were two novels and several short stories.

They went to Paris, where Fitzgerald introduced himself to Ernest Hemingway. He had followed the younger writer's work in literary magazines and encouraged Scribners to pick him up. (Fitzgerald would generously jumpstart the careers of many unknown writers.) From there he went to Rome where he churned out short stories to pay the bills. He had every faith that when *Gatsby* was published it would be a smash and solve their money woes for good, but when the book was released he received a dubious telegram from publisher Max Perkins: "SALES SITUATION DOUBTFUL EXCELLENT REVIEWS." Most critics called *Gatsby,* the story of a Midwestern boy who reinvents himself as a wealthy, mysterious criminal; a masterpiece and many of its biggest fans were other writers. Sales, however, were so poor that there were only two printings and neither sold out.

One of the writers who praised the book was Edith Wharton. She represented an older generation and a kind of literary elite. Fitzgerald was honored but nervous when she asked him to visit her Paris salon. En route he braced himself with gin and by the time he arrived, he was playing the role of a worldly rake who meant to shock the stodgy grande dame, but in the end the only one scandalized was Fitzgerald himself. He told Wharton and her guests that he and Zelda had once lived in a Paris brothel for two weeks, then he smugly waited for a disapproving silence that he could manipulate. Wharton said that she was waiting breathlessly for all the details of what went on. He was essentially a prude and he withdrew from the field, too embarrassed to go further, angry at having been bested at his own game.

Hemingway was convinced that Zelda was insane. Moreover he believed that she sabotaged Fitzgerald's writing with her relentless insistence that he provide her with a good time. At the same time, he knew that his friend was perfectly capable of undermining his work without his wife's help, and wrote, "Above all he was completely undisciplined and he would quit [work] at the drop of a hat and borrow someone's hat to drop."

Fitzgerald knew it too, and wrote a friend that, "I had my chance back in 1920 to start my life on a sensible scale and I lost it and so I'll have to pay the penalty." In a letter to Max Perkins, he wrote:

> You remember I used to say I wanted to die at thirty—well I'm now twenty-nine, and the prospect is still welcome. My work is the only thing that makes me happy—except to be a little tight—and for those two indulgences, I pay a big price in mental and physical hangovers.

In the summer of 1925, he partied with everyone while he left Zelda to recuperate from a painful operation—possibly another abortion—on her own. She was lonely and drank, and her epic unraveling began in earnest. She now wanted more time alone, but instead the couple headed for the South of France where they were surrounded by expatriate writers and literary figures as well as a host of Broadway types. One night in a café, Fitzgerald knelt at the feet of the legendary Isadora Duncan. Zelda watched on, and to everyone's horror, threw herself down a flight of stone stairs. Amazingly, she got up and walked away. At the end of the year they went to Hollywood, where he had been offered a job in the movies creating cinematic jazz babies.

At Pickfair, the home of Mary Pickford and Douglas Fairbanks, the Fitzgeralds gathered up the purses of all the other guests and threw them into a pot of tomato sauce on the stove. Another night they invited themselves to visit a fellow screenwriter in the middle of the night. When he let them in, Zelda took a pair of scissors and threatened to castrate him. They crashed a swank party by barking at the front door on their hands and knees.

Zelda was about to embark on a course that would challenge Fitzgerald's rule and exacerbate her growing mental illness. She decided to become a ballerina. The scenario was tragic. Zelda could not accept the fact that no amount of work or zeal could turn a woman of her age into a working classical dancer. It just made her try harder to master the grueling discipline of ballet, and her desire grew into obsession, then mania. Fitzgerald was jealous, resentful, and concerned.

It was morally important to Zelda that she pay for the lessons herself, so she turned to writing her own stories for cash. The stories and articles she wrote were usually published under a shared byline with her husband, and sometimes under his name alone. Much has been made, rightfully so, of his taking credit for her work, but it is also clear that she agreed to it willingly, in order to get the higher pay by thousands of dollars that a magazine would give for his name.

In 1927, the two were hosts to a never-ending string of parties and Fitzgerald developed an incapacitating case of the shakes. They pursued another geographic cure, sailing for Europe in the spring of 1928 where Zelda continued dancing lessons in France. She was practicing up to ten or more hours a day; it was as if she was unable to stop. Some of their friends saw the serious mental disturbance behind it, but Fitzgerald only knew that he resented it, and mocked her ambitions. Years later she defended herself: "You were constantly drunk. You didn't work and you were dragged home at night by taxi-drivers when you came home at all. You said it was my fault for dancing all day. What was I to do?"

That summer Fitzgerald turned thirty and was jailed twice for brawling and drunkenness. When they returned to America in the fall it was getting harder and harder to stall his publisher. Scribners had handed over several advances for the unfinished book. That November Fitzgerald delivered the first installment to editor Max Perkins. It would be another ten years before he sent another.

He was now the highest paid short story writer in the country, commanding $3,500 per piece. For years, he had complained about being forced to write for cash; now even the short stories stalled. Instead of manuscripts, the *Post* received dozens of telegrams that begged for further advances, and apologized for stories that were already over deadline. He became increasingly aware that his old friends were now avoiding him. Even Hemingway put limits on their company; an earlier visit had got him evicted after Fitzgerald used his porch for a bathroom and woke the landlord at three in the morning.

In the fall of 1929, they moved to the Riviera where Zelda slipped further into madness. She alternated between agitated excitement and moody silence. Sometimes she laughed at things that others couldn't see or hear, and she would go without food for days at a time. In lucid moments she begged Fitzgerald for help, but he mocked her.

He also rejected her sexual advances without telling her the reason: that drinking and fear had left him impotent. Her response was to tell their friends that he was homosexual and that he was having an affair with Ernest Hemingway. As Fitzgerald was homophobic, famously well-known for his intolerance of "fairies," he found this accusation unforgivable.

Zelda knew very well that her grip on reality was going. Hallucination was more real than reality, people on the street appeared to be one-dimensional, and she believed she could smell ants. But no one could get her to take a break from her frenzied dancing, even during a bout of bronchitis and high fever, and it hurried her final breakdown. When it came, Fitzgerald had her committed to a local hospital; she checked herself out so that she could make her dance lessons. A few days later she collapsed again and was sent to a Swiss sanitarium.

Zelda's doctors felt that if Fitzgerald quit drinking, she would stand a better of chance of recovery. He hated them for pressuring him to give it up. If he let them make him quit, then he was confessing that he had played a part in his wife's madness. Scott Fitzgerald never really admitted that he was an alcoholic. He certainly did not take responsibility for it. While he was perfectly aware that he was a laughingstock in the literary world and a social liability in every other one, he refused to give up or even limit his drinking as this would amount to an admission.

It would allow public opinion to direct his role, to take away his chosen façade of hell-raising genius and replace it with alcoholic wreck. Zelda was well enough to travel in 1931, and he took her to Alabama to be cared for by her parents while he went to Hollywood. He was hoping to make enough money to pay old bills and buy time to finish his novel. One night he was a guest at a party hosted by his boss, studio head Irving Thalberg. Aware that his reputation had preceded him and that he was being watched, Fitzgerald was very nervous and sneaked into the kitchen and bathroom for surreptitious drinks rather than accept the martinis offered around the room on trays.

Primed with gin, he insulted actor Robert Montgomery, who had specifically asked to meet him. He then asked his hostess, Norma Shearer, if he might sing a song. She politely offered him the floor and he proceeded to give a performance that would shorten his MGM contract by weeks. Standing at the piano, he began to sing a sentimental song to Miss Shearer's poodle.

The song had many, many verses and as time went on and it showed no signs of ending, the audience began to grow restless. Hollywood's biggest stars started hissing and booing, his boss jammed his hands in his pockets and ground his teeth, but Fitzgerald refused to leave the floor until a friend led him away saying, "Come on, Scott. We're going home."

When he returned to Alabama he was impressed, and a little unnerved, to find that Zelda had finished a novel of her own and submitted it to his publisher. At first he was amused, but when he was finally allowed to read the manuscript, there was hell to pay. She had stolen liberally from the incomplete manuscript he had spent years on. Her hero was named Amory Blaine, the name of the protagonist of *The Beautiful and the Damned.* To add insult to injury, she included true but painful and well-known incidents from their own life that were especially unattractive to Fitzgerald.

He convinced her, and their publishers to remove the offending sections. When *Save Me the Waltz* was released, the reviews were bad, but by then Zelda had suffered another breakdown and was living in a hospital in Asheville, North Carolina. Before he could get back to work on his novel, Fitzgerald first had to go on a bender, the result of which can be gauged by a post-visit apology to Edmund Wilson. "I came to New York to get drunk and swinish and I shouldn't have looked up you and Ernest [Hemingway] in such a humor of impotent desperation."

His ongoing efforts to appear sober were pathetic. He protested over his small glasses of wine while he disappeared into the kitchen for gin. When Edmund Wilson visited one weekend, he declined a drink with lunch and Fitzgerald went into a fury. "It seems so puritanical somehow," he yelled, "breaking off entirely like that!"

His treatment of Zelda degenerated. While faithful in his financial responsibility for her care, he resented it. Specifically, he hated the fact that it he was no longer in control of any part of her life. Her doctors were not necessarily up on their literature and he felt that they did not give him the respect—and moral leeway—that a great writer should have. This frustration was confounded by the fact that they treated Zelda's life and desire to create as if it could actually be as important as his.

Throughout 1933, he worked on his long anticipated novel, and finished it in November. When it was done he checked himself into John Hopkins for treatment of his alcoholism. He admitted now, at least to himself, that drinking had compromised his book and said, "I would give anything if I hadn't had to write Part III of *Tender is the Night* entirely on stimulant."

When the book was serialized in a popular magazine, the reaction was mixed. It was as if critics wanted to love it, but couldn't. It was a good story, but simply put, it lacked the craft they expected from the creator of *The Great Gatsby.* Fitzgerald knew they were right, but he was devastated all the same. Zelda was not helped when she read the barely veiled description of herself in the book, as a character who ruins her husband's life with her mental illness.

In 1935, he spent the summer in Asheville, North Carolina, ostensibly to treat his (nonexistent) tuberculosis. He convinced his doctor that he should reside at a grand hotel instead of a hospital. At the hotel he began an affair with a young married woman who admired his writing. He also slept with a high-class prostitute who walked around the hotel with a string of French poodles and an arm-load of unread books; she often met her clientele at the hotel's book shop. Fitzgerald played the whole summer for high drama, reading his lover's letters aloud to others and creating over-elaborate ruses for avoiding her husband. Since his health would not allow him to drink liquor, he limited himself to beer—thirty bottles a day.

As always, he was able to turn his life into literature, and the result was *The Crack-Up*. This powerful account of his personal breakdown and lapses into denial, especially where alcohol was concerned, was a brave, painful work. Unfortunately, the tell-all memoir was not in favor in 1936 and most of his contemporaries were disgusted with his exposure of the dirty laundry.

Now, at age forty, he had to drink in order to write. He had lost what was left of his self-confidence, what he called his "utter faith. Through a series of blows, many of them my own fault, something happened to that sense of immunity and I lost my grip."

He hired a nurse to help him stay sober. There was little she could do for him, including stopping an overdose of morphine while she was in the next room. Fortunately, he threw it up. Despite his well-publicized decline, he managed to get another job in Hollywood. He knew that this was his last chance, and managed to stay sober for brief periods. Drunk, he was all bravado and bluster, sober he was self-pitying and whiny. He did not know how to put his life back together but he was about to get some help.

The last chapter of his story began with journalist Sheila Graham. She was an English woman working in Hollywood, and she was beautiful, sound, and disciplined. She fell in love with Fitzgerald and would care for him until his death. Although he would fall off the wagon with spectacularly humiliating crashes that wounded her career as well as his, with Graham he was able to write again, and he began his final work. *The Last Tycoon* was a fictional story based on his former boss Irving Thalberg. It was never finished.

In 1938, he had a fight with Graham that ended with him waving a gun around and threatening to kill himself. After two years of gin hidden in the car, pills, nurses, and high-stakes game-playing, she told him to do it and walked out.

Instead of a gun, he chose a different, less direct method of self-destruction and returned to North Carolina where he checked the delusional Zelda out of the hospital and took her to Cuba, then New York. They drank around-the-clock and wandered the city picking fights; he was badly beaten twice. At last members of his family arrived and got him to a hospital.

In 1940, he returned to Hollywood and Graham. He was working on his novel and trying to find freelance scriptwriting work. For the first time in years he managed to stay sober, but it was too late. His reputation in the movie community was ruined he was all but forgotten by readers, many of whom believed he was already dead. That Christmas he felt a searing pain in his chest, but he would not let Graham call the doctor. The next day, he had a fatal heart attack.

There were a few things left behind. One was his novel, which even in its incomplete stage became modern classic. There was his legacy to literature that rose like a phoenix in the late 1940s. And there was Zelda. In the ten years after his death, she painted her pictures while living behind the walls of an Asheville hospital. In 1948, she and eight other inmates died in a fire caused by faulty wiring. Over the years her beauty and wildness have spoken to generations of youth, and today her following is just as large, and probably more intense, than that of her husband.

JACK LONDON

DRINK OF CHOICE

🙚 Although he was delighted when he
discovered the cocktail, a relatively, new
innovation in the twentieth century, he
usually drank whiskey.

"Alcohol was an acquired taste. It had been painfully acquired."

- Jack London

"It is easy for any man to roll in the gutter. But it is a terrible ordeal for a man to stand upright on his two legs unswaying, and decide that in all the universe he finds for himself but one freedom, namely, the anticipating of the day of his death…His feet are taking hold of the path that leads down into the grave."

- Jack London

Jack London's life story reads like one of his adventure novels. He was the illegitimate child of a mentally unstable mother who put him to work in a factory for up to eighteen hours a day. He was a teenage sailor off the coast of the Bering Sea; a gold miner in the brutal Klondike; a famous and wealthy writer; and he sailed around the world in a boat of his own design. He meant to "…adventure like a man, and fight like a man and do a man's work…lustfull roving and conquering by sheer superiority and strength." And he did, by the age of forty, when he died by his own hand.

London was born in California in 1876. The Civil War had ended only ten years earlier, and the West was still quite wild. His mother, Flora, was equally unstable. She came from a well-to-do family, and had been spoiled as a child. A bout with typhoid fever took her looks and a fair amount of her health, and left her the size of a child. She left home at sixteen and ended up in the arms of an older man, an astrologer who abandoned her when she became pregnant and refused to get an abortion. Flora left baby London with a wet nurse, Jennie, who would raise him the first eight months of his life.

In the meantime, Flora married John London, a widower with two daughters. The older one, Eliza, would be a mother and best friend to Jack, not like Flora, who was distant and cool to her son. She bullied her husband and was subject to frightening fits. His stepfather, John, bought and managed a small farm. He and his men were working in the fields on a hot day when they sent five-year-old Jack to bring them some cool beer. The tiny boy lugged a pail back from the pub. It was heavy and sloshed, and he didn't want to waste it, so he drank a bit. Then he drank some more. For the first time, but hardly for the last, Jack London was drunk.

The farm failed after a series of natural disasters and accidents, and John moved his family to Oakland, California. In his autobiographical writings, London would claim that his childhood was a hungry one, and that he stole food from other children, or grabbed it out of the dirt. While times were hard, his family was nowhere near starving.

Somehow the nine-year-old London discovered the public library. He could hardly believe there was such a palace that contained all of those stories, and it was free.

In *John Barleycorn*, he wrote:

> I read everything, but principally history and adventure, and all the old travels and voyages. I read mornings, afternoons, and nights. I read in bed, I read at table, I read as I walked to and from school, and I read at recess while the other boys were playing.

The next year, there was little time for reading. He went to work selling newspapers and doing odd jobs, like helping the ice man, to help support his family. His work often took him near saloons. "From ten to fifteen I rarely tasted liquor, but I was intimately in contact with drinkers and drinking places." High school was too expensive for the London family, so at age thirteen, London's education was finished, and he went to work full-time, one of the thousands of child laborers in California.

There were no child labor laws at the time, and London never put in less than ten hours a day, sometimes twelve and more, for ten cents an hour. The work was dull and grinding and left no time for play or reading, but his mother nagged continuously about his responsibilities. All of his wages went to her and the family. He managed to find consolation at Johnny Heingold's First and Last Chance Saloon. He discovered, to his pride, that he could hold his beer and rotgut whiskey as well as the older men.

He longed to be an oyster pirate, a poacher who stole from established shellfish farms and sold their fare on the black market. When he was fifteen, he heard that a small ship was for sale. His story of the *Razzle Dazzle,* recounted years later, is as unlikely as it is charming. Through the years he had remained friends with his old nurse, Mammy Jennie. Now she lent him the three hundred dollars he needed to buy the schooner. London, Jennie, and the boat's previous owner—a guy named French Frank—celebrated the new purchase. At fifteen, London preferred candy to liquor, but they filled his glass and he drank it as a matter of pride. "If I was only fifteen, at least I could not show myself any less a man than she…Was I a milk and water sop? No; a thousand times no, and a thousand glasses no."

He stood in the boat's companionway and managed to throw over most of his drink without notice, but he learned something that night. Drinking with comrades was pleasant and it opened doors. "The buying of drinks for other men, and the accepting of drinks from other men devolved upon me as a social duty and a manhood rite." It was part and parcel of a ritual, of drinking, singing, telling stories, and fighting.

"Always the life was tied up with drinking…Saloons are a congregating place…We celebrated our good fortune or wept our grief in saloons." It likewise worked with the authorities as well. When policemen boarded the *Razzle Dazzle* looking for illegal cargo, they were suitably bribed. "We opened oysters and fed them to them with squirts of pepper sauce, and rushed the growler [beer] or got stronger stuff in bottles." The teenage boy was running, smuggling, hoping to stay ahead of the law and his fellow poachers on the waterfront, where life was extraordinarily cheap.

Something of the boy remained in the notorious oyster pirate. His companions were men who lived from drink to drink but, as he wrote in *John Barleycorn:*

> I nursed a secret and shameful desire for candy. But I would have died before I'd let anybody guess it. I used to indulge in lonely debauches, on nights when I knew my crew was going to sleep ashore. I would go up to the Free Library, exchange my books, buy a quarter's worth of all sorts of candy...sneak aboard the *Razzle Dazzle,* lock myself in the cabin, go to bed, and lie there long hours of bliss, reading and chewing candy.

A few months later an oil lantern spilled on deck, and the resulting fire was the end of London's first ship. At liberty, he went to work for the police, trapping other oyster pirates. One night while drunk, he stumbled off a ship's deck into dark water. Instead of swimming, he let the current carry him out of the bay toward the ocean. "Thoughts of suicide had never entered my head. And now that they entered, I thought it fine, a splendid culmination, a perfect rounding off of my short but exciting career."

His life flashed before his eyes, and it was one of waterfront bars and the criminals and vagabonds met there. At once he felt degradation and relief. "The water was delicious. It was a man's way to die." He was awash of fantasies of his heroic death when he heard the rush of the water. Suddenly sober, he stripped off his clothes and swam, cross-current, for shore, where he was rescued by a Greek fisherman. He came away from this brush with death with a new fear—and hatred—for alcohol, but he had no intention of quitting. Drinking was a mode of communication in the world of hard work and the saloon. At sixteen, he drank every day and as much as he could get. He seldom ate, and woke hung over most mornings. It took a shot of liquor to get him going in the morning. At the same time, he recognized that booze was affecting his work ethic, his desire, even his curiosity. Liquor was about to offer him death again, in the form of a parade.

It was election night, and politicians entered bar after bar, offering free booze to anyone who would march and vote for them. London joined the parade. Afterwards the saloons of the town were thrown open. When bartenders couldn't serve fast enough, London went behind the bar and helped himself to bottles. Outside, he cracked one open on the curb, and drank. "I still labored under the misconception that one was to drink all he could get—especially when it didn't cost anything." The boy who believed he could drink older men under the table had no experience with straight whiskey. That night he drank at least two fifths of straight whiskey, maybe more; he was never sure.

A train was provided to take the revelers out of town at dawn. Making his way to the train with his companions, he realized from the depths of his stupor that he was more than just sick, he was dying. It was beyond horror. In his memoir, he wrote:

> [The men around me] thought I was merely an antic drunk. They did not dream that John Barleycorn had me by the throat in a death-clutch. But I knew it. And I remembered the fleeting bitterness that was mine as I realized that I was in a struggle with death and that these others did not know.

When he fell down, they laughed. On the train, he fought to smash windows, and hung outside of them for air and life. At home in Oakland he passed out, and lay comatose for seventeen hours. While men have died from far less alcohol poisoning, he survived. His next step was to ship out on a seal-hunting voyage. The seventeen-year-old London brought his books on board, and hid them when no one was looking. Once near the islands off the coast of northern Japan, he longed to visit the exotic paradise. But when he got ashore he never made it past the local bars.

It was, again, a case of drinking to keep up with other men, to save face, even if it meant deadly fights and wholesale destruction of local property. "I was part of it, a chesty sea-rover along with all these other chesty sea-rovers among the paper houses of Japan." The seal hunt itself was an unanticipated horror of slaughter and blood.

Back home in California, he took stock of his life, and found that all his waterfront cronies were dead or in jail. In an effort to settle down, he took work in a local jute mill: ten hours a day, ten cents an hour.

However unlikely, it was also his first, and last, adolescence, joining a friend in walks in the park, where they flirted with "nice" girls. The sailor Jack London had experienced sex, but he had never before felt the innocent, heart-melting infatuation that came with a look, a word, or a silence. He saved every penny from his work to afford the five-cent carfare and the candy that constituted a date in those days.

Eager to make more money, he wrote an essay called "Typhoon Off the Coast of Japan" and sent it to a local paper. While it earned him twenty-five dollars, he was forced to take a job shoveling coal for twelve or more hours a day, six days a week, for thirty dollars a month. The work crippled his body, but he believed that it was the key to an Horatio Alger beginning, until one day a co-worker told him the truth. In taking the job, he had replaced two other men who made forty dollars a month each; one killed himself when he lost his job. London quit in dismay. Unemployed, he joined Kelly's Army, a group of thousands of unemployed men who were making their way to Washington D.C. to demand jobs. The trip was long and risky. He sometimes grabbed a train by riding underneath its carriage. He joined hordes of homeless men sleeping in the cold, drinking whiskey, begging and fighting for food. In the talk around the fire, London heard about politics, and for the first time, about Socialism.

Halfway across the country, the trains ran out. The men traveled the rest of the way in handmade rafts. By the time they made it to D.C., the once mighty throng was a mere four hundred marchers. Separating from the shabby group, London hitchhiked to New York. There he saw firsthand the terrible suffering in the slums. He was sleeping in a park when police raided it and he was knocked unconscious by a nightstick. From there he made his way to Niagara Falls where he was arrested for vagrancy, and given thirty days hard labor. Jail was a terrifying ordeal, at the mercy of "the ruck and the filth, the scum and the dregs, of society." He turned to an older inmate for protection, becoming his "meat." When he regained his freedom, he made his way home by train and tramp steamer, careful to avoid the police.

He had seen the limitations of a future based on brute labor and aimless tramping. Now he wanted to go to school. At nineteen, he was far older than his high school classmates, but he persevered, bringing his famous work ethic with him. He worked as a janitor and took other odd jobs to pay for the school and help his family. In the library he discovered works of politics and philosophy, including *The Communist Manifesto*. (He would soon join the Socialist Party.) To improve his vocabulary, he bought a dictionary and memorized twenty new words a day.

He pawned everything he owned to pay for school, including his clothes and bicycle. He studied nineteen hours a day, pushing himself without a break. After high school he was accepted to a local college, but left after two semesters. He decided instead to pursue a career in writing. He applied the same fervor to words that he had to study, creating poems, essays, and stories for fifteen hours a day. Over and over he submitted pieces to publications and editors who did not respond. The silence was colder than rejection, and he began to wonder if there was anybody out there.

When he could no longer afford to be without a paying job, he went to work at the laundry of a local private school. It was hard, beast-like work for thirty dollars a month. In 1897, a prospector discovered gold in Alaska and London joined the rush to find riches in the new land. His sister Eliza mortgaged her house so that he could join thousands from all over the country who had gold fever. The money went fast, for tents, food, stoves, coats, and layers of warm clothing. It was only the beginning. Once there, travel was brutal and terrifying, climbing ice-covered mountains on horseback, and traversing snow filled crevices, covering mile after mile on foot. When he came to a lake, the twenty-one-year-old London felled his own trees and built a boat he christened the *Yukon Belle,* then he steered her through perilous rapids. He survived on skill, raw strength, and dumb luck.

He arrived in the Yukon too late to make a decent claim, and was forced to wait out the savage winter in an abandoned cabin, with temperatures of sixty below. There was a little company among the other prospectors, and London had his books: Milton, Dante, Karl Marx. Most importantly he kept a journal, where he recorded thoughts about the wildness of the ice and the hugeness of the land, and the characters around him who were rough or crazy enough to try to endure the Yukon. He could not help but note that men were judged by a different code in a land where whiskey was carried instead of food.

The basic fare was dried beans, bacon, and rough bread. Months without fruit or vegetables of any kind left London with a deadly case of scurvy. All of his teeth were loose and he could not heal from simplest cuts or sores. His life was saved when a stranger gave him some raw potatoes and canned tomatoes, which gave him enough strength to make the perilous journey home. He had lost all of his and his sister's money but he did not realize that he was carrying a treasure back with him: his journal and a head full of stories.

In Oakland he looked for work, investigating everything from advertising model to salesman. When nothing panned out, he worked odd jobs and wrote accounts of his travels. Again he sent the stories out into an unfeeling world. He was relentless in the face of rejection, but he was also at the end of his tether, beaten out and starved, when a story sold for forty dollars. Then another, and another, and slowly, but surely, everything was brought out of hock, and back bills were paid.

He set a goal of one thousand words a day, and he met it without fail, for almost every day of the rest of his life. There was no one to guide him, and so he created his own course for learning the craft of writing. He read everything, taught himself grammar, and studied the lives of successful writers. To understand their style, he copied famous stories by hand, again and again. "There was so much to learn, so much to be done, that I felt wicked when I slept seven hours. And I blessed the man who invented alarm clocks."

In November 1899, a Jack London story was accepted by *The Atlantic Monthly*. Soon after, Houghton Mifflin approached him for a collection of short stories. When *Son of the Wolf* was published, the critical response was good. At age twenty-four, he had arrived. He lost no time in promoting his own legend: Horatio Alger, rags-to-riches, self-mademan, and all that. Certainly much of it was true, but he himself freely admitted that he took dramatic license with his life history, giving the public what they wanted to read, and so began the cult of Jack London.

The legend wanted sons, and lots of them. When London went looking for a wife, he did so with a clinical eye to the right biological type to make a good mother. While part of him longed for a sexual mate and life companion, he disdained the notion of romance in marriage as much as he praised the holiness of motherhood. To this end, he chose Bess Maddern. She had been a friend, and sometimes tutor, for years. She was pleasant but conventional, grounded but prudish.

He believed this was what he wanted. "I shall be steadied, and can be able to devote more time to my work. I shall be a cleaner, wholesomer man because of a restraint being laid upon me instead of being free to drift wheresoever I listed." They married in April 1900. Bess tutored students; typed, corrected, and edited his manuscripts; and hoped that in time he would love her. London wrote his thousand words a day, and enjoyed his life as a public figure.

He was a star member of a group called the Bohemian Club. Poets, painters, and their unconventional spouses lived together in a community that was well known to the Bay area. Their pursuit of art garnered them respect that they did not always earn, and in time there would be a distinct aura of dissipation in the group. For now it was a symbol of the brightest and most creative talents in town, and London was its best-known member.

Bess disappointed London. She did not keep up with his glamorous role, nor did she want to. By the time she was expecting their first child, London hated her. He found her not just small, but microscopic. His resentment for the very restraint he married her for led him to accuse her of egomania, meaning, he couldn't believe that she had the nerve to expect him to attend to her needs, one of the most ridiculous of them being that he remain sexually faithful. Throughout his life, women would be wildly attracted to Jack London. He was unusually good looking, with eyes that bore through to the soul. Sensual, virile, and self-confident, he never lacked for women throwing themselves at his feet. He was also attracted to men. He and friend George Sterling, of the Bohemian Club, were devoted to each other. They were chesty men who drank and visited brothels together, but at the same time addressed letters to each other as "darling" and "dearest." They worked out together and London took pictures of George in the nude.

His first child was not a son, but a daughter named Joan. London adored her, but his treatment of Bess would eventually leave them bitterly estranged. The fact that Bess became pregnant again was evidence that he was still sleeping with his wife, which led his girlfriend to leave him in a huff.

For the first time in his life he had money, and he liked it. He loved to shop, and always bought the best. His entertainment was lavish. He wrote:

> It's money I want, or rather the things money will buy;
> and I can never possibly have too much. More money
> means more life to me. If cash comes with fame, come
> fame; if cash comes without fame, then come cash.

When William Randolph Hearst asked him to travel abroad and write for his paper, London agreed. He knew it was "yellow journalism" but the pay and the exposure were an offer he couldn't refuse. On his return, he was twenty-six with a bestseller on his hands, a second daughter, and an idea for a story that would not let him go. It became *Call of the Wild*, a breathtaking masterpiece, and one of Modern Library's "100 Best Novels" of the twentieth century. Unfortunately for London, he sold the manuscript for short money, two thousand dollars outright, and never saw a penny of royalties.

He was a celebrity now, the darling of critics and readers alike, which meant that at twenty-eight, he was fair game for the press. When he left Bess and his young daughters, it was a nationwide story. Wisely, he said little to the media. To his friends, however, he raged. It was her fault that they were getting a divorce, because she would not permit his philandering.

He began an affair with Charmian Kittredge. She was a figure on the edge of the Bohemian Club crowd, noted for her vegetarianism, and for the fact that she earned a living in a man's field, as a magazine editor. Even more fascinating—or appalling, depending on your mindset—was the fact that she was a proponent of free love. At the turn of the century this quaint phrase indicated the most shocking thing a woman could possibly believe.

London was intrigued. While his family was out of town, he was laid up with a knee injury, and Charmian was a frequent visitor to the sickroom. They were soon lovers. At first it was a simple, sexual affair, the most fulfilling and demanding one that he had ever had. Before long, it was much more serious. He was deeply and hopelessly in love. To protect Charmian from the scrutiny of the press after he left his wife, he let the world, and Bess, believe that he was having an affair with a different woman, one who in fact was a good friend. When Bess named her in the divorce papers, London had to tell her the truth.

He avoided coverage of his own life by reporting on the Russo-Japanese War. The hundreds of photographs that he took in Japan were groundbreaking, pictorial reporting. They also got him in trouble: he was actually arrested as a spy, but he was soon released. Most of the world's journalists had been denied access to the Japanese army and were cooling their heels in hotel bars for lack of information. Not Jack London. He spent two months working his way to the front line, riding a horse over the frozen mountains of Korea, surviving on rice and vegetables. It was long and hard, but when he arrived, he scooped the whole world, with interviews of members of the Japanese army and first hand reporting on its movements.

The Sea Wolf, published in 1905, is not only a great adventure story, it is also a psychological thriller, pitting an intellectual aesthete, Humphrey van Weyden, against the sadistic captain, Wolf Larsen, who rescues him at sea. It is wild, dark, and undeniably homoerotic. Van Weyden hates and fears Larsen, yet swoons when the stronger man undresses: "I had never before seen him stripped, and the sight of his body quite took my breath away…His great muscles leaped and moved under the satiny skin."

He found that potshots from the press were not the only liability of fame. He had everything he had ever dreamed of, but it didn't make him happy, and this was making him crazy. "I meditated suicide coolly," he wrote. "My regret was that there were too many dependent upon me for food and shelter for me to quit living. But that was sheer morality." He became so obsessed with dying that he gave his gun away for fear he would use it.

He medicated his despair with liquor, which he called John Barleycorn. "The so-called truths of life are not true." Drinking made it easier to stand the angst, and to put up with others. "A poor companion without a cocktail, I became a very good companion with one." Since childhood he had been subject to prodigious binges of so-called industrial drinking; now he began to imbibe slow and steady for the sake of getting through the day, although in his memoir he maintained, "I was not pessimistic. I swear I was not pessimistic. I was merely bored."

When he and Charmian married, it caused a national scandal. Speaking engagements were cancelled and his books were pulled from library shelves. Charmian was painted as a scarlet woman who had led America's favorite boy-writer from his wife and children. But she was tough and she could take it. In order to make London happy, she learned to sail and box, taking her blows like a man. Like Bess before her, she became his full-time secretary and editor, and unlike Bess, she agreed to let him wander from the marital bed.

The couple bought a farm in Glen Ellen, California. Over the years, London would add to it obsessively, until it was over one thousand acres. He bought pedigree pigs and prize winning horses and cattle, and eventually sixteen thousand eucalyptus trees. The thirty-year-old writer wanted to be a rancher, to cultivate the land using organic techniques and head a self-producing organization. He had another dream, one of sailing around the world in a ship of his own design.

The disaster of *The Snark* was an excruciatingly one. One of London's more foolish shortcomings was a gift for putting his life in the hands of the crooked and incompetent. Putting his sister Eliza in charge of the farm was an exception. When he got ready to build his own ship from the ground up, however, he chose Charmian's uncle, a man who knew absolutely nothing about construction or sailing. Consequently, *The Snark* took years to build, cost a small fortune, and was next to worthless in the water.

London was not to be put off. To make the perilous and demanding trip around the world, he hired an entirely novice crew. Before leaving, he put his literary affairs into the hands of Charmian's mother, a move that would bankrupt him. He said goodbye to his daughters, for what he assumed would be seven years, and in April 1907, shoved off, bound for Hawaii. Hours later, the boat began to leak. It was an inopportune time to discover that the anchor didn't work, the back-up anchor didn't work, the lifeboat didn't work, the sail was useless, and the navigator didn't know how to use a sextant. Charmian took the wheel, London taught himself to navigate, and they limped toward Hawaii. Still, he never missed his goal of a thousand words a day.

In Hawaii, he learned to surf and wrote an article about it, introducing the country to the little known island pastime. He and Charmian spent several days at a leper colony before moving on to the Marquesas Islands, following in the footsteps of his heroes Herman Melville and Robert Louis Stevenson. En route they became stranded in the doldrums for weeks, until water was running dangerously low. A rainstorm saved them and allowed them to collect enough water in a tarp to get them through the next two weeks until they finally made land.

London started drinking. Although no liquor had been brought on board, the ship's cook found some bottles of sweet wine that had turned in the heat into a kind of brandy. For London, the trouble was, "I had to share the stuff, and the length of the traverse was doubtful. I regretted that there were not more than a dozen bottles. And when they were gone I even regretted that I had shared any of it."

At their next stop, he stocked up. "I sailed with sufficient absinthe in ballast to last me to Tahiti, where I outfitted with Scotch and American whisky." They sailed on to the Solomon Islands and Melanesia, where the natives were not always friendly after their experiences with white colonialists and missionaries. Add to that life-threatening sunburns; epic and regular insect attacks and the infections that resulted from their stings.; add to that malaria; dysentery; and a mysterious disease that caused London's hands to swell to twice their normal size, his skin to rot and fall away in chunks, and his toenails to become infected.

Jack London's psychic and physical resources were tremendous, but he knew when he was at the end of them. When they reached Sydney, he went to the hospital and spent five months recovering. He was not going on. He sold *The Snark* for one-tenth of what it cost him and headed home to more disaster. Thanks to the negligence of Charmian's mother, his literary and financial affairs were in shambles. Crueler still, critics rejected his latest novel.

Although today *Martin Eden* is considered his greatest novel, with the possible exception of *Call of the Wild*, it was misunderstood in his lifetime. It tells the story of a young man who goes from uneducated adventurer to famous author in a few years, only to despair when he achieves fame. London was furious when critics wrote that this was simply not credible.

The book sold well and he tried to take the critical setback in stride. He got back to work and turned out his one thousand words a day. The quality of his work varied, as he was perfectly aware. "I have no unfinished stories. Invariably, I complete every one I start. If it's good, I sign it and send it out. If it isn't good, I sign it and send it out." He was in it for the money, now more than ever. He had debts to square, two families to support, a farm to run, and he planned a new house that promised to be opulent and expensive. The Wolf House was to have a dozen bedrooms, a game room, a separate wing for Charmian, and a library of fifty thousand books.

He worked hard, but at his pace it was inevitable he would run out of ideas, so he resorted to buying plots from young writers like Sinclair Lewis for five dollars apiece. His depression grew and with it his drinking. "Bourbon or rye, or cunningly aged blends, constituted the pre-midday drinking. In the late afternoon it was Scotch and soda." Soon he needed a drink to begin the morning's work, then a drink at the five hundred-word mark, two more when he reached one thousand. If he had company he sneaked two for their one. "What could I do but steal that every second drink, or else deny myself?" Then an afternoon's swimming and horseback riding, followed by two or three cocktails before dinner, and bottles of Liebfraumilch with his food.

His meals did as much, or more, to undermine his health than the alcohol. Against doctor's orders, he ate his meat raw, or nearly so. His digestion was already compromised by the beginnings of the kidney disease that would kill him, but he would not give up his cannibal sandwiches of uncooked hamburger and chopped onions, or his nightly duck, cooked for no more than twelve minutes and served bloody.

Although he was often in pain, he was cheered by the news that Charmian was expecting a baby. She was thirty-eight and it was her first, but they were both joyously optimistic. Their life took another downward turn when the baby died shortly after birth after the doctor damaged the child's spine during delivery. Charmian was shattered.

The couple remained close, camping and sailing together, although London's drinking was slowly driving a wedge between them. When they visited New York together, he went to the fights, played craps, visited burlesque halls and slept around, while his wife waited for him at their hotel. She could read about it in the papers, which followed his every move. One night he did not come home at all. The next day she begged him to put his house in order, and he turned on her, reminding her that he could come and go as he pleased.

Their marriage was given a reprieve when they shipped out as crew on a small ship. They drew close to each, talking, boxing, and reading together. One day they both climbed to the crow's nest, where she proceeded to do needlework all afternoon. At the end of three months, she was pregnant again. They both suffered when she miscarried at five months.

In 1913, they lived as if under a curse. Their eucalyptus trees were devoured by grasshoppers and a prize horse in foal was found shot. London took out another mortgage on the farm to pay for Wolf House, which progressed slowly. After a morning's writing, he entertained a variety of sycophants, hangers-on, and philosophical dilettantes; Charmian loathed them all. His health continued to decline in a dozen different ways and he treated the pain with both morphine and heroin.

He was pleased with a movie version of *The Sea Wolf*, the first of many films based on his writing. Movies were in their infancy, and copyright laws were roundly ignored, to his fury, so he traveled to New York to lead the fight to change the laws. While there he got drunk and heckled William Jennings Bryan during an after-dinner speech.

This scene was disturbing to many, in light of London's most recent bestseller. *John Barleycorn* was subtitled "An Alcoholic's Memoir," and it recounted in courageous detail his lifelong struggle with drinking. It was hugely popular, and would be used by both the Temperance movement and Alcoholics Anonymous as an important tool. One critic wrote, "That the work of a drinker who had no intention of stopping drinking should become a major propaganda piece in the campaign for Prohibition is surely one of the choice ironies in the history of alcohol."

In July, he was diagnosed with kidney disease. Doctors performed an emergency surgery, but in the days before dialysis, the condition was basically untreatable, and he remained in incredible pain. It helped that the Wolf House was nearly complete. There was still this last dream that had carried him through the last few painful years, but soon it would be lost in a fire. A drought had left the ranch with little water, and they watched in horror as the glorious mansion burned to the ground. It had not been insured. By dawn, London was nearly hysterical.

He turned to his work, and produced *The Star Rover*, a strange novel about a man who escapes torture by living in his imagination. He also looked for consolation in his daughters, and asked them to live with him and Charmian. When they chose to stay with their mother instead of going to the man who abandoned them, he was heart broken and angry. In an effort to settle his debts, he made several, hugely disastrously business investments, like Jack London Grape Juice. Equally unsuccessful were various land schemes. His health woes were compounded by dysentery, followed closely by pleurisy, and by the mercury based medicine that was meant to cure it.

His drinking frightened some of his friends, especially when he said things like, "In ten seconds I'll feel 'em crawling. The worms... The white worm, tunneling through our brains." Toward the very end of his life, he attempted to understand his alcoholism and other aspects of his personality by reading Jung, and teaching himself about the subconscious. This self-analysis sparked the idea of a new biography. Sadly, *The Dark Abysm of Sex* was never written.

At forty years old, Jack London was worn out, and worn very, very thin. His cult would have it that he died of a surfeit of life, of having crammed so much life into his first thirty years. It is certainly, an essential part of the picture. The immediate cause was easier to identify. At that time, the morphine and heroin that he self-administered for pain were legal. In a story written shortly before his death, he wrote of a hero in pain who took an overdose of narcotics. "An hour later, afraid of his thoughts and the prospect of a sleepless night, he took another powder. At one-hour intervals he twice repeated the dosage."

Uremia hadn't stopped him from eating two raw ducks a day. Now he vomited it up, and curled over in pain. He said to Charmian, "Thank

God, you're not afraid of anything." Then he sat up and wrote his daughters, asking them to join him for lunch and a sail. He sat writing into the night. When Charmian found him the next morning, his face was blue, and his body was folded in half. Two vials of morphine were by his side. There has been much debate, and little conclusion, about whether or not his overdose was accidental or deliberate, or if in fact his death was from kidney failure.

Charmian slept for two days, then oversaw his cremation. "Jack chose death, or shall we say another form of rebirth," she wrote. "He went with the illuminated smile of one who has chosen well." Her notion mirrors so well his own earlier writing:

> To me the idea of death is sweet. Think of it—to lie down and go into the dark out of all the struggle and pain of living—to go to sleep and rest, always to be resting...when I come to die, I will be smiling at death, I promise you...

ROBERT LOWELL

DRINK OF CHOICE

🐦 Vodka martini.

🐦 Vodka and milk.

"His depressions generally disappear with his second drink and reappear with his fifth. From that moment on, it's all downhill."

– Unnamed girlfriend, quoted in the biography
Robert Lowell by Ian Hamilton.

In a day when celebrity is assigned to those with the feeblest of qualifications, it is hard to imagine a more unlikely star than patrician poet Robert Lowell. At cocktail parties of the literary elite, he cultivated a reputation as a mentally ill alcoholic and womanizer. His notoriety livened up the profession and raised its profile. When his work turned confessional, he became a sex symbol for the intellectual set, and he knew it.

To be a Lowell in Boston was to be heir to American aristocracy. This was doubly so in Robert Lowell's case since his mother could trace her ancestors back to the Mayflower. Charlotte Winslow was a vain and manipulative woman, the kind who played what her son called "the fearfully important game of keeping the world guessing what was on her mind." She married to acquire the Lowell name and what she wrongly imagined to be an elevated social position. What she got instead was an unambitious and rather dim man who was content to be a naval officer. It was not in him to stand up to his wife's vicious nagging that the Navy was beneath them, and he eventually resigned. He failed in a succession of civilian jobs, falling from position to lower position for the rest of his life, and she hated him for it.

Their only child, Robert Traill Spence Lowell IV, was born in 1917, and was alternately pampered and ignored. Charlotte instilled in the boy a sense of entitlement, never allowing him to forget his rank in society, but at school he was a bully, shoplifting and stealing from younger kids. He described his child-self as thick-witted, narcissistic, and thuggish, which certainly explains the nickname he chose for himself. "Cal" was short for Caligula and short for Caliban, the perfect tag for a boy who tended to be a tyrant and a monster. It followed him all of his adult life.

In high school he pressured other boys into reading, thinking and eating what he wanted. One night he decreed that they should experience drunkenness, and that the medium would be rum and cocoa. "We got blind drunk in about twenty minutes," said a friend in an interview with biographer Ian Hamilton. "Next thing I remember I was staggering onto the porch outside—and how I didn't choke on my own vomit, I don't know." Eventually, Cal reinvented himself as an intellectual and started writing poetry.

It went without saying that he would attend Harvard, where his cousin was president. A college roommate said that he had the "intelligent habit of lying in bed all day. Around that bed like a tumble-down brick wall were his Greek Homer, his Latin Vergil, his Chaucer, letters from Boston, cast-off socks, his Dante, his Milton." He rarely bothered to attend classes. One day Lowell asked instructor Robert Frost to look at one of his poems. The older man's sole comment was, "It goes on rather a bit," a critique that convinced Lowell that Harvard did not appreciate him.

In 1936 he met an older woman who, like his school friends, was willing to be told what to think. She was sure they would marry and one night she allowed him into her bedroom. He told her that he had twice visited a brothel and "I can tell you what the whores do. I can tell you and you can try and do it." This met with about as much success as can be expected, and the experiment was not repeated. He did, however, announce his engagement to his parents. When his father tried to interfere, Lowell knocked him to the ground and ran away.

In order to distract her son from her idea of an unsuitable match, Charlotte had a friend introduce her son to writer Ford Madox Ford. He latched onto the older man and followed him to Tennessee, where a group of writers were staying with poet Allen Tate. When Lowell tried to join them, Tate tactfully turned him away, saying the house was so crowded that the only room was on the lawn. Lowell went straight to Sears, bought a tent, and installed himself in the yard for the next three months. In response to his parents' dismay at his having left Harvard, he wrote, "One can hardly be ostracized for taking the intellect and aristocracy and family tradition seriously."

Later that summer he followed Ford to the University of Colorado for its prestigious Writers' Conference. Working the event was a budding writer named Jean Stafford. She was smart, blonde, and beautiful, and Lowell found her worldly, which she was—she had contracted gonorrhea, and possibly syphilis, in Germany. She was also a heavy drinker. When he went to Kenyon College that fall, he courted her by letter.

In 1938 he invited her to Boston for winter break, where Charlotte Lowell took every opportunity to make Stafford feel unwelcome. Cal, an incompetent driver under the best of circumstances, had been drinking heavily at a party on Christmas Day and was driving Stafford home. He plowed the car into a wall.

There were conflicting reports, but one said that he walked away from the wreck and left Stafford alone. The crash shattered bones in her nose and face, and left splinters in the back of her skull. It took five operations to repair the damage, and her looks were never the same. Despite the fact that Lowell refused to admit he was to blame for the accident, the couple married in 1940.

After he finished his degree, Lowell was offered a fellowship at the University of Baton Rouge on the condition that his wife, a published writer with a masters degree, come with him and work as a secretary for the school literary magazine. While Lowell charmed the English department with his brilliance, Stafford became a drudge. She supported Lowell financially, came home daily to make his lunch, and typed his poems at night. Somehow, she found energy for her own writing.

In Louisiana, Lowell converted to Roman Catholicism, a faith he had once mocked as a religion for Irish servant girls. His mental illness was as yet undetected but in retrospect it was clear that his spiritual zealousness corresponded to a manic phase. He insisted on getting married again, this time in the Catholic church, then he stopped sleeping with his wife altogether. He censored her reading, conversation, and movie-going. One night while drinking and arguing, they fought and he broke her nose. Again.

There was a war on and he tried to join the army but was turned down due to poor eyesight. Months later, he was officially called up by the draft and would no doubt have been sent away again, but he took the opportunity to send letters to President Roosevelt (and the newspapers) announcing that he would not go. He was sentenced to prison for a year and a day, where he by and large enjoyed a monastic life. Upon his release Lowell told Stafford that he meant to be a soapbox preacher in the park. "And when I inquire of him how we will live," she wrote, "he points to the Gospels and says that we must not worry about that."

The mood passed, sort of, but he did take a job with a Catholic publisher and made an unenthusiastic Stafford do charity work. In spite of their chores and unsettled lives, they both published books in 1944. *Land of Unlikeness*, Lowell's first collection of poems, was released to small but critical success; his mother said it was nice, but valueless. Stafford's debut novel, *Boston Adventure*, came out at almost the same time and was an amazing hit, selling hundreds of thousands of copies, which only drove another stake into the marriage.

When Stafford used the proceeds to buy their first house, Lowell became even more of a bully. He told her he did not want a wife and they both drank heavily. Sometimes he went for days without speaking. Other times he encouraged a stream of friends and literary guests to use the home as a hotel, talking, drinking, and reading poetry late into the night, oblivious of Jean, who was expected to clean up after them. He did not bother to hide his emotional—soon to be physical—affair with one of the guests in the house, the ex-wife of poet Delmore

Schwartz. Jean rarely drew a sober breath and Cal was wild. Driven into a breakdown by alcohol and despair, Stafford checked herself into a hospital where she spent nearly a year drying out and conquering depression. While she was there, Lowell filed for divorce.

His second book, *Lord Weary's Castle*, came out in 1946 to incredible praise. One reviewer wrote, "A few of these poems, I believe, will be read as long as men remember English." The result was a Pulitzer Prize, a National Book Award, a Guggenheim fellowship, a photo spread in *Time*, the job as the Consultant in Poetry at the Library of Congress, and a spot at the Yaddo Artists' Colony.

At Yaddo he began to speed up, his expression for the manic enthusiasm that preceded his breakdowns. He decided that colony director Elizabeth Ames was a Communist and wrote a letter to the board demanding that they dismiss her. Along with the letter was a list of important friends he would call on to destroy Yaddo if they thwarted his wishes, but a defense of Ames led by writer John Cheever convinced the board to do nothing. Lowell was furious and proclaimed that Yaddo symbolized "the great evil of the world."

He spent some time visiting friends around the country and preached to them with what he later called pathological enthusiasm. He believed he was connected to the Virgin Mary and the Holy Ghost. "I believed I could stop cars and paralyze their forces by merely standing in the middle of the highway with my arms outspread," he wrote. While staying with Allen Tate, he turned over a list of Tate's former lovers to his wife, then held him out of a second story window by his ankles while reciting poetry in the voice of an imaginary bear. The police were called, and when they arrived he begged them to cut off his testicles. What he got instead was a padded cell and shock treatment.

Lowell's disintegration followed a basic pattern from now until his death, starting with weeks of speeding up during which he conducted brilliant, non-stop monologues that went on for days. At times he believed himself to be Jesus, Hitler, or Napoleon. Often he would become obsessed with a young woman he barely knew; it had to be someone so inexperienced that she wouldn't know better than to be flattered. When asked to support Lowell's candidacy for professorship of poetry at Oxford, his friend W.H. Auden said yes, but—"I think, however, that his supporters should be aware, if they aren't already, that Cal has times when he has to go into the bin. The warning signals are three: a) He announces that he is the only living poet; b) a romantic and usually platonic attraction to a young girl; and c) he gives a huge party."

The sometimes result of one of these parties was time in jail or the hospital. Aid for his condition was extremely limited, and he was usually released after a few weeks of shock treatment. While his bipolar condition was an untreatable result of disturbed brain chemistry, neither the mania nor its subsequent depression was helped by his heavy drinking. To some extent alcohol was his method of self-medication.

Late in 1949 he married writer Elizabeth Hardwick. They had met at Yaddo earlier in the year and Hardwick had been a regular visitor after his breakdown. Although she witnessed his attack on Elizabeth Ames firsthand and was warned by his own friends that he was dangerous, she wanted to believe Lowell when he wrote, "How happy we'll be together writing the world's masterpieces, swimming and washing dishes."

After his recovery they spent several years in Europe and in 1953 Lowell started teaching at the University of Cincinnati. He was habitually rumpled and his drunken performances at parties and readings were the talk of the town, but students and administrators alike had their idea of what a brilliant poet should be and Lowell gave it to them. He insulted his colleagues and seduced their wives, and made conspicuous, daily visits to a local strip club. The more outrageous he was, the more they liked it, and not for the last time did a community close ranks to protect Lowell from Hardwick's care. They called her fast enough, however, when their pet genius finally spun out of control—when he jumped from a moving taxi because he couldn't afford the fare; when he lectured to his class that Adolph Hitler had been misunderstood.

During the ensuing hospitalization and ones that followed, doctors suggested that he put his problems into poetry as a kind of therapy. Previously his work had been in classical form with strict observance to rules of meter and rhyme. Now, influenced by the emerging beat poets, he began to create a new verse form—the confessional poem. Its subject matter was unheard of in the 1950s: insanity, family hatreds, drinking and adultery. The works were savage and brilliant and stripped away the false veneer of the era in a way that grabbed the attention of the nation.

The piece "The Drinker" describes in painful detail one too many morning-afters:

> Stubbed before-breakfast cigarettes
> burn bull's-eyes on the bedside table;
> a plastic tumbler of an alka seltzer
> champagnes in the bathroom.

While a wife wants to know in an early draft of "To Speak of the Woe That Is in Marriage":

> What can I do for you,
> Shambling into our bed at two
> With all the monotonous sourness of your lust,
> A tusked heart, an alcoholic's mind,
> And blind, blind, blind
> Drunk? Have pity...

In 1959, he had a new book, *Life Studies*, and a two-year-old daughter, Harriett. While Hardwick remained steadfast, she worried about her child's health and safety around her husband. He made efforts to stay on the wagon. "I feel pretty used to not drinking now," he wrote, "though a little grudging and unsociable around six o'clock as I swig my bottle of concentrated grape juice." More often, however, he drank heavily on top of medication and Hardwick watched carefully for signs of mania and violence, such as his attack in 1960.

He was working in New York, creating a libretto for an opera based on a Herman Melville story, when friends noticed the signs: the sweating, lighting cigarettes, talking nonstop, the beautiful, naïve young woman. This time he went so far as to rent an apartment for them to share. Hardwick was worn down and returned to Boston with Harriet. A chastened Lowell soon followed.

He was a guest at the Kennedy White House in 1962, and a few months later he went to South America on behalf of Congress as an official representative of the American arts. When he met his assigned liaison in Argentina he took him to a six (double) martini breakfast. By lunch Lowell was taking off his clothes and insisting that he be allowed to climb equestrian statues and sit on the horses. Friend and fellow poet Elizabeth Bishop—who had fielded repeated proposals from Lowell despite the fact that he knew she was a lesbian—lived in Brazil and was on hand to help him get home to Hardwick.

Lowell spent much of the 1960s teaching at various universities. At Harvard he made quite an impression as the casually, coolly disheveled professor prone to drinking, chain smoking, and sleeping with eager undergraduates. If his appearance was confused and shy, his demeanor was dangerous and sometimes abusive. One who acted as a de facto caretaker told Ian Hamilton, "He woke earlier and earlier, and he felt worse and worse about the cruelty he had handed out the night before, and drank earlier and earlier in the day to forget it, so that in the end he was drinking vodka and milk at half past ten in the morning."

Although he won remarkable praise for 1964's *For the Union Dead*, he was unable to write for several years afterward. In 1966, after he was given a new drug called lithium, he was soon turning out up to four sonnets a day. That winter, for the first time in almost twenty years, he did not have a breakdown, and his hopes were high that "now for the rest of my life, I can drink and be a valetudinarian and pontificate nonsense." Sanity did not, unfortunately, mean peace, and his marriage was continuously assailed by his repeated affairs and alcohol abuse.

In a letter to Hardwick he wrote:

> I have been hard going the last couple of years, tho when haven't I been? I am going to do everything to cut down on the drinking, even stop if I must. You know it's hard, I seemed to connect almost unstopping composition with drinking. Nothing was written drunk at least nothing was perfect and finished, but I have looked forward to whatever one gets from drinking, a stirring and a blurring[.]

Hardwick loved her job as an instructor at Barnard, but when Lowell accepted a position at Oxford, she gave it up and took Harriett out of school so that they could join him in England. He went on ahead while she finalized arrangements, but before she could complete them, he announced that he was having an affair. Lady Caroline Blackwood was an heiress whose famous beauty was beginning to be betrayed by the ravages of lifelong drinking, but who retained an erotic quality that had captivated artists in the past. The very fact that she was older, had three children and abundant life experience indicated to many that this was different from his usual manic infatuations.

Blackwood was pregnant and Hardwick was furious. In addition to her pain and humiliation, she found that she could not get her job back nor find a decent school for the daughter he had left behind. "My utter contempt for both of you for the misery you have brought to two people who had never hurt you knows no bounds," she wrote him. There were more letters, as well as telegrams and phone calls, full of raw, revealing pain and even his most loyal friends were shocked when he used them in his next collection. *The Dolphin* won him a second Pulitzer Prize, critical praise, and the personal scorn of almost everyone who knew him.

Even after they married, life with Lowell and Lady Caroline was messy. "If I have had hysterical drunken seizures,/it's from loving you too much. It makes me wild," he wrote in a poem. Their world was littered with madness, neglect, drunkenness, pills and broken glass. "They were very much alike," said a friend. "They were both drinkers, and clever, and had tons to talk about. And both lived very near the cliff edge." A young and impressionable Lowell cousin observed, "Empty liquor bottles were scattered everywhere on the floors. Lady Caroline sat elegantly with a liquor bottle at her feet that she did not even try to kick under the couch. To me, this made her an aristocrat."

She was not, however, a saint, and was soon exasperated with Lowell. He was notorious at the university where he patronized his co-workers and slept with their wives. Lady Caroline's ex-husband threatened to take her children away after witnessing one too many violent scenes with Lowell. When he had another breakdown, he managed to charm his way out of the hospital and into a pub, still wearing his pajamas. He told her he wanted to go back to Hardwick, but he never really could make up his mind. Instead, he staged several reunions with both women. He needed one and wanted the other, and died trying to have them both. In 1977, on his way home to Hardwick from a visit to England, he died in the taxi of a heart attack. He was clutching a portrait of Lady Caroline.

PART FOUR

PARTS SOUTH: CHEERS, Y'ALL

James Dickey

Carson McCullers

Tennessee Williams

JAMES DICKEY

DRINK OF CHOICE

🐦 Jack Daniels

🐦 He could also mix a mean Ramos Gin Fizz
2 ounces gin, 2 ounces cream, add lemon
and lime juice, with a few drops of orange
blossom water, egg white, 1 teaspoon
powdered sugar. All of the items are given
a long shaking in a cocktail shaker until
frothy, and topped off with seltzer.

"I am crazy about being drunk...I like it like Patton liked war, more than my damn life."

- James Dickey

"Drinking is an artificial joy, but an artificial joy is better than no joy at all."

- James Dickey

Writer James Dickey had a problem with fellow poet Theodore Roethke. While he admired the man's work, he hated his dishonesty, and he hated it in a strange, strange way. "My own disappointment was not at all in the fact that Roethke lied," Dickey wrote, "but in the obviousness and uncreativeness of the manner in which he did it." Roethke's lies lacked style, imagination, panache. James Dickey never had that problem.

He was, in fact, a liar's liar. At one time or another he claimed that he: was raised in the mountains without a pair of shoes; was heir to the Coca-Cola fortune (he was upper-middle class); was a U.S. clay court tennis champion; had been quarterback at Vanderbilt (wingback, really, and rarely off the bench); played basketball in college (didn't); shot a 450-pound wild boar with a bow and arrow (was drinking while someone else did it); was the child of divorced parents (they were married until death); was married to a former nurse and a former prostitute (she worked for an airline); taught at Oxford; piloted over a hundred bombing missions in World War II (he was a radio operator); was a night-flyer in Korea (served state-side); was a one-time roommate of Philip Roth (they never met); had lunch with T.S. Eliot (they never met) and drinks with William Faulkner (they never met); once cheered up Samuel Beckett (never met); slept with Anne Sexton (nope); received over four hundred letters from Ezra Pound (more like a dozen); was given a Corvette as a bonus from *The New Yorker*; won the Congressional Medal of Honor and a Pulitzer Prize…and so on.

His boyhood was hardly shoeless. This self-proclaimed "hillbilly" was born in 1923 into a socially prominent family in Atlanta, Georgia. He was raised in an antebellum mansion with a cook, a nurse, and a chauffeur who drove him to school. His money came, not from Coke, but something called Triple-S Tonic, a popular patent medicine; Dickey received money from Triple-S for the rest of his life.

His mother, Maibelle, was a talented woman who could have been a writer, but her parents would not permit a career. She passed her love of words on to her children. Dickey's sister wrote for several national magazines and his brother co-authored books about the Civil War. After her first child died of polio, Maibelle doted on Dickey, and the two were unusually close. His father was nominally a lawyer but practically more of a scoundrel who spent his time breeding and fighting cocks. To his disappointment, the boy hated these bloody battles.

From the beginning, Dickey was intelligent and loved reading; he wrote his first book at five. But he was also competitive and wanted to be popular, so he did everything he could to look dumb in school. He ran track and played football, and although he did not excel in either, he perfected the role of jock. In 1942, he enrolled at Clemson A & M as a solid, unexciting engineering major. There he played football, but was never All-Southern or good enough to consider a professional sports career—two fabrications that were part of his standard repertoire.

In World War II he joined the Army Air Corps with hopes of becoming a pilot. A near crash during a test flight, ended his career behind the controls. Instead, he became a radar operator and assisted bravely and ably on many missions, winning many awards for his work. One of them, however, was not the Purple Heart, as he often claimed.

Life on base could be boring, and he filled the time reading an impressive array of writers, from the classics to the popular, making up for the education he neglected at school. Besides reading, he stood out from his peers in the fact that he rarely drank. "Almost everyone in the squadron but me drinks like mad. Anyone ruined by liquor must really be a weakling," he wrote his mother.

Dickey was a tall, brawny blonde who shaved his chest to increase his resemblance to a body-builder. He was a good-looking man in uniform, and he got a lot of mileage out of it with the women. Less than eager to ship out, he tried his best to avoid combat. When he was eventually sent to the Philippines, he performed his duty, which did not, however, include being shot down by the enemy, rescued by submarine, picking off stray Kamikazes, or firebombing Japanese cities. Perhaps his most bizarre invention was a fictional, Australian bride. He claimed she died near the end of the war, except when he claimed she died of a mysterious infection or sometimes suicide. But die she always did, which allowed him to grieve for her in a very pretty fashion for decades.

He wrote his mother often and their connection remained strong, perhaps too strong: "I find myself debating the merits of this girl or that girl, and am finally and always driven back to the only yardstick I ever had, my own mother," he wrote. "I do not think I could ever love any girl more than I love you." In addition to letters home he wrote poems, and in 1945 he had his first collection. It was primarily sentimental work influenced by World War I poets such as Siegfried Sassoon and Rupert Brook.

After the war he returned to Atlanta. He knew now that his future was in writing, and he enrolled at Vanderbilt, home of the so-called literary Fugitives, such as Allen Tate and Robert Penn Warren. He also studied the world of mythology and ancient symbolism; the subconscious, science and spirit, the "animal faith" of the world, totems and such show up in his work for the rest of his life.

In Tennessee he met Maxine Syerson, the local Miss American Airlines. She was beautiful and feminine, but Dickey recognized something else in her, something that he needed if he was going to succeed: she was very capable. They married, and Maxine became his typist, business manager, agent, and caretaker. Her devotion allowed him to be a great poet, and it allowed Maxine to be in charge of the life of a great poet. They would both pay a heavy price for the deal.

After their marriage, he got a job teaching at Rice University in Texas where he established his trademark teaching style that would last to his death. From a chair on top of a desk, he held forth, charmed and offended, baited and praised, and performed as much as instructed. He frequently lured female students to his office with attention to their work that they did not always deserve. One told biographer Henry Hart that once there he asked her, "Have you thought it would be interesting to have sex chained against a wall?"

In 1951, America was at war with Korea and Dickey taught radar instruction in Texas and Mississippi. It was good work, but hardly as exciting as the hundreds of missions he falsely claimed to have flown over Asia. In fact, most of the time he simply read and worked on poems, sitting around a swimming pool in the smallest, possible bathing suit.

He denied—but did little to hide—the affairs he was having while away from Maxine. He wrote her that he would not be bound by middle-class morality. "I want to come back to you from other people and find you the same, always," he said. The "same" meant she was not to play around herself. When she did once, he exploded in self-righteous, masculine fury. He returned to Rice in 1952. The *Sewanee Review* published a few of his poems, and in 1954 gave him a fellowship, which he used to take his wife and new son Christopher abroad. While there he taught himself French so he could study their literature in the original. When he returned home, he started working at the University of Florida.

On campus, Dickey and Maxine became known for both their flair and their drinking. Dickey made passes at faculty wives, and courted their attention by lifting weights in public in skimpy outfits. He created a more impressive scandal by reading a risqué poem to a women's group and deliberately using bad language. The University demanded an apology, which he refused. Instead he simply left Florida in the middle of the night, leaving others to grade his papers and Maxine to face his boss.

His sister helped him get a job writing advertising copy for Coca-Cola. It wasn't art, but the money was good. For the rest of his life, he creatively transformed the steady, low-level job into a more exciting scenario, one where he was a self-described player who ran the Atlanta end of the business.

When he worked in the New York branch, he took in the Greenwich Village literary scene and met writers like Norman Mailer, Allen Ginsberg, and Jack Keruoac. He also took advantage of the fact that Maxine was still in Florida to pursue women. One girl he dated did not know he was married until he took photos of Maxine and Chris out of his pocket. He ripped them up and threw them in the water saying, "That's my wife and my son." The young woman, clearly not as worldly as he had hoped, ran away from him.

When he was transferred to Coke's home offices in Atlanta, he was something of a character, doing push-ups on his desk and pull-ups in the bathroom stalls. He usually lunched alone on soup and double martinis. The fact that he spent most of his time at work writing poetry did not go unnoticed by his co-workers or his boss. Maxine continued to raise their son, run the house and manage their finances. Her dedication allowed Dickey to claim with pride that, "I'm the world's oldest living adolescent."

In 1958 a second son, Kevin, was born. The next year Dickey signed a coveted "first-reader contract" with *The New Yorker*, giving them first shot at any poem he wrote. His first book-length collection, *Into the Stone*, was published in 1960, when he was thirty-seven. The literary world sat up and took notice. At a time when the fashion was for the Beats, he brought out classical work that portrayed the world as a dark miracle. His topics were unashamedly virile, his style moving and revealing, often tinged with mythology and mysticism. It won a Guggenheim fellowship, just in time, as he was finally fired from Coke, though he claimed he quit.

To make money until the grant began, he taught a writer's workshop where he began an affair with one of his married students. He forbade the young woman to use birth control, and while she did not become pregnant, he spoke with glee about the possibility that she would have his baby and raise it as her husband's.

The Guggenheim paid for a second trip abroad. On his return in 1962, he found work at Reed University in Oregon. His second book, *Drowning with Others*, was published and nominated for the National Book Award. Reed was pleased with their new literary star, but the liberal school did not know what to do about his aggressive, pseudo-conservative antics in the classroom, asking students questions like, "Don't you agree that niggers smell worse than we do?" Acting out guaranteed that everyone would talk about him, and certainly it gave him the reputation, for better or worse, for having a gutsy, appearances-be-damned outlook.

His poems were serious, dramatic work—direct, primal accounts of soldiers and backwoods men searching for meaning. He wanted all the attention he could get to help promote them. Unfortunately, readers and critics alike found it increasingly hard to separate the man from his behavior, and it would ultimately damage his reputation as an artist.

For the time being, he was a very entertaining reader of his own work on short tours to other colleges, which he called "barnstorming" for poetry. On the road his behavior seldom varied: one faculty wife told Henry Hart that Dickey acted in one of three ways: sober and charming, drunk and obnoxious, or sober and ornery. Women, whether students or his hosts' wives, were treated with an obnoxious *droit de seigneur* for which Maxine threatened to divorce him, but didn't. She did, however, drink more, and the couple had painful fights in front of their boys.

Dickey made universities pay for his performances. At a time when most poets were willing to take two hundred dollars or less, Dickey demanded fees up to three thousand dollars a weekend. He traveled first class. Unfortunately, his transgressions seemed to grow in proportion to the money he made. He made comments like, "Did anyone ever stop to think that maybe the Blacks are inferior?" which caused colleagues to call him the southerner-in-residence.

His affairs with campus women added to the gossip: a young professor had a nervous breakdown when he found that his wife was sleeping with Dickey. One couple divorced when the wife claimed that she was carrying Dickey's child. Another female student had to go to

Mexico for an abortion. Maxine had a very understandable bout of hysterical blindness.

In *Summer of Deliverance*, Christopher Dickey wrote, "My father was drunk onstage, and disoriented. It was difficult to watch him, but I knew the old friends would make excuses. They always did. We always did." That was the day that Dickey smirked and unveiled a new confessional poem, "Adultery," in front of an audience that included his wife and sons. Maxine took the public blow with grace.

Dickey's next collection, *Buckdancer's Choice*, won the National Book Award in 1966. In spite of this and other awards, one reviewer said it sounded like a sort of Georgia cracker Kipling. Cracker or no, in 1966 he was made Poetry Consultant to the Library of Congress, the highest honor America gives to a working poet.

Dickey took the tribute, and the job, seriously, but approached it in his own way. One of his goals, he said, was to "get every guy to sit down and have a beer with his soul." He was a sensitive artist in a Corvette Stingray who regularly greeted female students with lines like, "Hi, honey; fuckin' anybody regular?" Poet Donald Hall described dinner with Dickey before a televised reading: "He had a bunch of Manhattans without ice, and then champagne, and when we were all finished he got another bottle of champagne, drank a good bit of it, and stuck the bottle in his pocket while we walked from the restaurant."

Dickey's celebrity continued to grow with the publication of *Poems 1957-67*. He charged more than ever for his readings, but conference organizers frequently found that he cost them more than cash. At a college in New York he told his host, professor Kelsie Harder, that, "I am a legend in my own time." On the drive to the conference, Harder's wife felt Dickey's hand on her breast. He demanded a bottle of Jack Daniels before each reading, and drank dramatically throughout. While it made for a good theater, it did not improve his judgment: the conference director was Hindustani; Dickey called him a nigger.

His relationship with his oldest son degenerated. He was a loving father when home, but he clearly went out of his way to avoid home as much as possible. As Chris grew into adolescence, Dickey seemed determined to turn him into a drinking buddy. When he was fourteen his father told him that he had fucked over a thousand women. The year after that he got the boy drunk. They argued bitterly over his plans for school and a career.

After the Library of Congress, Dickey became writer-in-residence at the University of South Carolina in Columbia. As his popularity grew, so did his need for attention, often obtained by baiting faculty and audience. When Reynolds Price and John Cheever accepted an invitation to read at University of South Carolina, they not were not prepared for Dickey's inquiry into their personal masturbation practices. Or that he would make a strange but rather sweet pass at Price. (Price was actually fond of him, and referred to his friend's alter ego as Dickey Berserk.)

He agreed to be interviewed by James and Barbara Reiss. The young literary couple tried to keep up with his drinking: martinis and Bloody Marys in the morning, Scotch by the tumbler-full at lunch. When their tapes were transcribed and edited into a book, Dickey elbowed them out of the way and worked behind the scenes to keep their names off the finished book, which he called *Self-Interviews*. He made the singularly grandiose claim that the book would cause a shock that "will cause a certain revaluation of poetry, and, yes, of existence in this time and place."

The existence of time and space notwithstanding, his books were big sellers. In a field where most poets have to settle for prestige instead of cash, Dickey, ad-man and promoter extraordinaire, was offered a $25,000 advance for his next two volumes. It did not stop him from being cheap. While he owned a Corvette, Jaguar, and Cadillac, he always made someone else pick up the check, even if they were students, out-of-work friends, or a woman he was hoping to seduce.

After seven years of work, the novel *Deliverance* was published in 1970. The story of four Atlanta businessmen who get in over their heads in the Georgia wilderness was an instant bestseller, selling almost two million copies in two years. It also garnered considerable critical praise and no small amount of controversy. Some women found it to be misogynistic. In towns where the story was deemed pornographic, it was pulled from schools and libraries and burned.

Deliverance resulted in celebrity that gave James Dickey a scope for his personal theater. "It seemed to me then and for a long time afterward that forces of self-indulgence and self-destruction, which were always there in my father but held in check, were cut loose," wrote Christopher Dickey. Under the influence of fifteen bourbons he went on television and claimed that the story was true and he had lived it. At a writers' conference he prowled around the women's dorms yelling for a sacrificial virgin until security took him away.

In 1971, *Deliverance* was made into a movie, and Dickey haunted the set, attempting to micro-manage the production, to the dismay of director John Boorman. After a breakfast of bourbon or martinis, he would criticize Boorman or one of the film's stars for not catching the moment that he had written. Rehearsals were almost impossible, and when actual shooting began he was banned from the set, although he returned toward the end to play the small role of a local sheriff. In a magazine interview, actor Burt Reynolds said, "He is a wonderful poet, a wonderful poet. And the kind of man that after he has four martinis you want to drop a grenade down his throat…"

When the movie was released in 1972, Dickey was in his glory. At the New York premiere, he paraded up and down the line of ticket-holders and introduced himself as one of the stars of the film. When the movie started he yelled out commentary like "Hot Damn!" and when the lights came up he was in his sheriff's costume. He announced to the audience, "I did everything in this movie…but direct it, and I even did some of that, too."

For weeks at movie theaters in South Carolina, he walked up and down the aisles shouting out dialogue, or stood in front of the screen and lip-synched with his character's lines. In restaurants, he would walk up to strangers, especially good-looking women, and say, "I wrote *Deliverance*." His classes became little more than a forum for his accounts—real and imagined—of his importance during the making of the movie. He bragged to the boys and put down the girls, and slapped one in the face when she contradicted him.

Dickey was sensitive about not having a PhD, and now his worldly popularity made him seem less of an academic figure. To shore up his image, he began to pressure colleges to give him honorary degrees, using everything from wheedling to coercion. Through his hard work he eventually garnered a dozen, then he pretended they didn't matter.

In 1971, *Sorties* was released. It is a collection of Dickey's essays, opinions, and inexplicably nasty put-downs of almost everywriter he knew, including Norman Mailer, Anne Sexton, Sylvia Plath, John Berryman, Elizabeth Bishop and Robert Lowell. Criticism of other writers was rapidly becoming part of Dickey's stock-in-trade: he called John Milton "a great stuffed goat;" in class he called the poetry of T.S. Eliot a lot of bull; in an interview he called Robert Frost a "sententious, holding-forth old bore who expected every hero-worshipping adenoidal little twerp of a student-poet to hang on his every word."

In the biography *The World as a Lie*, Henry Hart recounts a story of Dickey and Al Braselton. Their friendship went back to their advertising days in Atlanta. For the past few years, however, Braselton had been battling life-threatening alcoholism, a struggle that Dickey relentlessly undermined, pushing drinks on him, saying, "You're no more an alcoholic than I am." In 1973, Braselton and his girlfriend visited the Dickeys. When he asked for a Tab, Maxine brought him one laced with bourbon.

The next night the foursome dined at a nearby restaurant. Dickey and the girlfriend left early, leaving Maxine and Braselton to follow. When they did, they found their partners in bed together. In front of Maxine and Braselton, Dickey slapped the woman and asked, "Who's your man?" On the drive home, Braselton grabbed the steering wheel from Dickey's hands and tried kill them both before Dickey got the car under control.

In an unlikely turn-about, Dickey almost took the controls away from a pilot who was flying him to a reading. Heading for the University of Georgia, bad weather kept them from landing. The pilot, who was a professor at the college, wanted to turn around. Dickey knew the man was aware of his reputation as a World War II ace, and insisted that he take over. The offer was refused. At the reading that weekend, Dickey spoke long and loud about how he single-handedly landed the plane of a panicked pilot and saved his life.

Whether barnstorming or on tour, his actions were out of control. He was rude in interviews, and when he read his poem "Blood" on the radio, he dedicated it to "all the menstruating women out there." His appearance on *The Tonight Show* was marked by drunken rambling. He started an appearance at a formal luncheon with, "Alright, you assholes, I'm going to read you some literature." In 1975, he wrapped his Jaguar around a tree and tried to fight the police officers who rescued him.

He drank beer or scotch for breakfast. For lunch he had soup and double martinis followed by beer. Maxine was also drinking heavily. Christopher Dickey wrote of the "tinkling of ice cubes in the kitchen at six in the morning" that meant that she was up, and "the whisky she had at her right hand all day long every day until she died."

Life with Maxine, however, was almost over. The couple regularly threatened to kill each other and went at it with arrows, skillets and words. Chris begged his parents to get a divorce before it was too late. In 1976, Maxine was diagnosed with cirrhosis, and lost half her blood from a burst esophagus. She survived the night, but not the next collapse, which came two weeks later. Maxine Dickey died of alcoholism at age fifty.

In practical matters, Dickey was as helpless as a child, and he was angry with Maxine for deserting him, accused her of a death that was a virtual suicide. Christopher Dickey felt that it was more like slow murder on his father's part. The night before the funeral, Dickey hurt his children even more by saying that he did not want to see "the stuffed crow remains of Maxine" in her coffin.

His estrangement from his sons was almost complete. The gap widened when Dickey's book *The Zodiac* was released, and he tried to pressure Christopher, then an editor at the *Washington Post Book World*, into giving it a glowing review it did not deserve. But nothing pushed their relationship off the cliff like Dickey's marriage, eight weeks after Maxine's death, to a student less than half his age.

He told reporters that he did not care for liberated women and expected his wife to be a slave. And while Deborah Dickey gave up her academic pursuits to care for him, from the beginning she made it clear that she would not play by the same rules as the long-suffering Maxine.

She put her foot down about other women, and soon after the wedding beat both Dickey and one of his lovers in a confrontation. The next year, she hit him for talking with another woman. Once she stabbed him with one of his arrows.

While his writing still commanded high advances, magazines that courted him a few years earlier now rejected his poems. The demand for his readings declined dramatically as did the fees that he was offered for them; at age fifty-five, his public persona had become a liability. He never quite came around to the fact that his racist remarks, his macho posturing, and his relentless criticism of fellow poets from the podium weighed heavily against his diminishing talent and inferior recent work. He got another harsh dose of reality when he shopped his private papers to different universities with a $350,000 price tag, and there were no takers.

His past began to catch up with him in an unexpected way. Although his status was slipping in some quarters, there were some students from the next generation who wanted to make a documentary about his life. Dickey knew that any earnest filmmaker would expose a lifetime of lies, especially those that were part of his established legend, his role in World War II for instance. Now, instead of welcoming celebrity, he had to find ways to hold it at bay.

In 1981, his daughter Bronwen was born. He was thrilled and doted on the girl. Deborah, however, was depressed and refused to continue as the ad hoc secretary, typist, and manager that Maxine had been for decades. She was angry and unbalanced, and not quite the slave Dickey thought he was getting. In an interview with *People* magazine, she mocked him, saying, "He wants to captain the ship, my ship as well as his."

When she went back to school for her masters degree, Dickey fought her every step of the way. She got him back by beating him, and with a heroin habit that would soon rule their lives. To pay for drugs, Deborah pawned items that meant a great deal to Dickey, and he would trudge to the pawnshop to redeem them. For years he had told dramatic lies about his poverty—now it came close to the truth, as much of what he earned went to pay for her drugs. Worse still, she became involved with the criminals who were selling her heroin. They beat her up, broke the windows out of her van, and threatened Dickey and their daughter.

He reacted with petulance to the changing times, and seemed almost confused about feminism and racial equality. He commanded a far smaller fee than in his heyday, but he could still get readings at colleges. Schools, however, now knew to send handlers, usually a faculty member, to make sure that he made it to the podium relatively sober. Their efforts often failed, and university department heads found themselves increasingly embarrassed by his racist comments and his inclination to tell jokes about women or sex, and his habit of telling faculty wives that they needed a real man.

As time went on, he depended on, and manipulated, the kindness of those who would write about him. He followed one reporter to his car and said, "When you get back to the typewriter, you can say that I'm nothing more than a broken-down old drunk. You can say anything you want. I can't stop you. But don't do it."

While Dickey's current writing was considered to be inferior by some, he continued to win awards and accolades, and to be sought out for screenwriting jobs; Robert Redford visited with Dickey at the University of South Carolina about a possible project. That he continued to write at all was heroic, now that he was raising his daughter single-handedly and dealing with the desperate characters who regularly threatened his wife's life.

In 1986, Deborah hit Dickey with a heavy object, possibly a paperweight. At the hospital, a CAT scan showed a blood clot in his head, and immediate surgery was performed to release the pressure on his brain. Being James Dickey, he got plenty of mileage out of the situation, changing the story to one where he took a blow from a tire iron while trying to protect a child at a gas station who was being beaten.

Why did he put up with this abuse? Psychologically, there may have been many reasons, but his most practical excuse was that he wanted to keep his young daughter. For all his faults, he understandably feared that an official investigation would cause the authorities to take her away. He also held a real, however improbable, conviction that marriage was somehow inviolate.

In 1987, his novel *Alnilam* was published. It was far darker than his previous works: the story of a war hero turned murderer. The book was informed by his obsession with serial killer Ted Bundy, who he claimed—dishonestly—to have met. Parts of it were very well written, but it could not rise above its violently misogynistic bent. When he finally copped to the fact that this was hurting sales, he publicly backpedaled the he-man image he had cultivated for decades.

Even so, he often managed to act down to the world's worst expectations of him. At one reading, a woman professor was sent to get deliver him to the show: he told her, "You're too pushy. What you really want me to do is fuck you," then fell off a podium. One night in a crowded local honky tonk, he gave an impromptu poetry reading dressed in fishnet underwear.

Despite the critics' off-hand response to *Alnilam*, he was given a $500,000 advance for his next novel, but life was not letting up on the sixty-six-year-old Dickey. Biographers were on his trail, forcing him to unravel a lifetime of lies. He was letting friends take more and more responsibility for Bronwen. Deborah was attacked by her supplier in a downtown restaurant. When she was arrested on a drug charge, it made the newspaper. In 1991, they both had car wrecks involving driving under the influence.

In the early 1990s, his collected poems were released, but they attracted little attention from critics or readers. His third novel, *Toward the White Sky*, was published in 1993 but found few fans. He continued to receive awards and tributes from schools, but they were smaller and less frequent.

In 1994, his health took a dive. He staggered across the campus to a group of long-time lunch companions and gasped, "Help me." They got him to the hospital where he was diagnosed with hepatitis. He quickly went from 230 to 160 pounds. Deborah called for Dickey's sons, who came despite their years of separation. With their help, he found the courage to push Deborah away and file for divorce.

He tried to return to readings but life and culture, caught up with him. For the first time, his classroom comments about women were reported to the school as harassment. This, and ill health, circumscribed his teaching duties. During the last three years of his life he gave up drinking. His writing became stronger, and he continued to teach. In 1995, USC hosted a tribute to Dickey. The same year, pulmonary fibrosis was found in his lungs. He lived for a little more than a year, increasingly frail but sober, until his death early in 1997.

CARSON MCCULLERS

DRINK OF CHOICE

🐦 Bourbon and Sherry.

"Emily vowed that never again would she touch liquor, and for a few weeks she was sober, cold and downcast. Then gradually she began—not whiskey or gin—but quantities of beer, or sherry, or outlandish liqueurs; once he had come across a hatbox of empty créme de menthe bottles."

- Carson McCullers, *A Domestic Dilemma*

I have more to say than Hemingway and God knows, I say it better than Faulkner."

- Carson McCullers

"An hour with a dentist without Novocain was like a minute with Carson McCullers."

- Gore Vidal

When Lula Carson Smith and Reeves McCullers got married they made a deal: they would take turns at being writers. Carson would write for one year while Reeves supported her, then they would switch, and so on, year after year until they made it. "It was going to be a marriage of love and writing for both of us," she wrote. Neither the deal nor the marriage turned out as they planned. What they got instead was a life of cruelty and betrayal, selfishness manipulation, bisexual affairs on both sides, and years of drunkenness.

They met in 1935, in Carson's hometown of Columbus, Georgia. As a child, her mother had given the girl an incredibly strong sense of entitlement; she was forbidden to play with neighborhood children. "I'm sure I missed certain social advantages by being such a loner but it never bothered me," she wrote in her memoir. A tall and eccentric looking child, she didn't hesitate to accentuate her outsider status by wearing boy's clothes.

When she was fifteen, two things happened that changed her life: she received a typewriter, which she loved, and she got very sick, which she underestimated. Her illness was misdiagnosed as pneumonia. It was actually rheumatic fever, an infection that can often causes damage to the heart and other vital organs. In Carson's case it silently set in motion a series of strokes that would leave her paralyzed before the age of thirty.

By age eighteen she had already spent a year in New York where she took writing classes at Columbia University. She was home for the summer when she met Reeves McCullers at a friend's house and got "a shock, the shock of pure beauty, when I first saw him. He was the best looking man I had ever seen." The twenty-year-old Reeves brought her flowers, cigarettes and beer. As the summer went on in drink and endless hours of talk, they thought themselves to be psychic twins. When she returned to New York, they had an understanding.

A professor took notice of the strange, tall girl and her writing and helped her place her work into the prestigious *Story* magazine. She was paid twenty-five dollars which she spent on chocolate cake, wine, and a book. When Reeves joined her in New York, they became lovers. "The sexual experience was not like D. H. Lawrence," she wrote. It did bring them closer, however, and to celebrate, "we treated ourselves to pink champagne and tomatoes out of season."

That fall she was sick again with what was thought to be tuberculosis. Reeves brought her home to Columbus for a lengthy recuperation during which she began writing a novel. The fact that she believed herself to have a deadly lung disease did not stop her from smoking three packs of cigarettes a day.

The couple wanted to marry but jobs were scarce during the Depression. Eventually Reeves found something at a credit company in Charlotte, North Carolina. They had already agreed on their writing pact and that Carson would go first. After a year she would get a job and Reeves would be the writer. In 1937, twenty-year-old Carson Smith, wearing a green velvet suit, white socks and Buster Browns, married twenty-two-year-old Reeves McCullers in her parent's living room. They were happy in Charlotte, living in a two-room apartment overrun with books. In the evenings they listened to music and played chess, or Carson would read that day's writing aloud. They bought sherry by the gallon and tried to make it last a weekend. As time went on it did not, and their nights were increasingly filled with tension and drunken arguments.

Carson's novel-in-progress had already earned an advance from Houghton Mifflin, so even though they moved into Reeve's year, he continued to work while she finished the book. Since Carson was a slovenly housekeeper, he also had to clean and cook. In spite of this, after his death she wrote, "I don't know why I felt I owed such devotion to him." On some level she did know, because in the same account she wrote, "My husband wanted to be a writer and his failure in that was one of the disappointments that led to his death."

The Heart is a Lonely Hunter, was published in 1940, and was an immediate success. Carson was twenty-three and looked much younger, almost childlike, which added to her popularity. Her mother had prepared her for such a moment since early childhood and she had no problem living up to her image as the toast of New York. "I became an established literary figure overnight, and I was much too young to understand what happened to me or the responsibility it entailed. I was a bit of a holy terror," she wrote.

One group fascinated by this southern gothic *wunderkind* was a community of exiled artists and intellectuals who had come to America fleeing Nazi Germany. This worldly band was held in thrall by the girl's self-confident lack of sophistication, her white socks and baseball caps, and her long, slow drawl. Writer Klaus Mann shrewdly described Carson as "a strange mixture of refinement and wildness, 'morbidezza' and naiveté."

She would soon be sharing a house with Mann and his sister Erika, composer Benjamin Britten, writers Paul and Jane Bowles, and poet W. H. Auden. Another member of their circle was a beautiful and androgynous Swiss writer, Annemarie Clarac-Schwarzenbach. Carson was desperately attracted to her. "She had a face that I knew would haunt me to the end of my life," she wrote. At first the older woman returned McCuller's admiration and there may have been an affair, but soon Clarac-Schwarzenbach was on the run.

She wrote Mann:

> [Carson is] seriously ill and lives in an imaginary world
> so bizarre, so remote from reality that it is absolutely
> impossible to get her to listen to reason. I thought I
> had acted with all due caution and had treated her
> gently, but she is waiting for me to arrive from day to
> the next, convinced that I am her destiny.

Much has been written about Carson's sexuality. While she
certainly had a tendency to pursue a certain kind of woman, it is telling
that these were usually women who did not want her attention. She
recognized this quandary and analyzed it in her later writing:

> The curt truth is that, in a deep secret way, the state of
> being beloved is intolerable to many. The beloved fears
> and hates the lover, and with the best of reasons. The
> lover craves any possible relation with the beloved, even
> if this experience can cause him only pain.

Over and over Carson would bring herself this kind of pain by
chasing women who gave her no encouragement, forcing them to
reject her in awkward public encounters.

One day she saw Greta Garbo on the street. Carson boldly
approached the reclusive beauty and offered her love and devotion.
When Garbo politely declined, Carson wrote her a love letter several
hundred pages long. Another time she carried a bottle of champagne to
the house of writer Djuna Barnes and attempted to introduce herself.
Barnes' firmly refused the acquaintance from the other side of the door
with: "Whoever is ringing this bell, please go the hell away." Carson's
obsessions did not exclude men and all heck broke loose when she and
Reeves fell for the same guy, who happened to prefer Reeves. Poet Louis
Untermeyer told McCuller's biographer Josyane Savigneau that they
had a fling, a platonic affair intensified by not-so-platonic embraces.

Her second novel, *Reflections in a Golden Eye*, added to her
homosexual mystique. Published in 1941, it dealt with the sexual and
psychological confusion among the inmates of a Georgia army base.
It's a dark novel even by today's standards, and in its time it was almost

too hot to handle. Carson was visiting her family when the book was released, an occasion that prompted a visit from the local Ku Klux Klan, who told her "we don't want queers in this town."

It was the summer she suffered her first stroke. She was twenty-four years old and felt fine, until one day she wanted to check the time. When she looked at the clock she could see the numbers but no longer understood what any of them meant. She sat down fast and said, "Daddy, I'm afraid I'm sick." Over the next few weeks she endured blinding headaches, blurred vision, and confusion, but she slowly recovered and returned to New York with Reeves.

She spent the summer of 1941 at the Yaddo Artists' Colony working on a new novel, with a thermos of sherry and tea—heavy on the sherry—at arm's reach. Katherine Anne Porter was also in residence, and Carson decided that she was in love. She lay on the floor outside Porter's door for hours, crying and begging. When the evening dinner bell rang, Porter opened her door and stepped over the prostrate body of Carson McCullers without a word, effectively ending the obsession.

She wrote and sold several short stories that summer. *The New Yorker* bought one and when the check came, Reeves forged Carson's name and cashed this and several other checks made out to her. She filed for divorce and left Reeves in New York while she headed for Georgia. In 1942, she learned that she had won the prestigious Guggenheim grant. Reeves enlisted in the army.

He wrote Carson letters from his base in Tennessee, apologized and explained, "After I was with you I coasted on your identity until I became disgusted with myself and became alcoholic that year in New York. But the shock of our being apart straightened me out quickly and I have been of right mind since last spring." Carson responded and in May 1942 they met in Atlanta. That fall she returned to Yaddo and Reeves was transferred to nearby New Jersey and they spent several days together. By the time he shipped out in November, they were discussing marriage.

From Europe, Reeves wrote often, describing army life and the French countryside. His letters were those of a brave soldier away from home and Carson's responses were of a worried woman keeping the home fires burning. While their communications contained true tenderness, they also exhibited an element of role playing, to say nothing of denial: "When I was with you, you were the best wife a man could have—coming home from work, in the evenings, in the bed or hurried early mornings, at the market, in times of trouble—you were the most considerate, lovely and compatible person I could ever hope for as a life companion."

"My Reeves, do you know my love?" she wrote. "I want you to feel my tenderness for you every instant—I want you to feel it in each nerve and muscle and bone. I feel your love for me in that way."

He was slightly wounded as part of the D-Day landing at Normandy. Soon he was going about the French countryside "liberating" any Calvados—the strong, distilled apple cider of the region—that he could find. When he was wounded again in 1944 he was sent to England to recover and then on to the U.S. and Carson. Without her, Reeves would earn three Bronze Stars, a Silver Star and a Purple Heart. He would write letters that showed he could be a storyteller, stories that might have been a jumping off point for his long delayed writing career. Without her he had a second chance to live his life. Instead, he remarried Carson in 1945 and sealed his fate, putting into motion a marital disaster of epic proportion.

He returned to his base in Georgia while she worked at Yaddo completing her third novel, *The Member of the Wedding*. This story of an adolescent girl reluctantly coming of age was published in 1946, and contains some of the best descriptions of the pain and loneliness of child life ever written. After fifty years it remains part of the American literary canon, testament to the fact that however shortened by illness and self-destruction, Carson possessed enormous talent and skill.

Playwright Tennessee Williams read and loved *The Member of the Wedding*. He believed himself to be dying (a lifelong hobby he would pursue until his death at the age of seventy-three) and wrote Carson a fan letter inviting her join him for his final days. She spent a month at his home in Nantucket, cooking his meals and playing the piano while Williams read aloud from Hart Crane. They wrote every day from ten until two, and spent the rest of the day swimming, riding bicycles, and drinking hot rum and tea.

Carson also drank whiskey. Williams told interviewer Rex Reed, "She would go out and buy Johnnie Walker and sit in a straight-back chair at the foot of the steps and after my friend and I went to bed she'd sit up all night mooning over this romance in her head. I'd come down in the morning and the bottle would be empty."

She met fellow southerner Truman Capote and took the twenty-two-year-old writer under her wing. Together they spent May 1946, at Yaddo, writing, drinking, dancing, and in McCuller's case, wearing out her welcome. With its constant stream of ambitious artists, the colony often had its contentious moments, but Carson was in a league of her own, exhibiting a relentless, aggressive need to be the center of attention, demanding the love of other residents in a way that left them drained. It was the kind of behavior that writer Gore Vidal, in an interview with Virginia Spencer Carr, called, "vain, querulous, and a genius—alas, her presence in a room meant my absence: five minutes of one of her self-loving arias and I was gone."

In the summer of 1946, she won a second Guggenheim and used the money to go to France with Reeves. They were quite a couple: he was a returning war hero, full of self-confidence and covered in medals, and "Carson burst like a tiny bottle of glass on Paris," wrote Janet Flanner. "Melodramatic, a genius." Genius, probably, but melodramatic, definitely. French editor Andre Bay arrived at her hotel for a lunch date to find her in bed with a bottle of cognac. He told Josyane Savigneau that "She did not seem to comprehend me very well," so he put a coat over her nightgown and carried her to the restaurant. "I got something to eat. She drank." He said she was in "something of fog, as people who drink constantly from morning till night sometimes are."

Reeves was out the night that Carson fell. When he got home he found her on the floor where she had been for eight hours, conscious but unable to move. He rushed her to the hospital where they diagnosed her second stroke. It left her, at the age of twenty-nine, paralyzed on her left side for the rest of her life.

They flew to America for treatment and were met in New York by his-and-her ambulances—Reeves had DTs and had to be strapped down. Her family met them to help with her long recovery. Carson was unable to perform even the simplest tasks, and depended on them to cut her food, help her dress, and climb the stairs. A letter from Carson to Tennessee Williams read, "Last week, I was in the deepest depths of hell. I am still very sick. There is almost no respite from the pain." It is little surprise she self-medicated, or as her cousin and close friend Jordan Massee said, "The doctors told Carson she could have two cans of beer every evening and one large drink—or two small ones. Unfortunately, they didn't define 'large' or 'small.'"

In early 1948 Carson and Reeves separated again. Soon after she cut her wrists and had to spend a month at the Payne Whitney Psychiatric Clinic. Reeves joined Alcoholics Anonymous and found a job, and they reunited over the summer and returned to Carson's rambling house in Nyack, New York. Despite the fact that she was suffering from nausea, convulsions, and migraines, she worked on a theatrical adaptation of *The Member of the Wedding*. In December, it opened in Philadelphia.

Shortly after the opening, she discovered she was pregnant. In *Illumination and Night Glare* she wrote that she was "surprised but pleased." Her mother, however, was sure that a baby would kill her and told the doctor "I won't let Carson have this baby." Her mother arranged for an abortion but before it could be performed Carson miscarried.

In her unfinished autobiography *Illumination and Night Glare*, she wrote:

> The miscarriage was not easy. Mother who had some outlandish fear that either they might put the baby back or do something that would kill me in the end, would not call another doctor. So I suffered until Monday, when a taxi took me to New York. The blood was all over the car by the time I got there.

In 1950, *The Member of the Wedding* went to Broadway and was a huge success. This could not be said of the marriage, and the couple separated again. Carson went to Ireland where she stayed with novelist Elizabeth Bowen. At first they were strangers, but as Bowen got to know her houseguest she found her to be a destroyer, and a terrible handful. Carson continued on to London where she wired Reeves to join her, luring him away from his precarious stability. He did, but when they returned to New York that August, they separated again.

The next year *Ballad of the Sad Café*, a collection Carson's stories, was published to excellent reviews. Reeves was a weekly guest in Nyack, in spite of the separation, Carson was in a constant whiskey haze while Reeves was on the wagon, but his sobriety was short-lived. When Carson left for England on the *Queen Elizabeth*, he got drunk and stowed away. What must have seemed like a charming idea at the time soon became an awkward reality of no ticket and no passport. When they arrived some strings were pulled and he was allowed off the ship with two weeks to return home. He spent the time notoriously drunk in the lovely country homes of Carson's literary friends.

She remained in England when he was sent home, and there she fell in love with a doctor. She wrote her husband a letter that read, "I miss you beyond telling," even as she sent him details of her latest crush. "One more thing, darling. I want to thank you for your understanding. Of course this won't last long." In the fall of 1952 she rejoined him in America and they headed for Italy where they made spectacles of themselves, aimless and constantly drunk. Even old friends were put off, and she began a nasty feud with Truman Capote. Writer Gore Vidal was there, and later said that he would have spent the night running around the Coliseum had that been the only way to avoid Carson McCullers.

Her relationship with Reeves began its final, sorry descent. They began to physically abuse each other; one night he tried to throw her out of a window. In France they stayed with an old friend, John Brown, but it wasn't long before he asked them to leave. Their screaming and drunken fights were too much for his children. He told Savigneau that "Those two had an abominable, cannibalistic relationship. But she was the vampire. She had a colossal power of destruction."

They moved to a farmhouse in the French countryside. For anyone else it would have been idyllic, with fruit trees, dogs sleeping in front of the fireplace, and a village woman to make them soufflé and vegetable soup; not so for a couple who drank straight gin out of tumblers. One night Reeves tried to strangle Carson, who bit him. When he saw the blood he released his grip.

They returned to Rome. In a letter quoted by his biographer Gerald Clark, Truman Capote wrote, "Sister (the famous Carson McCullers, you remember *her*?) and Mr. Sister are frequently to be observed *staggering* along the Via Veneto but of course Sister and Mr. Sister are too exalted, and usually too drunk, to recognize my poor presence."

In the fall of 1952, they tried France again. Isolated in the farmhouse, their despair deepened and in the spring of 1953, Carson fled without warning, leaving Reeves alone and penniless. Broke and depressed, he stopped eating, but when friends wrote to Carson about his condition, she responded by asking for her records and silverware. They rescued Reeves themselves, gave him money and installed him in their hotel, but it was too late. One night in November 1952, the forty-year-old Reeves McCullers got very, very drunk, took too many pills, and threw them up. He suffocated while unconscious.

They had been together for eighteen of Carson's thirty-six years. When she was told of her husband's suicide, she asked for a drink, then proceeded to finish a bottle while making phone calls to friends and family. Contrary to the wishes of Reeves' family she did not bring his body home, perhaps feeling he would have preferred France. At the burial of his ashes were Janet Flanner, Truman Capote, and several war comrades. Absent was Carson.

Tennessee Williams, Carson's most loyal friend, told biographer Virginia Spencer Carr, that "Reeves died, ultimately, out of great love for Carson. His was a desperate loneliness." Williams was uncharacteristically critical when he accused her of "casting off Reeves as she did and showing no feeling for him or his memory after he was dead. She spoke of him in the most unkind terms, and it always upset me." She likewise wrote of Reeves in unkind terms in her memoir when she said, "I had to handle him like a spoiled brat, conceding to everything, so that the dignity of our marriage was quickly being destroyed."

In the 1950s she lectured at universities. Once, believing she saw her arch-nemesis Truman Capote in the audience, she started screaming from the stage. Visiting Yaddo she was constantly drunk and often cruel. She went to Florida and drank tumblers of gin with Tennessee Williams and worked on a play called *The Square Root of Wonderful*, about a man who wants to be a writer and kills himself when he fails. It opened in 1957 and gave Carson her first-ever negative reviews. She acknowledged them: "In 1954 I began to write a disaster not on purpose, God knows, but day by day, inch by inch, I was falling into chaos. Why I wrote this crap is hard to realize; of course, I had no idea it was so bad."

In 1958, she began work with psychiatrist Mary Mercer. For Carson it was another impossible crushes—"I not only liked Dr. Mercer immediately, I loved her"—but Dr. Mercer was able, after a year of therapy, to relieve a considerable amount of the psychic pain that was getting in the way of Carson's writing. Surgery partially restored mobility to her left arm, although more and more she relied on a wheelchair to get around. In 1960 she published her last novel, *The Clock Without Hands*. Although it was a bestseller, the reviews were mixed. No matter; if a critic or reporter came to interview her, she would meet them in her nightgown and wheelchair and offer them a drink, with "A little toddy for the body?"

In 1961, the public library of Columbus, Georgia, asked her to give them her original manuscripts. She responded furiously, damning them for the fact that the library was for whites only. "How can I, in all good conscience, deposit these works of love in a place, where all mankind is not permitted to read, enjoy and use them?" she wrote.

In 1962, she had a mastectomy to remove breast cancer. She was weak and tired, but continued to write, working with Edward Albee on another theatrical adaptation of her work. There was also a book of children's poems. In 1967, following the filming of *Reflections in a Golden Eye*, director John Huston invited Carson to his estate in Ireland. By now she was an invalid and in great pain, but she enjoyed the trip and the attention from the Irish press.

Her decline did not stop her from smoking and drinking bourbon from a special silver cup. Amazingly, she was planning a book of short stories and writing letters, when in August 1967, she suffered another stroke. This time it was the right—the good side of her body—that was paralyzed, and she never regained consciousness. She died a few weeks later. Her funeral was attended by Truman Capote, Janet Flanner, and W. H. Auden.

TENNESSEE WILLIAMS

DRINK OF CHOICE

🕊 In the late 1940s, he drank gin and grape juice. In the late 1960s, he drank gin with Seconal. On his visit to New Orleans, he discovered a bar called Victor's Café and a drink called the Brandy Alexander: mix one ounce crème de cacao with one ounce brandy, top with heavy cream. Shake with ice and strain.

"I've read stories about Hemingway sharpening twenty pencils every morning to get himself started, but I don't believe them. I take a martini in with me."

- Tennessee Williams

"I have a reputation for immorality, but I know that I'm [t]he most goddamn fucking puritan that ever was."

- Tennessee Williams

"Tennessee was utterly doped. He says the only way he can face being with the family is to put a Seconal in his drink every evening."

- Christopher Isherwood, *Diaries, Volume One*

Tennessee Williams said, "I'd like to live a simple life with epic fornications." By all accounts the American playwright got only half his wish, and it wasn't the simple part, for his fornications were indeed epic, as was his drug use, liquor consumption, and capacity for cruelty. Hundreds of sexual partners, and pills and booze took their toll on his talent and life, although the man who was arguably the twentieth century's greatest playwright was forced to live his personal drama off the stage.

He was born Tom Lanier Williams in Columbus, Mississippi. As a boy he learned self-dramatization at his mother's knee. Edwina Williams would faint when vexed, but only if in proximity to a convenient couch. She played the lifelong role of a proper southern belle with a desperate pertness and non-stop chatter. Gore Vidal called her the last of the great room-emptiers. Tom and his sister Rose were brought up under a shadow of forced elegance and delicacy. They were not allowed to have friends, and together they formed a deep and troubled bond that would last their entire lives. Rose, frail and neurotic to begin with, wilted under her mother's efforts to make her into a vivacious belle. Tom learned an unlikely helplessness and unbounded hypochondria.

Their father Cornelius worked for a shoe company. His was on the road a lot, which made it easy for him to pursue his womanizing, gambling and drinking. When he was home he browbeat his son, and called him Miss Nancy. When Tom was seven, Cornelius moved the family to St. Louis, Missouri, where shy and possessed of a deep southern drawl, he was unable to make friends. Instead he withdrew into Rose's company, and books. When Edwina bought him a typewriter for his homework, it became "my place of retreat, my cave, my refuge."

His poems and stories were printed in his school paper, and when he was seventeen, his first story was published in the national magazine *Weird Tales*. These small but real publishing triumphs caught the attention of his fellow students, giving him new status and self-confidence.

He began to seek out the attention of girls, but his mother bitterly discouraged these friendships. There was consolation, however, in his first trip to Europe with his grandparents. In Paris he had his first cocktail, a Manhattan, and a glass of champagne.

On his return he enrolled at the University of Missouri. In college, he felt confusing feelings towards some of his fraternity brothers. He was deeply in love with his roommate, but neither of them knew what to do about it. It would be a few years before he found out. In the meantime, he had other problems. The Depression caused a dent in the family finances and this, combined with his lackluster grades, had him living at home again and working for his father.

He studied typing and stenography at night, and expected to be a secretary, but he continued to write. Although he did not yet depend on the alcohol that would dominate much of his life, he was addicted to coffee and cigarettes, and relied on them instead of sleep. The pace brought on his first nervous breakdown in 1935. His grandparents welcomed him to their home in Memphis for the summer, to rest and recover. While there he haunted the local library, and discovered for the first time the plays and stories of Anton Chekov. The Russian writer became an obsession, and a determination to be a playwright was born.

He returned to St. Louis with his mind awakened and a goal that would become all consuming. He lived at home and attended classes at a city college. Of this time, he wrote in his journal that he considered himself "egocentric, introspective, morbid, sensual, irreligious, lazy, timid, cowardly." History finds him guilty as charged on every count save one—he was never lazy. "Tom had fanatical and inexhaustible energy in his writing," said a fellow student years later. "His persistence was almost grotesque. It was Dionysian, demoniac. He wrote because it was a fatal need."

Rose's condition was degenerating. She was in her late twenties and of a precarious mental state in general. Her lack of an outlet for her sexual feelings made things worse. One doctor actually prescribed that Rose have sex, to the horror of her mother, whose Victorian prudishness exacerbated the whole situation. Edwina had coached Rose in restless, endless talk, meant to indicate a bubbly charm that would put others at ease. It never did; a man seldom called on Rose more than once.

In 1937, doctors diagnosed her with schizophrenia, while some members of her family accused her of having delusions of sexual immorality. Rose was committed to a local mental hospital, where for the next six years she would be treated with cold water and shock treatment. The same year, twenty-five-year-old Tom failed to graduate locally, and enrolled in the University of Iowa. He was under increasing pressure from his father to get a real job but Tom had no intention of obliging. When he left school a year later, he changed his name to "Tennessee." It was a gesture meant to sever his connection to the conventional world.

Through the years, when asked about the origin of the unusual soubriquet, he told a charming lie: "The fellows in my class could only remember that I was from a southern state with a long name. And when they couldn't think of Mississippi, they settled on Tennessee." In fact, no one at the three colleges he attended remembers him by that name. In his wonderful biography, *The Kindness of Strangers,* Donald

Spoto writes that it is more likely that Tom was searching for a word that would symbolize his fresh beginning, and liked none better than the name of the state where he had been happy with his grandparents, and where he first discovered great works of drama in a Memphis library.

He wandered to New Orleans looking for work, taking on a variety of odd jobs to pay for a room on Royal Street. Some people find their soul mate in a person, for Williams it was in a town. The Crescent City spoke to the part of his mind that he called the rebellious Puritan. It was there that on New Year's Eve 1938, he had his first gay experience with a stranger he met at a party.

Soon he headed to California in hopes of finding work as a screenwriter. What he got was a job plucking chickens. Rescue came in the form of a hundred-dollar prize, an award from a New York theater group for one of his plays. The one-act work was forwarded to agent Audrey Wood.

After reading it, she signed the unknown playwright sight unseen. For the next thirty years she would sell his work and take care of him in a hundred practical ways. In the meantime, he lived off the odd ten-dollar bill from his mother or grandfather.

Sometimes he got by on fifty cents a day. Sometimes he just starved. "His primary need was survival," wrote Wood. "It was unending struggle to stay alive and fed until we could find a producer who would give his work a production." Once he had to hock his typewriter, so he borrowed one from a friend to write with, then pawned that one as well. "Not a red cent and no credit, no groceries but dried peas and a few potatoes. But I will survive somehow," he wrote. In a letter he told a friend that he was down in Mexico "without fucking penny twixt me and the hairless chihuahuas."

When bad finally went to worse, he made his way home to St. Louis, which, for him, was a circle of hell. In a letter to Audrey he wrote: "My life is hopelessly circumscribed by the wholesale shoe business on one side and the D.A.R. on the other." His father drank and mocked his grown son with no job. His mother tired him with her relentless genteel airs. Writing play after play kept him sane, and helped ease the pain of seeing Rose in the hospital.

Years later, their younger brother Dakin Williams recalled a medical report. Rose Williams "smiles and laughs when telling of persons plotting to kill her. Masturbates frequently. Memory for remote past is nil. Appetite good." Her doctors wrote that "Rose is generally cooperative. She believes that her doctor is related to her and that everyone in her ward are her relatives." After an afternoon with her in 1939, Williams wrote, "Visited Rose at sanitarium—horrible, horrible! Her talk was so obscene—she laughed and talked continual obscenities."

A few months later he won a Rockefeller Grant for one thousand dollars, which Audrey, having found that Williams was hopeless in money matters, prudently doled out in small installments. With this he was able to finish his first long play *Battle of Angels*. With Audrey at work finding a producer, he visited Provincetown, Massachusetts. In the 1940s, as now, the city was a haven for artists and had a notable gay community. While he still entertained the mental notion of heterosexuality, physically he threw himself into a binge of promiscuous sex with men. He changed partners nightly, and for the rest of his life he would seem unable, or unwilling, to deny any impulse, whether sex, liquor, or drugs.

Battle of Angels opened in Boston in early 1941. Its mixture of adulterous desire and religious conflict and imagery garnered a public outcry. Critics and public alike felt it was indecent. When it closed after two weeks, Willliams was exhausted and discouraged. Soon he was broke and working as hard as ever, but one friend noticed a change in Williams. Before he had always "had this great sweetness and charm and humor." Now he could turn "and be cold and abusive as ice," said Fritz Bultman.

Bultman was also concerned about his friend's reckless drinking and sexual behavior, such as nightly trips to the waterfront or Central Park in search of anonymous encounters. The inevitable results were an occasional beating, robbery, or threats at the end of a knife. But sex was one of the ways he self-medicated both physical and mental pain. A persistent cataract in one eye kept him out of service in World War II, and required several painful, frightening surgeries. A year after his first play, he was thirty-one years old and working as a waiter, elevator operator, and movie usher. It is hardly surprising that he suffered emotionally from the "blue devils," the darkest kind of depression.

It was nothing compared to the horror he would soon face. Rose had been institutionalized for six years. Treatment for mental illness in this era was extremely limited, and Rose's condition had responded to nothing. Now her doctors wanted to try a new brain operation in hopes of restoring her sanity. Instead, it was a disaster. During the lobotomy, certain nerves in her brain were severed, which left her calm but hopelessly confused. Time stopped for her, and for the rest of her life it would be 1943.

Williams held his mother responsible. He himself, however, was perfectly aware that his mother had been advised to this extreme move by their family doctor and other professionals. The damage was done. He would write Rose's story, in one way or another, into almost every play he created.

His extreme poverty came to an abrupt halt when agent Audrey Wood told him he was on his way to Hollywood. MGM was offering $250 a week for the up-and-coming playwright. The drawback was that he was obliged to write something stupid enough for a Lana Turner or Margaret O'Brien movie. He had a strategy, though: he would work on his own plays at his hotel, and collect the studio check anyway. Surprisingly, this sometimes worked.

He was making headway on the play that would become *The Glass Menagerie*. For the first time, he could help out at home by sending a portion of his check to St. Louis, to be spent on Rose and his grandmother, who was dying of cancer. This meant that he could spend little on himself, a fact that did not seem to cramp his personal life. In a journal he wrote, "New lovers every night, barely missing one, for a month or more," and "Had a pretty satisfactory 'roll in the hay' this evening—then a long, dull round of the gay places to kill time. I have nothing to say to these people after I've been to bed with one of them."

In the fall of 1944, his contract with the movies was finished, and so was his play. With the help of Wood, it soon had a backer and producer. It opened in Chicago, where no one had seen anything like it before. Arthur Miller later wrote, "It is usually forgotten what a revolution his first great success meant to the theatre." The story was deceptively simple: two children who are suffocated to near madness by their mother and her illusions. Amanda Wingfield, a dead match for Edwina Williams, tyrannizes her children with the memory of her own fantasy childhood as a southern belle, a role that her neurotically shy daughter can never live up to. If Williams stole painful characterization from his mother and her shortcomings, he made up for it by giving her half of the royalties from the play.

It opened to a small audience and a few days later producers had a closing notice ready to post. Two Chicago critics, however, were not prepared to let this work pass so easily. They wrote rave reviews in their respective papers, and came back night after night, and continued to champion the work in print. It slowly built up speed. By the end of the month, it was sold out every night. When it opened in New York, lines were around the block. At thirty-three, Tennessee Williams had been a failure living with his parents. At thirty-four, he was an overnight success.

He was already working on *A Streetcar Named Desire*. It would become a centerpiece of American theater, an account of a faded southern belle struggling to tell her lies and keep her sanity in the face of her earthy brother-in-law. It was a fabulous story, and at the same time an allegory of the Old South striving against the demanding brutality of the new world. As in all of his best plays, Williams himself is imbedded in the heroine, Blanche du Bois: fragile, cruel, promiscuous, and hungry for acceptance, lying to herself as much as others. In her delicate tottering to insanity, there was also another depiction of Rose.

When it opened, it was hailed as a masterpiece, and would soon win the Drama Critics Circle Award—the first of four for Williams—and a Pulitzer Prize. When it was up and running he fled to Italy, where he found a country recovering from war and its aftermath, and men who were hungry and willing. His endless, faceless encounters with such men would inspire his novel *The Roman Spring of Mrs. Stone*. The movie of the book would be Williams's favorite film adaptation of his work. He began to mix pills into his substantial liquor intake. In August he returned to New York for rehearsals of *Summer and Smoke*.

Williams began to earn his reputation as a world-class hypochondriac, insisting on his imminent death to anyone who would listen. The blatant fact that he wasn't sick was no consolation; he honestly believed that this indicated an affliction so obscure that treatment was impossible. The obsession eventually altered course, so that he believed friends and strangers alike were plotting to kill him.

It was around this time that he met Frank Merlo. They lived together for the next fourteen years, during which Merlo cared for the writer in every way, creating a relatively stable domestic life that would shore up Williams's ailing mental health and make it possible for him to not only survive "the catastrophe of success," but create some of his greatest works. "[Frank] was at home with everyone, easy to be with, uncomplicated and understanding. And he loved and protected Tenn and did everything for him," said a longtime friend.

When the couple visited Hollywood, producer Jack Warner asked Frank Merlo what he did. "I sleep with Mr. Williams," he answered. "He was no goody-goody," wrote Christopher Isherwood. "He was just plain good. And he wasn't just some kind of faithful servitor. He was a lovable man with a strong will." Another friend said, "He took no nonsense from him—and Tennessee could ladle out nonsense—and he was a man of sense and good taste."

Williams was rich and famous before he turned forty. *Streetcar* had been sold to the movies for a half-million dollars, and critics agreed that he was genius. He bought a house in Key West. While it was a base of operations, he continued to travel a great deal. At least with Merlo, his wandering was grounded in something safe and sound. Privately, however, Williams complained to friends that his sex life was limited by Merlo's desire for a quiet home life. Williams crammed in as many lovers as he could whenever Merlo was out of town,

Merlo could not persuade Williams to settle down, neither could he slow his increasing drug use, like barbiturates washed down with gin. The combination increased Williams's incipient paranoia, even his envy of Merlo. Straight and gay friends alike called Merlo the "Mayor of Key West" because of his easy popularity, and Williams resented it.

His latest play, *The Rose Tattoo*, was another popular success, and won a Tony Award for Williams and its two stars. With its run established in 1951, he visited Rome, where he totaled his Jaguar in a drunken crash that he miraculously walked away from. He was often drunk these days, and was arrested in Key West for driving while intoxicated.

Williams went from New York to Florida to Rome to London to Denmark. Some think that he was just running, trying to stay ahead of—or outside of—his adult responsibilities: sobriety, self-knowledge, obligations of art, and Merlo's love. He lied and told friends that Merlo was cheating on him to gain their sympathy and avoid judgment for his own infidelity. More and more he surrounded himself with an entourage of sycophants to assure him he could do no wrong.

Theatrically, he still had the ability to take chances. *Camino Real* was his biggest failure from this era—one reviewer wrote that it was the worst play yet written by the best playwright of his generation—but this non-linear juxtaposition of poetry and fantasy was close to his heart. For the rest of his life he would take its failure hard, but on opening night he managed—with the help of heavy drugs—to hang tough. When most of the audience walked out between acts, he turned to a crew member and deadpanned, "Well, I don't think they are really taking the play to their hearts, would you say?"

In 1952 there was a revival of *Summer and Smoke*. The 1948 version had not fared well, but this time it starred a little-known actress namedGeraldine Page as Alma Winemiller. Miss Alma is a tragically inhibited character, and her struggle with longing and repression made her the one character out of all of his plays that Williams related to the most.

In New Orleans, he scheduled surgery, then cancelled it when the hospital wouldn't let him drink in his room. In New York, Williams and fellow writer Carson McCullers drank their way through a pitcher of martinis at a reading at the Young Men's Hebrew Association; both writers remained blissfully unaware of their audience's embarrassment. (When French writer Françoise Sagan visited Williams and McCullers in Key West a few years later, she was surprised to find the tumblers of water they carried around with them were actually full of gin.)

In 1955, *The Rose Tattoo* was sold to Hollywood for $100,000. Both Williams and Merlo had cameos in the film. The same year he won a second Pulitzer for *Cat on a Hot Tin Roof*. By now, audiences knew what to expect from Tennessee Williams's writing: poetry, humor and examination that went deep into the human soul, packed into a great story, and this play was no exception. A family gathers on a Mississippi plantation for the birthday of patriarch, Big Daddy. Maggie the Cat, his desperate daughter-in-law, does not intend to be bested by either him, her drunken husband or her greedy in-laws. (The ending for this original version was somewhat darker than the ultimate movie ending.)

Williams was at the top of his game, artistically, financially, and critically. He had the company of a good man who loved him for himself, but his slow, downward spiral became a landslide, soon to be an avalanche. When he left for Europe that summer, it was without Merlo. He moved from city to city, from hotel to hotel, with no plan or order, possibly due to his increased intake of double martinis and Seconal, which was also beginning to affect his famous work ethic.

That fall, Williams was supposed to join director Elia Kazan for the demanding work of shaping and reshaping the play *Baby Doll*. Kazan had collaborated with Williams on several plays and their movie counterparts, and he knew that something had changed when Williams left him to take care of the revisions himself. Moreover, there was no ending to the play, and the director, brilliant as he was, could not write it for him. Not only was Kazan worried about his colleague, his own reputation as a director was at stake. Williams eventually finished the play long-distance, and mailed it to Kazan on location.

By 1956 he admitted that he drank too much, but justified it on the grounds that he had to medicate his anxiety attacks. He told friends that Merlo did not care about him and only wanted his money. He accused Merlo of taking drugs, although in fact his strongest drug of choice was tobacco, four packs a day, and the occasional cannabis. "I never really knew what [a paranoid personality] meant until I saw it in Tennessee in the 1950s," said Maureen Stapleton. "He would accuse Frank of something—in Frank's presence and mine—and Frank would prove Tenn wrong. But even then Tenn wouldn't believe him." It got worse. Another friend remembered that "More than once, we sat at a restaurant table and he would overhear someone nearby say something uncomplimentary—and invariably Tenn thought it was about him."

In the summer of 1957, he started seeing a psychotherapist. The doctor suggested he try heterosexuality, ending the partnership with the doctor. Williams had Rose moved to a private hospital in Ossining, New York, and when he was nearby he spent most of his time with her. He came away from one visit with a ten-dollar bill in his hands and tears in his eyes. Rose, whose comfortable home, treats, clothes, and vacations were paid for by her millionaire brother, had scrimped to save ten dollars for him and pressed it into his hands saying, "Tom, I know how hard you are working at the shoe warehouse. I have been saving some change for you, and I hope this will help things to be a little easier."

He turned a year's worth of analysis into a play about insanity and therapy. The 1958 play *Suddenly Last Summer* chronicles the story of a young woman. She has witnessed the horrifying death of her manipulative cousin, and his mother tries to bribe local doctors to perform an unnecessary lobotomy and erase the memory. Writing this play, with its themes of sex, homosexuality and cannibalism, he knew he was playing into the hands of those critics who felt that he was writing for shock value.

He had already run into this wall over the film *Baby Doll*, when near hysterical charges of immorality were launched nationwide; it just wasn't as "nice" as *The Glass Menagerie*. In an interview with Don Ross, he responded to the notion of perversion in his work: "Sordid is just a term used by a second-rate reviewer." He also said, "I want to shock people but not to have a *succes de scandale*, not to shock per se, but because I want to give people a jolt, get them fully alive. I never do it for commercial reasons."

The accusations surfaced again in 1959 over his play *Sweet Bird of Youth*. He was called "a dirty minded dramatist who has written of moral and physical decadence as shockingly as he can." There were other challenges to his popularity. Williams had been on top for over a decade. It is rare for any artist, regardless of talent, to stay at the pinnacle, and there is nowhere to go but down. The sixties were coming, and with it the dramatic era of the "Angry Young Man." The growing popularity of television would further change public tastes.

But quite simply, his ability to create a long, sustained play was being eroded by his drug and alcohol use.

Night of the Iguana, in 1960, would be his last major work. It had its share of sex and tortured souls, but also looked to an unexpected spirituality in the characters of an elderly poet with slightly roguish qualities—an homage to his beloved grandfather—and his granddaughter, the understanding Hannah. The play and the subsequent movie were popular, but Williams continued on his personal descent.

Stalwart supporters like Audrey Wood and Frank Merlo were disturbed by his connection to damaged, alcoholic writers like McCullers, Jane Bowles, and William Inge. Even more frightening was his inclination to surround himself with members of the aimless jet-set, down-at-heels aristocracy, and a dismaying coterie of beautiful losers. They told him anything he wanted to hear, especially that his old friends, and old love, only wanted his money.

He became more and more estranged from Frank Merlo. Years later, Williams would say, "Frank would also put me down like a prize shit when I deserved it, and I often did. One loved him for it." Perhaps, but apparently one preferred courtiers who did not say no. Williams left Merlo at home while he picked up willing men in bars, or held court with adoring women. Now that Williams could afford the best help and all the adoration that money could buy, Merlo was just someone who limited his life, who dared to pass judgment on his performance as a human being.

Williams made Merlo the villain. He told anyone who would listen that Merlo was using him, so that he could leave him and in doing so, gain more pity and support than ever. Frank Merlo would not be the only friend to fall in this fashion.

Cheryl Crawford had produced his plays for years, with devotion to his vision. Without warning, he gave his newest play to someone else, then wrote Crawford to criticize her for dropping the work. He greeted her, if at all, with coolness, from then on. In *Esquire*, he gave an interview that all but dismissed agent Audrey Wood. In 1961 he admitted that the only thing keeping him going was liquor, pills, and swimming. The first two contributed to the scene he made with Merlo when he was bitten by his own dog, Satan. He ranted and claimed that Merlo had turned the dog on him in order to kill him for his money. Close friend Maureen Stapleton told Williams's biographer Donald Spoto, "It was Tennessee who brought it on. He was paranoid about everything—his health, the opinion others had of him, Frankie's intention...the craziness began with those awful crazy pills he was getting."

After *Night of the Iguana*, his plays were flops. In the years to come, he would damn critics and audiences alike for being unwilling to let him change his voice and style, to take chances. He played the role of misunderstood visionary, when in fact, his vision, or lack thereof, was the result of drugs. His confusion and the disreputable hangers-on who surrounded him shielded him from realizing that there was nothing brave in producing a non-linear play without form or narrative, just because the playwright is too stoned to face the work of producing a narrative. "I must continue to dare to fail," he said. "That is my life."

There is controversy surrounding the behavior of Tennessee Williams at the death of Frank Merlo. When his chain-smoking lover was found to have lung cancer, Williams took him to Key West to recuperate. At the same time, he kept himself at an arm's length to make room for writing and other partners. It is likely that something inside his wounded psyche had to distance himself from the death of his lover and the illusion of a grounded home life that Merlo had given him. "With Frank ill, Tennessee just couldn't cope for himself with the details of real life...He was incapable of relying on himself or his own strengths, and I think this is why he turned to those bereft souls who provided him with easy distractions and no challenges," said friend Frank Corsaro.

The night of Merlo's death, he waited until the end of visiting hours, then went out for drinks. His best friend died while he was at the bar. The only positive thing that seemed to come from his passing was that Williams gave up smoking.

For the next few months he retreated to Key West and saw no one. He took more and more drugs, and surrounded himself with yes-men who would let him get away with any petty behavior, as opposed to friends and colleagues who might demand something more of him.

"Whenever he encountered old friends, he felt a compulsion to make them suffer as he was suffering," said Donald Windham. The man who had written so beautifully of the kindness of strangers was becoming an expert in deliberate cruelty.

In 1964, Williams wrote friend Paul Bowles: "I now rely mainly on drink and pills. My intake of liquor is about a fifth a day—half Bourbon, half vodka. To pep up, I take half a Dexamyl, and when I find it's necessary to smooth things over I take one and a half Seconals." He came under the sway of the infamous celebrity "doctor" Max Jacobson, who made his name by giving "vitamins" intravenously to an array of stars. (The Beatles would write a song about him.) His vitamin-B shots were laced with a healthy dose of speed to move things along. As his patients became addicts, he was happy to supply them with their own syringes and vials of amphetamines to administer to themselves; for years Williams carried such a pack. He was also taking Nembutal, Seconal, Phenobarbital, and other Schedule II narcotics, and drinking heavily. He had doctors in many cities and was able to fill multiple prescriptions.

Windham, who had collaborated with Williams years before, believed there was a change, when "his raw material begins to veer away from being an isolated individual's reaction to life and toward being an isolated individual's reaction to himself and his condition." Shorthand, it was all about him. Williams himself admitted, "I wrote on speed, and my mind started going too fast for the typewriter."

By 1966 he needed higher doses of amphetamines to get an effect, which contributed heavily to his paranoia. He was also taking a sedative called Doriden. A usual dose was 1/4 gram, twice a day. Williams took five grams a day. Audrey Wood had tried to stay out of his personal crises, as he clearly wanted her to, but in 1967 she asked him to quit seeing Dr. Jacobson. He refused, repeating over and over that the doctor was "a lovely man."

During this self-proclaimed "Stoned Age," he frequently misplaced pills or forgot how many he had taken. One night he screamed at his new companion, William Glavin, and accused him of stealing them and of plotting to hurt him. Summoning what dignity he could, Glavin left the restaurant. Williams asked the waiter for some paper, and wrote: "If anything of a violent nature happens to me, ending my life abruptly, it will not be a case of suicide, as it would be made to appear. I am not happy, it is true, in a net of con men." He signed it Tom, and mailed it to his brother Dakin.

The man who was honored by the National Institute of Arts and Letters that summer could not feed himself. "When he knocked over a liquor glass, he accused others of doing it to embarrass him. Seconal tablets were still washed down with gin," wrote biographer Donald Spoto.

He traveled to Japan with actress Anne Meacham, where he had Italian food with Yukio Mishima. Drug possession was a serious crime in this country, and Meacham panicked when he accused her of stealing his needles and pills. She called Dakin for backup, who managed to get Williams to return to America.

He collected William Glavin, who was recovering from surgery, and they made their way from San Francisco to New York to Key West and back to San Francisco in a matter of weeks. Now Williams believed that people in nearby hotel rooms were planning to murder him. He complained to the management that other patrons were laughing at him and plotting against him. He was asked to leave.

Back in Key West, Williams had an accident and burned himself. His told to Rex Reed, "Baby, I was out of my skull. I could no longer remember how many pills I had taken, and the liquor I washed them down with had a synergistic effect. I woke up at two A.M. pouring a pot of scalding hot coffee all over my body." Dakin was called in, and took advantage of the situation to get his reluctant brother into a hospital, and from there to St. Louis.

> It's almost the last thing I remember before they committed me to the loony bin...the next thing I knew, my brother Dakin was in town and we were at the airport; and next I was in the basement of the house in St. Louis with a bottle and Dakin had brought me a typewriter and I couldn't hit any of the right keys, and I told him the typewriter was no good and he said, 'Tom, you really must check into the hospital now.

Inside the psychiatric ward of the hospital, doctors took him off of his drugs cold turkey. The shock of the withdrawal caused three convulsions and two heart attacks in a matter of days. He was released in a few weeks, but the paranoia remained—he believed that television shows were plotting against him. He never forgave Dakin. As soon as he was able to talk again, Williams bitterly accused him of trying to kill him for his money. "My incarceration in the bin was nothing less than an attempt at legal assassination," he told *Playboy* in 1973. Close friend Maureen Stapleton said, "I called Tennessee later and told him he should be grateful to his brother and when I said that, he turned on me for a time, too."

In 1970, he acknowledged his homosexuality on live television. Asked about it by host David Frost, he answered, "I don't want to be involved in some sort of a scandal, but I've covered the waterfront." Frost hastily called for a commercial, and Williams said, "I should think you would." The audience loved it. He was disarmingly honest about his drug use and illness to the media. It was a way of striking first, while choosing what to include and what to omit and his bravado won him points.

His Key West parties were full of drinking and strangers. He accepted the admiration of a crowd who "gave him nothing but took whatever they could get," said one director. Friend David Greggory observed, "If you live at the top of fame and material success, of course, it's hard to live anywhere else. At this time he began to group people in terms of those who believed [success] would happen again and those who didn't."

In 1971, *Two Character Play* was being staged. This work would always mean a great deal to him. It was another try at working out the dynamic between himself and Rose, through a brother and sister embroiled in madness and confusion. While rewriting and rehearsing the play, he returned to heavy drug use. He shot up Ritalin for the rush, then popped Nembutal to help him sleep.

Audrey Wood had reservations about this experimental play, but when *Life* and *The New York Times* wrote about Williams's strange behavior, she came to his defense in public editorials. This woman whose livelihood depended on the good will of the press, walked out on a very public limb for his sake. Then she flew to Chicago to help him get through what promised to be a rocky opening. The audience on the night of the preview was indifferent to the play, and Wood reported that he "swiveled about to stare at me, and with the vigor only he possessed, shouted at me, 'And as for you, you have wished I was dead for the last ten years!' As I exited, I heard him say, 'That bitch! I'm glad I'm through with her!'"

He wanted a play to keep him from "sinking into shadow and eclipse of so much of everything that has made my life meaningful to me." If he could not have this, then he would settle for attention, which he got when he agreed to act in *Small Craft Warnings*. He played to type in the role of drunken doctor, but mugged and spoke directly to the audience in comic asides, and ad-libbed so much that his fellow actors were confused. For publicity, he went on a local news show and gave a weather report that warned "small crafts" of an impending storm.

For the rest of his life, his work would bear a similar and weary stamp. Running through his plays now were the themes of a fading artist facing insanity, guilt, and sex.

In his great plays, he had explored these topics through the psychology of various characters and a complex weave of narrative and poetry. Now he tossed them around as a series of images, barely connected vignettes, and stream of consciousness that made the audience his personal therapist. More and more they balked at having to buy a ticket for the privilege.

He acknowledged the change in style, but rationalized: "As my life became more desperate I had to change the style, because the conventional pattern of a play no longer contain that kind of frenzy." At the same time he told reporters that critics wanted to cut him down to size. As his theatrical reputation declined, he sought the spotlight in other ways.

Memoirs, published in 1973, offered a rambling, self-indulgent, but dishy, view into his personal life. The same year, he told *Playboy* less about his craft than his masturbation history and feelings about "anal eroticism." Readers also learned that "I find women much more interesting than men, but I'm afraid to try to fuck women now" and that, "I can't get it up without love."

In the late 1970s, he barricaded himself in his hotel room and refused to work on rewrites of *Clothes for a Summer Hotel*. A press conference was arranged to publicize the play. When he didn't show up, the play's press agent took journalists straight to Williams's hotel and demanded entrance. One reporter remembered, "Williams answered the door half-naked and very coquettish." Inside his room writers and photographers found filth, broken glass, and unflushed toilets.

In the next two years he was honored by the Kennedy Center for his lifetime achievement, and given the Medal of Freedom by President Jimmy Carter. In 1980, Edwina Williams died. Williams covered her casket with two thousand violets.

His paranoia continued unabated. In 1981, while as working on out-of-town try-outs in Chicago for his last full-length play, *A House Not Meant to Stand*, he turned on his new agent Mitch Douglas. "He came up with the notion that I had been dealing with the airlines to put him on a depressurized airplane to cause him to die of a heart attack. And he threatened to make this publicly known," Douglas told Donald Spoto. "I, for one was more and more unwilling to be a doormat for him."

He was proud to accept an honorary doctorate from Harvard University in 1982, but he was also tired and confused. Still, he wrote every day. "Gallant is the word to describe Tennessee at the end" said Elia Kazan. He roamed ceaselessly, from Cambridge to Key West to London to Rome and back to Key West. One day he got on a bus alone, with no fixed destination, got off in Key Largo and wandered to a bar. A young couple befriended him and drove him back to Key West. In return, he gave the husband, a writer, his typewriter.

Williams ate very little now, and lived mainly on wine, coffee, and Seconal. On Christmas Eve, he was found unconscious and rushed to the hospital. He announced that he was suffering from "a sufficiency of life." Between Christmas and February 1983, he traveled from Florida to New Orleans, then to Italy and finally came back to New York. There he stayed at the Hotel Elysee. He was accompanied by a paid companion, but he kept to himself, and on the night of February 24, he went to bed with a bottle of red wine, a little cocaine, and a bottle of pills. He somehow managed to choke on the cap of the pill bottle, fell from his bed, and died.

Tennessee Williams loved the work of Hart Crane, the young poet who committed suicide by jumping off a ship and into the ocean. For years, Williams maintained a codicil in his will that he be buried at sea, as close to that point, "twenty-four hours north of Havana," where Crane leapt to his end. Instead he was buried in St. Louis, where his tombstone reads from his play *Camino Real*, "The violets in the mountains have broken the rocks."

PART FIVE

TAKE IT OR LEAVE IT:
LOVE ME, LOVE MY BOTTLE

Dashiell Hammett

Kingsley Amis

Marguerite Duras

DASHIELL HAMMETT

DRINK OF CHOICE

꒲ Martini

꒲ Johnnie Walker Red

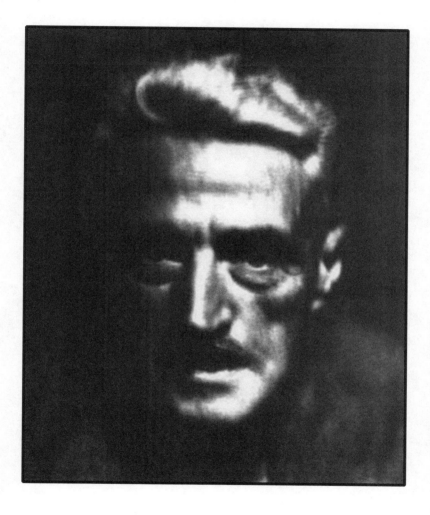

"In one bar, he gently removed a glass from a woman drinking a martini, and threw it over the bar, where it crashed at the bartender's feet. 'Mix baby a Dashiell Hammett special!' he ordered. Into a brandy snifter the bartender then poured all manner of liquors."

- Joan Mellen, *Hammett and Hellman*

**There are relatively few biographical works on Dashiell Hammett, largely due to the interference of Lillian Hellman, who devoted herself to preserving her version of his legend. To this end she ruthlessly frustrated writers and filmmakers who were interested in his story, instead promoting her own largely fictional memoirs, *An Unfinished Woman* and *Pentimento*. While much of these accounts are untruthful, they do give an interesting flavor of what life with Hammett must have been like.

In his heyday, Dashiell Hammett was often confused with the characters in his novels. Like Sam Spade in *The Maltese Falcon*, he had been a detective and lived by a hardboiled code. Like Nick Charles in *The Thin Man*, he dressed well and was attractive to women. And, like his literary creations, he was a heavy drinker, but while Spade and Charles could more or less hold their liquor, Hammett was more likely to pass out in a gutter.

Of course, he could afford to. His detective stories had made him both rich and famous and with good reason. He almost single-handedly brought the mystery genre from lowbrow to literature and he did it in five, bestselling novels written in four years. Readers were hungry for more, but from 1934 until his death in 1961, he would write nothing. His brilliant output followed by decades of silence has turned into one of literature's enduring questions: did he stop writing because he drank, or did he drink because he couldn't write?

He had his first drink in a Baltimore railroad yard where he had been working since age fourteen. In 1908 he left school to help support his family, who were perpetually on the edge of debt. Working as a clerk at the B & O gave him an education of sorts: he learned to play dice, bet on horses, drink, and visit prostitutes. By age twenty he was nursing a venereal disease, the first of many that would keep him temporarily out of commission with women. It would be the only thing that ever would.

When he was twenty-one, he went to work for the world-famous Pinkerton Detective Agency where he learned how to shadow a suspect, use a blackjack, and more importantly, how to wait out the tedious hours between action. He saw corruption first-hand and learned the hard way that the line between the good guys and the bad is sometimes blurred.

In 1917, mineworkers in Montana were striking for better wages and safer conditions. Hammett was one of several operatives Pinkerton sent to break up the strike, using intimidation tactics to force the desperate miners back to work. (He may have witnessed the murder of labor organizer Frank Little.) He was young and did his job but it didn't make him feel any better about himself. Years later his role in this injustice would influence his ill-fated decision to join the Communist party.

Like many other young men, he enlisted in the army during World War I. Before he could ship out, however, he was struck down by the 1918 influenza epidemic that would kill over 600,000 Americans. Hammett lived, but contracted tuberculosis in his weakened state and his lungs were permanently damaged. He was discharged in 1919, but soon his health was in total collapse and he was forced to live in a veterans' hospital in Washington state. He was weak and coughing up blood, but that did not stop him from complaining that the hospital didn't give him enough free cigarettes.

The twenty-seven-year-old patient saw a lot of nurse Josephine Dolan. Their affair was fun and friendly and after Hammett was transferred to another hospital, she asked him for a favor. She was pregnant—which had cost her her job—had no other family and was in a tight spot. She was honest about the fact that the baby wasn't his.

He genuinely liked Jose and appreciated the devotion she had shown him during his illness. He also held a high regard for people who told the truth when it might cost them. Besides, after years in the hospital with bleeding lungs he was sure he would die young. So in the summer of 1921 they married and moved to San Francisco.

Their apartment was small and they were poor, but they were happy together. Hammett tried detecting again but the outside work in the bay area fog was hard on his lungs. Instead he spent most of his time in the library, reading anything and everything, getting the education he had missed as a child. Eventually he found a full-time job writing advertising copy. It was unexciting, but it was steady.

He also wrote stories. More than anything he wanted his work to be in H.L. Mencken's *Smart Set* magazine. It was the last word in sophistication and highbrow commentary and when one of his pieces was accepted in 1922, he knew he could make it as a writer. But he needed quick money for his new family and to get it he turned to a different Mencken publication, the pulp magazine *Black Mask*. It was one of the first and best mystery magazines, popular and well read. Hammett studied the format and began to write to formula for easy sales. His style was unique, however, and he soon had a following.

Up to this point, most detective fiction had been intellectual and urbane, of the Sherlock Holmes or Philo Vance variety. Hammett's stories introduced a new kind of sleuth, one whose experiences mirrored his own at Pinkerton. The Continental Op (short for Operative) was given no other name. Short, balding, and overweight, he had a personal code that was tough but honest. The Op appeared in twenty-six stories and two novels. Not only was the hero new, so was the writing. The prose was lean and spare. No writer of mere detective fiction had ever used sentences so sharp and clear. This may have been genre writing, but he wrote it, he said, after reading Henry James and Dostoevsky.

As he turned thirty, a second daughter—his—was born, and he was still writing at the kitchen table in a two-room apartment. His stories were popular but he was only making two cents a word. He had to write a novel if he was going to make enough money for the girls. When his tuberculosis flared up again, he was coughing up blood, and he believed that there wasn't much time left. The disease was contagious, and he made his wife and daughters move out. While he visited them often, he was sick, broke and alone with nothing to do except write.

The result was his first novel, *Red Harvest*, which was eagerly accepted by publisher Alfred Knopf in 1928. It featured the Continental Op and was full of murder, corruption, and lots of double-crossing. It was an immediate success and was followed months later by the deliciously wicked *The Dain Curse*. He was already at work on *The Maltese Falcon*.

The books were popular with readers and critics. One reviewer wrote, "There are detective-story writers, and then there is Dashiell Hammett. I can think of no one in the world who is his match." No one had written anything quite like it, crime stories that read like literature. He sometimes had to fight for that quality. Knopf wanted to cut two scenes from *The Maltese Falcon* that the publisher admitted he would have allowed in conventional fiction. "I should like to leave them as they are, especially since you say they 'would be all right perhaps in an ordinary novel,'" Hammett wrote. "It seems to me that the only thing that can be said against their use in a detective novel is that nobody has tried it yet. I'd like to try it.'"

When he moved to New York in 1929, he was an instant celebrity. It's hard today to realize how popular he was. In two years he had come out with three best-selling books that were already affecting the American literary voice. As for Hammett himself, he was lean and elegant. He had always been handsome but now he had the money for hand-tailored clothes, and he wore them with style. After New York he headed for Hollywood. In the early 1930s it was the place to be, the heady days of Irving Thalberg and *The Last Tycoon*, and of early talking pictures. Here Hammett was strange enough to be exotic—classy, urbane, and tough. Everyone wanted him to create something for their studio. He was the talk of the town when he met the woman who would co-star in his life for the next thirty years.

Lillian Hellman was unknown when she spotted him in a restaurant. The New Orleans belle was tough and smart and accustomed to getting what she wanted. She was far from a beauty but she shrewdly cultivated what she did have: wit, sex, intelligence, and the sense to wear only the most stylish clothes. Her husband was a nice guy but she didn't want a nice guy. She wanted someone like Hammett, hardboiled and sexual, who could be cruel and cutting after a few drinks. Without hesitating, she crossed the restaurant and introduced herself. Within weeks she moved in with him, to the dismay of her husband and other lovers.

Winning his love was a prize but there was a catch. He made it clear that he would not curb his voracious womanizing. "In every relationship there's a winner and a loser, but the winner ought to be careful," Hellman later wrote. She was jealous of the other women, especially the beautiful ones; she was jealous of his distant affection for his daughters and even of his wife, whom he now saw only as a friend. Hellman's response was to sleep with her husband and lots of other men.

For months Hammett tested her. He wanted her to sleep with him and another woman, to see how far she would go; Hellman complied. She learned to play poker "like a man" and she started to smoke as heavily as he did. It was not as easy to keep up with his drinking. He went from club to club, vomited in the street, and passed out in gutters. One night James Thurber threw a drink at Lillian and Dash slammed him into the wall. Another time he beat up an actress at his hotel; when she sued him and won, he accepted the blow to his pocketbook and reputation with ironic grace.

He was riding high when *The Glass Key* was released in 1931. It was his fourth novel in four years, and is today considered to be his best. The movie rights went for $25,000, but this did not stop the money problems he had begun to make for himself. He borrowed against the advance of a fifth novel. No one knew that it would be his last.

Hammett was about to stop writing and Hellman was about to start. He supported her financially but much more importantly he did for her what he could no longer do for himself: he reviewed, slashed, rewrote, and revised. He shamed and browbeat her into creating dozens of drafts until one was acceptable to him. With his collaboration she would become a great playwright.

In Hollywood he was wild, drinking with writers and sleeping with actresses. When Lillian went to New York he wrote her letters that were newsy, affectionate, and cruel. He wrote that he missed her, but he also wanted it understood that he was sleeping around. "God knows I'm doing my best to keep celibacy from rearing its ugly head in Hollywood!" he wrote. In 1932, he returned to New York. He met William Faulkner and found the southern writer with his courtly manners and ruthless way with words and bourbon to be a perfect drinking buddy. Once, after a day of drinking, they paid a call on Hammett's publisher. Alfred Knopf was hosting a formal party for author Willa Cather, and they both wanted to meet her, so they crashed the dinner. Hammett proceeded to pass out in front of New York's literary finest, while Faulkner, the future Nobel Prize winner, yelled at Knopf for not being more understanding.

There were other signs that Hammett was coming apart. He repeatedly missed deadlines for his fifth novel and was dodging his publisher. Knopf, on the other hand, received a letter from Jose Hammett asking for help. Hammett had sent her only one hundred dollars in seven months and the girls were hungry. During a drunken fight with Hellman he ground a lit cigarette into his cheek.

Unable to pay his hotel bill, he sneaked out wearing all the clothes he could manage. Writer Nathaniel West gave him a room and Hammett got to work. Letting his children down was as close to bending the Hammett code as he was going to get, and he finished *The Thin Man* in short time; it was published in 1934. Nick Charles, the story's detective, has lost something of himself in marrying a wealthy woman, Nora. Their affection and banter are based on Hammett and Hellman's, and is the most memorable part of the book, aside from Charles' drinking. All of Hammett's previous heroes had a bottle in the desk drawer and could handle a slug or two at any time, but none of them drank like Nick Charles, in a hopeless, defeated way.

The Thin Man was a huge success. Movie rights were sold pre-publication for over $20,000. Publicity photos were taken of Hammett looking very Nick Charles-like, dapper and sophisticated in white fedora and cane. Magazines interviewed him; one asked about his hobbies. "Let's see, I drink a lot," he answered.

He took Hellman to Florida for a few weeks to fish and get drunk. They worked on her play and he bullied her and her work; he would let her get away with nothing. His idea of a compliment was to tell her that her writing would be good one day. He returned to Los Angeles and she traveled on to New York.

Money rolled in, as it would for years, from reprints and radio and movie adaptations. He devoted an incredible amount of energy into disposing of it. Some went to Jose and the girls. He was also quick with generous loans and handouts to anyone who asked. It was his own lifestyle, however, that kept him in precarious financial condition: a six-bedroom, six-bathroom suite at the Beverly Wilshire; handmade clothes; parties to which he invited ladies and prostitutes alike, and presents—a fur coat here, a diamond watch there—showered on both.

Biographer Joan Mellen wrote, "These were the years when in his rough working-class way he would ask virtually every good-looking woman he met to go to bed with him. Many took him on." He preferred, however, to hire his female companionship, and it became one of his substantial expenses. He especially liked Asian or black women he would pick up in Harlem, although he kept an open account with a local brothel that made house calls.

During one week long bender he wrote Hellman that he had been "hitting the booze pretty heavily, neglecting studio, dignity, and so on." In another letter he wrote lightly of getting "very—not to say disgracefully—drunk." He wrote that he loved her and that she should come to California to take care of him. She couldn't have even if she had wanted to. Her first play, *The Children's Hour*, was about to open on Broadway and when it did, there would be a new star in the family, and this time it would be Miss Lillian Hellman.

He asked Knopf for more money against his non-existent book. His studio, waiting in vain for overdue scripts, sent a secretary to his suite every day to take dictation. Many days he would not come out to meet her. When he did he sat in silence or read or asked for her help on a crossword puzzle. She never saw him eat solid food. One day she found only a note that read, "I feel too lousy to work today—thank God. See you tomorrow."

At night he made the rounds of cocktail parties where he was increasingly nasty and insulting, mocking friends to their faces.

Biographer Diane Johnson reported that one night he began "scooping up handfuls of knives, forks and spoons from the table and throwing them across the room." Another time, while leaving a club, he took a gun from a police officer's holster and started waving it around, shooting at nothing. When he got angry with a lover who criticized his alcohol-impaired sexual performance, he put a knife to her throat.

In 1936 he flew to New York and on arrival had to be hospitalized for exhaustion, which was another way of saying alcohol poisoning. He was also suffering again from gonorrhea. This time the disease resisted the traditional treatment and the doctors were forced to give Hammett a very painful fever therapy that raised the patient's temperature in order to burn the disease out of the body. It worked, but left him scarred in body and spirit.

He continued to lie to his publisher, assuring a new novel was on its way. In reality, he read, drank, whored, and wrote nothing whatsoever. Life had become a non-stop drunk or hangover and even in Hollywood, a city that loves a spectacle, his reputation was beginning to suffer.

In the late 1930s, it became fashionable among artists and intellectuals to join the Communist Party. Hammett signed on in 1938, writing letters and sponsoring fundraisers. He spoke on behalf of groups that sought to organize writers, circulated and signed petitions, and worked on the editorial board of *Equality*, a political magazine. His ideals were real, but naïve and unfocused; he was a Marxist living in a luxury suite, who wore tailored suits and employed a full-time chauffeur. Hellman joined him at rallies wearing mink.

When Hellman discovered she was pregnant with his child, he reacted characteristically. First he asked Jose for a divorce so that he and Lily could marry. Then, to guarantee that Hellman understood, he staged a scene for her benefit: she walked in on him and a prostitute, caught in the act. Not about to be bested in a power struggle, she aborted their child.

In 1939, Hammett managed to stay sober for fourteen months; when he fell off the wagon it was with a mighty crash. A friend found him at his hotel, pale and emaciated, sprawled over the bed, unable to speak or move. She knew she had to get him to a hospital, but the hotel manager refused to let him leave until he paid his bill. It was over eight thousand dollars. She managed to smuggle Hammett out and onto a plane where, fortified with whiskey, he made his way to Hellman who checked him into a hospital. There he lay for weeks, gaining weight and recuperating.

In 1939, his publishers optimistically told the public that a new Hammett novel was imminent, while he wrote to his new editor, "To answer your questions…No, I'm not drunk…Yes, I am plugging away at it." When friends asked him what the book was about, he made things up, spreading rumors about a wide variety of plots and titles, none of them true. He drank. More money came, which he spent and gambled away with a frantic prodigality.

In 1939, Hellman bought a place in Pleasantville, New York, called Hardscrabble Farm. Hammett was often in residence there, and their life together was a mixture of the painful and the sublime. He loved the acres of land and the pond where he fished or trapped turtles. He could hole up in the house and read or help Hellman with her plays. But they both drank, sometimes all day, and fought. Afterward he would head for a brothel. She took lover after lover.

In 1942, a few months after the bombing of Pearl Harbor, forty-eight-year-old Hammett enlisted in the army. He was six-feet-two and weighed only 141 pounds, was improbably frail, and had scarred lungs, but they took him. At the time, however, the army was inclined to keep suspicious characters, like card-carrying Communist party members, in exile. When he shipped out later that year, it was to the Aleutian Islands off the coast of Alaska.

It was no-man's-land, but he loved it. He started a paper for the ranks, and taught them to write and edit their own work. He drank less and read constantly. Away from Hellman, his letters were loving, affectionate, and intimate in a way that he could never say to her face. He even asked her to buy him a ring, then wondered how he had ever lived without one. In 1943 he was promoted to sergeant.

The next year he was transferred to the mainland where he was to travel the Alaskan coast lecturing soldiers in an effort to raise morale. His carefully guarded island world was replaced by no-holds-barred hell-raising. In a letter to Hellman, quoted in Johnson's biography, he describes "a procession of bars and liquor stores. Smashed, crocked, jugged, loud, boisterous, talking nonsense, then eloquence, then just four-letter words. The gamut, including weeping."

When he was reassigned to the island base he continued out of control. He still contributed to the paper but was often too drunk to walk or talk and had to be carried by his comrades to his bunk. One of his youthful commanding officers was forced to give the older man a gentle dressing down. "Do you really think you are doing right for this unit and the country?" He only meant that Hammett should sober up, but humiliated and angry, he resigned the same day.

He headed for the farm where he spent Christmas with Hellman, then got his own apartment in New York. He wandered through his work for the Communist party in a thoughtless way, signing petitions and attending functions. He managed to teach a course in mystery writing for a Marxist school once a week but mainly he drank, beginning a three-year descent into the darkest realms of alcoholic despair.

He was mean in restaurants, yelling at waiters and humiliating other patrons. One night he ordered everything on the menu, and to the embarrassment of his date he got it, delivered by a line of waiters. He slid under tables, passed out on floors, slobbered on women, and fell in the street. When he visited Jose and the girls he was, for the first time, cruel to them. Toward the end he would shut himself in his apartment with cases of Johnnie Walker Red, refusing to see anyone. He no longer bothered to get out of bed and there were times when he almost couldn't make it to the bathroom.

The one person he would see was his housekeeper. One day she called Hellman and asked her to come. Lillian refused, but the housekeeper insisted that Hammett was dying. When Hellman arrived she saw to her horror that it had been no exaggeration. He was gaunt and weak and screaming uncontrollably. She called a doctor who, after examining him, told Hellman that he had two months to live if he did not quit drinking, something that she and the doctor believed he could not do. But he promised the doctor he would quit and he did. He would be sober for the rest of his life. It was not always easy being clean, especially when the writing did not come back. Biographer Joan Mellen reported his yelling a bitter rant about "reformed drunks who should have stayed drunk, so that they don't wake up to find out they haven't any talent."

In 1949 he realized that the FBI was following him. For some time he had been a chairman of New York's Civil Rights Congress, an activist group that made bail for several Communists. When four of them jumped bail and became refugees, Hammett was called before the House Un-American Activities Committee and asked to turn over a list of thousands of Civil Rights Congress contributors.

He was also asked to inform on the whereabouts of certain individuals. He knew nothing of the four fugitives and Hellman asked him why he didn't just say so. His answer was angry: "I don't know why. I don't let cops or judges tell me what I think democracy is."

On the stand he refused to answer questions and was arrested for contempt of court. Denied bail, he spent the next six months in jail. Hellman, who feared for her own arrest and its effect on her career, went to England until it was over. When he was released, she met him at his plane and was shocked to see how thin and sick he looked as he stumbled down the steps.

The government was not finished with Hammett. They claimed he owed over $100,000 in back taxes, and for the rest of his life his income would be attached. He was broke. He was also demonized in the press, described as a traitor and a threat to the American way of life. His books were removed from libraries and were even burned.

In 1952, still sick and feverish, he moved to a cottage in the country near Pleasantville and worked on an autobiographical novel called *Tulip*. He was still sober and would sometimes visit Hellman at her new home in Martha's Vineyard, where he would fish, read, and sleep. He allowed himself one martini a day; if he wanted more he walked in the woods until the craving passed.

In 1955 he was called again to testify before the HUAC. He was older now and some of the bravado was gone from his testimony; he was afraid of going back to jail. A heart attack later in the summer weakened him further, but he continued to smoke heavily. Over the next few years he lived as a near-recluse, making little effort to get out but seeing people when they came, including Hellman who made the visit once a week. He was exhausted all the time. He began to ignore his phone and let the mail pile up. When he wrote letters, they were cryptic and worrisome. Ashtrays filled and ran over, dust gathered on the typewriter.

Finally he confessed to Hellman that he had been falling down and could no longer live alone. It was an agonizing admission. Hellman, who had long avoided taking on any responsibility where he was concerned, took him home to live with her. He moved slowly and tried very hard not to ask anyone for anything. In spite of her care, he grew thinner.

One night he refused his nightly martini, and Hellman knew it was a bad sign. The doctors told her that he had inoperable lung cancer. She decided not to tell him, although she once asked him, obscurely, if he wanted to talk about "it." With angry tears he answered, "No. My only chance is not to talk about it." She watched and waited as he struggled with emphysema, lung cancer, and pneumonia. She took him to the hospital on New Year's Eve, and on January 10, 1961, he died.

The man who changed the face of the mystery was one himself. Why didn't he ever write again? Why would an artist with his talent and drive retire from the field so early and leave us with nothing more? It is commonly said that it was because of "writer's block," which is a simple answer.

The truth may actually be simpler still. In her biography of Hammett, Diane Johnson quotes a letter of writer and drinking buddy Nunnally Johnson: "He had none of the usual incentives that keep writers at their typewriters for as long as they have the strength to hit the keys. He had no ambition to accomplish more as a writer." Nunnally Johnson believed that Hammett honestly thought he didn't have long to live, and wrote only to get his pile. After that he had no interest in writing and only wanted to spend his last days having a good time. When Hammett realized that he wasn't going to die anytime soon, "it was too late to sit down at the typewriter again with much confidence. When the end approached, it was thirty years later than he expected it, and Death owed him a genuine apology when it eventually made its tardy appearance."

KINGLSEY AMIS

DRINK OF CHOICE

❧ Macallan's whiskey with a splash of Evian.

❧ Cock ale: a concoction of smashed rooster, cloves, and beer that steeps for ten days before being bottled.

❧ The perfect martini: fifteen parts gin to one part vermouth. Add cucumber juice for a "Lucky Jim."

*"Alcohol meant many things to Kingsley. These things included oblivion...
but there were innocent gradations along the way."*

- Martin Amis, *Experience*

*"Just the thing for the funk at the typewriter, except that when one has one
little one, one wants one little one more."*

- Kingsley Amis, *Memoirs*

Kingsley Amis did not care what people thought of his drinking. He
was a grand old man of English letters, a comic master, recipient
of the Booker Prize, a Knight of the British Empire. So what if "Now
and then I become conscious of having the reputation of being one of
the great drinkers, if not one of the great drunks, of our time." So what
if he fell over on the way out of pubs? If you didn't like it, you could
piss off.

He wasn't born to such fame but rather to the solid middle class
of Norbury, a drab, down-at-heel London suburb. He hated it, and
resented his family, which suffered from a false sense of superior status
and a fear of losing a rank it never had in the first place. The only
child of older parents, he was forbidden neighborhood friends who
were deemed too common. While he was loved and pampered, he was
also smothered. His mother did everything for him, down to feeding
him by hand, even when he was thirteen, setting the stage for a man

who was hopelessly helpless. He could neither drive a car nor use a telephone.

Other adult peculiarities sprang from his childhood. As a man he would have a violent loathing for stinginess that began with a grandmother who was so cheap that, although she paid for servants, she gave her family paper bags to use as toilet paper. When he was ten, a short, nauseating trip in an airplane left him with a morbid fear and inability to fly, no matter how great the distance. And as an older child, he encouraged his parents to go out without him, but when they did he was so sure that he had been abandoned that, for the rest of his life he was incapable of being in a house alone.

On the other hand, his mother was a beautiful and fun-loving woman who enjoyed reading and encouraged her son to do the same. His father, an executive at Colman's Mustard, was brilliant at storytelling and making funny faces, a gift his son absorbed and used in becoming one of the twentieth century's great raconteurs. As a father of his generation, however, he enforced middle-class strictures that seemed ridiculous to the boy. In *Memoirs*, Kingsley Amis remembered, "reading in public was deemed rude, while reading in private was anti-social." It left little in between.

Both parents devoted themselves to keeping their son in the dark about sexual matters. His mother forbade a friend to use the word "honeymoon" in front of the fourteen-year-old boy, while his father vigilantly tried to root out any attempt at teenage masturbation, saying, "every ejaculation thinned the blood and the victim eventually fell into helpless insanity." He was forbidden to lock the bathroom door, and grew to expect his father creeping around the house and popping into rooms, hoping to catch him in the act.

His school career was unremarkable until he was ten and a new teacher introduced him to Shakespeare and poetry. Amis wrote a poem of his own and found that he liked it. When he was twelve, he attended the City of London School where boys wore uniforms and striped pants, and read Greek and Latin. There he discovered G.K. Chesterton and American jazz, and continued to write poetry that he later called pieces of appalling pretentiousness and affectation. His wickedly funny impersonations of teachers and other boys guaranteed his popularity.

He won a scholarship to Oxford and started there in the spring of 1941. War cast a low-key atmosphere over the school, not like he had expected from novels. Rationing made all sorts of things scarce, from sugar to gasoline, and he stood in long lines for extra food and cigarettes. In one of those queues he met fellow student Philip Larkin. The two discovered they shared a love of movies, jazz, and drinking. More importantly they were savagely uninterested in the same things, and the two became lifelong friends.

Despite rationing, Amis managed to find enough sherry to get drunk for the first time in his life, an event which left him vomiting into a chamber pot. He also arranged for his first sexual encounter, through a friend who knew a woman who was willing but had a couple of requests: that he first read a marriage manual, and lay in a supply of condoms. If Amis's fictional hints are to be trusted, the experience was less than a success, due to the fact that he did not follow the book's advice.

By the summer of 1942 he could no longer put off joining the army. Basic training and military routine were tedious, but eventually he was transferred to the Signal Corps where he fared a little better. Years later he described a fictional counterpart who hardly fit in:

> He philandered in public; he talked freely of his homosexual friends in Oxford; he spoke of intercourse between the sexes much as the rest spoke of football, eating or drinking; he wrote poetry in the Signal Office.

Eventually he was sent to Normandy, where he served as a radio operator, dispatching and receiving messages. He wrote that there was "no sex to be had there, or none that I could find. There was no beer, and of course no whisky even if I could have afforded it. But there was some stuff called burgundy."

Like other soldiers he took soap to the local farmhouses to trade for extra food, which was how he discovered some stuff called Calvados, the strong apple brandy native to the countryside. While in Belgium, he drank a cocktail called Gin and French, three parts gin to two parts vermouth.

At the end of the war he was demobilized and returned to London anticipating a life "full of girls and drinks and jazz and books and decent houses and decent job and being your own boss." In addition to resuming classes at the university, his agenda included not working, getting drunk and pursuing young women. In 1946, he was focused on one young woman in particular.

Hilary Bardwell was a seventeen-year-old art student when he saw her in a tearoom. "Hilly" was very beautiful and had no lack of male company. She was not at all sure that she was interested in the threadbare English student in the baggy suit, but she allowed herself to be pursued. Soon Amis wrote Larkin that "she does really like jazz. And she likes me." Discouragingly, she was "not nearly so depraved as I had hoped."

Although talk was one of Amis's great joys, he had little use for women's conversation, which he felt was indiscriminate. Years later, a character in his novel *Jake's Thing* explains that women "don't use language for discourse but for extending their personality, they take all disagreement as opposition, yes they do, even the brightest of them." Amis liked the fact that Hilly spoke little and listened well.

She was also incredibly understanding. In the late 1940s, a man would have always escorted a woman home. Not so for Kingsley Amis. His terror of riding a bus alone and entering a dark room meant that Hilly took him to his place first then saw herself home. When he felt the relationship was growing too close, he put distance between them, then pursued her again when he saw that this didn't bother her. The result was that Hilly was pregnant late in 1947. Both sets of parents reluctantly attended a short wedding service in January 1948, then took the couple to tea.

They soon had a cottage, a dog, a cat, and a son, Philip, named for Larkin. While Hilly stayed home with the baby, Amis took the bus to Oxford where he attended lectures by J.R.R. Tolkien ("repulsive") and C.S. Lewis ("the best lecturer I ever heard"). Hilly, however, was isolated with no transportation, a baby, and another soon on the way. She also had a husband who described himself as "selfish, self-indulgent, lazy, arrogant and above all inextinguishably promiscuous by nature." This was putting it mildly. A little more than a year after their wedding, she found that he was cheating on her, not with one woman, but with many, some of them her friends.

While he obtained a degree, he failed to defend his thesis for a higher degree to an antagonistic examiner he had insulted. It had actually been an unintentional slight, which is more than can be said for the time he wrote that a bunch of dons had less dignity than a "procession of syphilitic, cancerous, necrophilic shit-bespattered lavatory attendants." He took the defeat of his thesis in stride, as he already had a job and his first novel was finished.

Lecturing at the University College of Swansea was secure, but the pay was so small that he had to grade extra papers on the side while Hilly worked cleaning up the local theater. Their house was small, with primitive furnishings—their new baby, Martin, slept in a drawer—and Amis was forced to ration his cigarettes. Even though he was a popular teacher, his views on literature confounded his colleagues. He hated Chaucer, Keats, *Beowulf,* Jane Austen, and had little use for Charles Dickens, a controversial stand for any English teacher. Even more outrageous, he criticized Swansea's beloved native son Dylan Thomas.

In 1951 Hilly inherited some money and they bought a house, a car and a refrigerator. The demands of teaching left Amis with little time and his first novel had failed to find a publisher, but he was determined to keep writing. The new house had a room for him to work in where children were not allowed. In his funny and moving account in *Experience,* Martin Amis wrote that it was from this point that his father "managed to abolish all responsibility for the domestic side of life. Other people looked after all that for him."

A new novel was born on a visit to Oxford in 1948. Philip Larkin was teaching there, and one morning Amis accompanied him to the staff common room. The scene stuck in Amis's brain and while it may not sound hilarious, it became the classic comic novel *Lucky Jim.* (In 1999, National Public Radio chose Jim Dixon as one of the greatest literary characters of the twentieth century.) It was published in January 1954, the same month his daughter Sally was born; Amis was thirty-two. The book was a huge hit with readers and critics, including one who wrote that Amis was a "novelist of formidable and uncomfortable talent." It was performed on radio, made into a movie in 1957—and 2002— and would eventually be translated into twenty languages. America, however, did not know what to make of the book. Its distributor in the states offered a money-back guarantee to readers who did not find it funny, and the company lost a fortune.

Many people assume, wrongly, that *Lucky Jim* is autobiographical. Amis did draw some characters from life: Jim Dixon is a lecturer at a small college who rations his cigarettes due to economy and whose hatred of pretension tends to get him in trouble with authority. He also has a genius for making really outrageous faces. Jim Dixon shared one other trait with his creator, the love of drink. "Kingsley has written often and poignantly about that moment when getting drunk suddenly turns into being drunk," wrote Martin Amis, "and he is, of course, the laureate of the hangover." To wit:

> He [Jim] stood brooding by his bed…The light did him harm, but not as much as looking at things did; he resolved, having done it once, never to move his eyeballs again. A dusty thudding in his head made the scene before him beat like a pulse. His mouth had been used as a latrine by some small creature of the night, and then as its mausoleum. During the night, too, he'd somehow been on a cross-country run and then been expertly beaten up by secret police. He felt bad.

One of the by-products of success was the opportunity for frequent trips to London, which meant sex and lots of it. Finding partners was no problem. He simply compulsively tried to seduce almost every woman he met. He described a typical adulterous scene in one of his poems:

> Drinks on the tray; the cover-story pat
> And quite uncheckable; her husband off
> Somewhere with all the kids till six o'clock
> …What about guilt, compunction and such stuff?
> It'll wear off, as usual.

Heavy drinking affected his judgment, but not, apparently, his performance. A few days into a weekend party with friends, he was compelled to be especially attentive to every woman at breakfast, as he had been drunk the night before and couldn't remember which lady he had slept with. In Swansea, he insisted that students make their apartments available for his extra-marital trysts, reminding them that they had to stand by the married man, and he regularly solicited alibis for anticipated absences from home. This was referred to as "a little chore I'd like you to do for me," and he always promised to return the favor.

These efforts at discretion were fairly half-hearted, and Hilly continued to find out. She was beautiful, lonely, and hurt, which led her to have moments of her own. One of them was serious, and threatened to break up the marriage. Regarding this possibility, Amis wrote in a letter, "Having one's wife fucked is one thing; having her taken away from you, plus your children, is another, I find."

They survived that round, but when Hilly found some letters from his mistress, she gave him an ultimatum. He agreed, with reluctance, writing, "I am to give all that up, it appears. Trouble is it's so hard to give all that up, habit of years and all that, and such bloody fun too." His terror of really losing his wife, however, was strong, especially as his psychological fears grew more peculiar in a way that a lover might question. After he saw the movie *Psycho*, for instance, he was too afraid to go to the bathroom at night unless Hilly went with him.

In 1955 he won a literary prize that carried the painful condition that he spend three months abroad. Amis hated being abroad. He saw it as nothing short of exile against his will, but in the end he accepted to make Hilly happy and to avoid looking too eccentric. The family settled on Portugal.

While many would enjoy the simple, fresh food, the local wine, and the opportunity to work on a new book at a nearby beach or chalet, to Amis it was all "[b]loody terrible, man." Instead, he worked on his goal—"to draw as few sober breaths as possible"—and succeeded by "drinking a lot of local gin and a kind of applejack-cum-Pernod that they go in for a lot hereabouts," he wrote Larkin. The only writing he got out of the trip was a piece called "Lusitanian Liquors."

That fall his second novel, *That Uncertain Feeling*, was published to good reviews. More and more he was asked to write journalistic pieces and reviews, many with a characteristically contrary tone. The public gave a collective literary gasp when he panned Evelyn Waugh's latest novel. He dismissed a collection of Dylan Thomas' prose with, "someone ought to give Dylan a bouquet of old bogwort before long."

Nothing was sacred, including England's most cherished symbols. In *Life* magazine he was quoted as saying:

> I would abolish the aristocracy and, naturally, the House of Lords. As for the royal family, it serves a purpose as a sentimental glue for the Commonwealth and probably has to be preserved, but just as a personal feeling of my own I would like to get rid of them, queen and all.

In Swansea, the university administrators were horrified, but wary of firing their celebrity faculty member. They got rid of him when he sailed—not flew—to Princeton, New Jersey, to teach creative writing. Amis loved the United States and its amiable, hard-drinking populace. In a letter to England he wrote:

> All very jolly here, settling in fine, with the smell of bourbon and King-size Chesterfields over all: cirrhosis and lung-cancer have moved into an altogether more proximate position relative to me.

He was unnerved, however, by the fact that no one cursed, ever. America liked him, too. He was hired by *Esquire* to review foreign movies, and asked to share the stage with Jack Kerouac, where he presented a gentlemanly contrast to the antics of the homegrown writer. Recreation was abundant, in the shape of female students and faculty wives, and he wrote to Larkin that he was "boozing and fucking" harder than any time in his life. Somehow he found time to teach classes and give a series of lectures on science fiction, a genre he enjoyed, which would eventually become the book *New Maps of Hell.*

He returned to England and a job at Oxford in 1960, although he almost didn't get the post. In spite of his best-selling novels and popular columns, he was not deemed to have published the right sort of thing. Needless to say, he had no use for this limited attitude nor the stuffy atmosphere of the academic elite. Compared to the freewheeling pub scene of Swansea, it was stultifying dull, but a bored Kingsley Amis could be counted on to show up drunk and liven things up.

The accepted method of instruction at the university was for a lecturer to feed students the correct interpretations of what was good or bad in literature. Amis made many of his colleagues, and some of his students, uncomfortable by encouraging his scholars to think for themselves and develop their own ideas about the work of even the most revered of masters. Furthermore, he drank with students, which was frowned upon, lest it lead to homosexuality, a possibility which hardly seemed likely with Amis.

While he enjoyed teaching, it was demanding and drained him of the energy he needed to write; he eventually left Oxford to write full-time. By the end of 1962, he had published six novels, all of them strong sellers. That fall, he—along with as an extremely drunk Carson McCullers—was invited to speak at a literary festival whose topic was "Sex in Literature." While there, he explored the subject by conducting an affair with one of the festival directors, novelist Elizabeth Jane Howard.

What started as casual turned serious and they continued to see each when the festival ended. Jane Howard was sexy, beautiful, and well-respected in English literary circles. She was also from the upper class, which appealed to the latent status-consciousness left over from Amis's childhood. He told Hilly that he was taking Jane to Spain for the summer. Hilly used a lipstick to scrawl "I fuck anything" on his bare back.

He left for Spain on her birthday, leaving her a present of a nightgown Jane had picked out. When he returned from his trip, he was furious to find that Hilly was not waiting. She had taken the children to Majorca and abandoned him to his fate. Although he did not want a divorce, for Kingsley Amis it was impossible to avoid. He would need "someone to make all the bookings, someone to get him to Southampton, someone to share his cabin on the boat, and someone to lead him from Palma to Soller and right up to our front door," wrote Martin. It was easier to simply return to Jane.

For the time being, Amis and the twice-divorced Jane lived together in London, where they were joined by the boys. The couple married in 1965, and Jane told the press, "I admit it. I'm really dotty about Kingsley." There was a cost, however. Like Hilly, she was expected to take care of all the practical matters while Kingsley wrote. She was the one who did the real parenting of his children—enforcing discipline, overseeing schools, the everyday grind. Amis's idea of being a good father was to turn his boys into his drinking buddies. In a gesture that was part bravado and part economy, he bought the fifteen and sixteen-year-old brothers a gross (144) of condoms.

In 1967, the family sailed to America where Amis was going to teach at Vanderbilt in Nashville. This trip to the states was not as successful as his previous one. He was unprepared, for instance, for a colleague who announced, "I can't find it in my heart to give a Negro or a Jew an A." Almost as disturbing as campus racism were the local laws which made it impossible to buy a drink in a bar or restaurant. He had to bring his own liquor to bars and order a set-up instead. Local laws notwithstanding, he managed to be hung over every day.

The couple returned to England via Mexico, where Amis discovered "a kind of tequila Bloody Mary with a hell of a lot of Tabasco and so on in the bloody part," which he described as very sustaining, and that the "tequila is murder but local gin is good. Food excellent, wine awful piss but beer drinkable."

Back home they moved into a Georgian country house the size of a small mansion, with two staircases and twenty-something rooms. Although she loved their new home, Howard found herself maneuvered more and more into the role of housekeeper, with increased duties such as cooking and cleaning as well as raising the boys, at the expense of her writing. Then Amis turned around and complained that he felt isolated, and that she wasn't doing enough to make friends for the two of them.

When they moved back to London, it was to please him—the country did not have enough pubs—although Jane was left to move the entire household herself. The only part Amis helped with was finishing off the half-empty liquor bottles around the house so they wouldn't have to be transported. He now had a lot in common with the protagonist of his 1969 novel *The Green Man*: a self-absorbed alcoholic, prone to an eating disorder, hypochondria, and neglect of his children and wives who feels that "the only time I can be reasonably sure of not feeling bloody awful is a couple of hours or so at the end of a day's drinking." In 1971 he published *On Drink*, along with *How's Your Glass* and *Everyday Drinking*, both published in the 1980s. The trio of books allowed him to play with his enthusiasm for his favorite hobby; as his son wrote, his delight with:

> ...the heated wine glass, the chilled cream poured over the back of a spoon, the mint leaves and the cucumber juice, the strips of orange peel, the rims of salt, the squeezers and strainers.

His son also believed that he "wrote about booze to salvage something from all the hours he devoted to it." If so, then the hours were salvaged delightfully, with recipes, history, advice on surviving the perils of drinking abroad, and "The Mean Sod's Guide," a fabulously funny and somewhat nasty chapter of instruction on how to be a stingy host. Also described is his suggestions for the "Boozing Man's Diet," which begins with a caveat. "The first, indeed the only, requirement of a diet is that it should lose you weight without reducing your alcoholic intake by the smallest degree."

There is even an improbably gleeful return to the hangover, now broken down into two basic types. The first is the physical hangover, for which he suggests a variety of palliatives, such as the Polish Bison— a combination of Bovril beef paste and vodka—or a tumbler of Grand Marnier for breakfast. He admits to trying baking soda with a vodka chaser, but ultimately does not recommend it. The metaphysical hangover is trickier:

> When that ineffable compound of depression, sadness (these two are not the same), anxiety, self-hatred, sense of failure and fear for the future begins to steal over you, start telling yourself that what you have is a hangover. You are not sickening for anything, you have

not suffered a minor brain lesion, you are not all that
bad at your job, your family and friends are not leagued
in a conspiracy of barely maintained silence about what
a shit you are, you have not come at last to see life as
it really is.

Unfortunately, that feeling about the family being in a conspiracy
was more than a hangover in his own life. His marriage to Jane was
disintegrating. He was no longer able to perform sexually, possibly
because of his drinking. They attended sex therapy, where he endured
forced masturbation, the clocking of his erections, and deliberate
foreplay, all of which he hated, but turned to hilarious use in his novel
Stanley and the Women.

Alcohol destroyed more than sex. When he misplaced an article
he was working on, he accused Jane of destroying it. Another time
he started a nasty argument about some guests that upset him at one
of their parties. The problem was that there had been no such party,
except in his imagination. There were repeated instances of calculated
rudeness to others that he later could not remember. Then there were
the physical indignities: the shoulder broken in drunken fall, a broken
hand in another, the necessity of going upstairs on all fours when
walking was impossible.

It was beneath Kingsley Amis to deny his drunkenness, but it was
likewise part of his bravado that he was unable to admit that it was a
factor in the death of his marriage. He did not believe in seeing another
person's side of things; he was proud of taking sides, and to this end
he was compelled to blame the whole mess on Jane and Jane alone. In
1980, she left him, but made an offer to come back if he would give up
drinking completely. Her request was met with anger, and he offered it
to his friends as an example of her overweening egotism.

It wasn't that he couldn't stop drinking. When he fell and broke
his leg in 1982, he underwent an enforced withdrawal, during which
he claimed he experienced "nothing spectacular, just a few voices and
non-existent cats," and then remained sober for six months. It was
more to the point that he was incapable of believing that drink was a
problem in his life or in his marriage, and Jane had no right to pretend
it was. The grounds for divorce were "unreasonable behavior," and he

considered contesting it. He accused Jane of being grasping about the settlement and was incredulous when she told the press that he made her keep house and kept her from her own writing, even though he admitted that it was her job to be domestic because she was good at it. Even so, he claimed that the divorce almost killed him. "Stopping being married to someone is an incredibly violent thing to happen to you, not easy to take in completely, ever."

After eighteen years together, he felt abandoned, and was simply more terrified than ever of being alone. While he had sought professional help for his phobias, psychiatry had failed him, and at the age of fifty-eight he enlisted his grown children as companions.

While he had been an imperfect father, he had also been a loving one, and they rallied around him. They realized, however, that permanent dad-sitting was not going to work, so Martin and Philip put their heads together and came up with an odd-shaped solution to an odd-shaped problem.

Hilly was now married to Alastair Boyd, Lord Kilmarnock, a member of the House of Lords. The marriage was happy but money was sometimes tight. Amis, on the other hand, needed company and protection, and was rich. Scarcely knowing what to hope, their children arranged for Amis to move in with his ex-wife, her husband, and young son, in a living arrangement that proved a great, if unlikely, success. After his second divorce, he swore-off women sexually and was no threat to Hilly's marriage. He leaned on her, however, and depended on her as if she was a wife or a mother for feeding, cleaning, even buying his clothes. Lord Kilmarnock did his bit too, making up Amis's bed every morning before he headed to Parliament.

With such devoted caretakers on hand, he drank more than ever. He also continued to write. Between 1983 and his death he wrote seven novels, a collection of short stories, a book of English usage, and scores of articles, essays, restaurant critiques, and reviews. His fiction grew increasingly misogynistic, and his journalistic pieces were markedly cantankerous. This quality was trademark Amis, and it could run the gamut from honest and unflinching criticism of hypocrisy to inexplicably cruel and public barbs at the expense of his friends.

These barbs showed up in his disdain for feminism, menus in

French, friends who did not offer cocktails at lunch, and Nelson Mandela whom he said should be hanged. Anyone that he considered a bore was treated with an almost single-minded contempt, yet he loathed snobbery. His conservatism was rabid, even as he railed against convention. Most of this was done in the interest of taking sides. He believed that an argument had to have sides, or discourse would suffer, so it was morally necessary for him to provide adamant opinions. "How I hate all that talk of moderation and reasonableness and flexibility, especially the last," he wrote. In reviews of other writers, he used such terms as "little twit," "fucking fool," "pompous buffoon," and "that little turd." He was aware that somewhere along the line he had become, in his words, a "curmudgeonly old shit." Friend and writer Christopher Hitches said it was a slow evolution, and that from "being a tease of the politically-correct he had become a bit of a droning old club-man."

The club where he did his droning was the Garrick, and as time went on it became the center of his social life. Every morning he would write at home for three hours, then take a cab to the Garrick where, according to Eric Jacobs, his biographer and sometimes companion, Amis would have:

> …three large Macallan's to be spread carefully through the hour or so between his arrival by taxi and the necessary chore of eating. There would be wine, both white and red, the bare minimum of food then a digestif before he caught another taxi home.

In the past, collapsing under the influence had been responsible for broken limbs, but now "falling over…was all he ever did," wrote Martin.

> There were the slow and majestic subsidences…And there were other types of trips, tumbles and purlers, usually performed in his rooms at home…To hear my mother tell it, some of these collapses sounded like a chest-of-drawers jettisoned from an aeroplane.

Hilly and Alastair rarely interfered, however, unless he got stuck and then he would bang on the floor for Alastair's help. One day after lunch with Martin he took a particularly spectacular dive, and his son was tempted to intervene. "Dad, you're too old for this shit, I might have said to him. But why bother? Do you think he didn't know?" he wrote in *Experience*. In 1995, while visiting friends in Swansea, Amis fell and hit his head hard on the concrete. Eric Jacobs was on hand to drive him back to London, where it became clear that something was wrong.

Words got mixed up in his speech, and when he was well enough to sit at a typewriter, he would get up before dawn and produce pages covered with the word "seagulls." In one of his novels, an Amis character says, "The rewards for being sane may not be very many but knowing what's funny is one of them." To Martin, the most frightening result of the fall was that his father could no longer understand what was funny. He no longer knew when or how to laugh.

He continued to drink while in the hospital. Upon his release, he visited the Garrick where he drank himself paralytic. His kept his medication jumbled in a shoebox, from which he would grab a handful and toss it back with whiskey. One day he yelled at Philip, "Kill me, you fucking fool!" The end came a few weeks later.

His final words were "Come on," but maybe it makes more sense to look back at his final sentence of the book *On Drink* and his admonishment to readers on their health and well-being: "Well—if you want to behave better and feel better, the only absolutely certain method is *drinking less*. But to find out how to do *that*, you will have to find a more expert expert than I shall ever be."

MARGUERITE DURAS

DRINK OF CHOICE

🍷 Wine

"When I was writing The Lover...*It was more or less as I've described, and the process of writing it down was so smooth it reminded you of the way you speak when you're drunk, when what you say always seems so simple and clear."*

- Marguerite Duras

"What stops you killing yourself when you're intoxicated out of your mind is the thought that once you're dead you won't be able to drink any more."

- Marguerite Duras

Marguerite Duras was sexy, gorgeous, and determined. If she wanted to twist life to her terms, life would oblige. If her writing was wildly narcissistic, it was also the work of an artist emptying herself into her prose. She wrote, "all the women in my books [are] imprudent, improvident. They all ruin their own lives," which is telling since most of her books were about herself. If her life was a ruin, it was a fabulous one.

She was born in Indochina—now Vietnam—in 1914, to French civil servants. Her father's death when she was seven left the family low on the caste system in colonial society. Her mentally unstable mother tried to run her own rice plantation but, in spite of hard work and privation, it never produced enough to support them. It was here as a child that Duras began drinking. She was skinny, and her mother said, "Where I come from in the north, when girls were thin like you we gave them beer to drink." So she did.

Her brother and mother abused the teenage Duras. She wrote:

> Mother would often beat me, especially when she went to pieces. She just couldn't help it. As I was the youngest and the most amenable of her children, I was the one she beat the most often. She'd send me spinning, she'd hit me with a stick. Anger would give her such a rush of blood to the head that she'd say she was having a stroke.

She was forced by her mother and brutal brother to encourage the attentions of an older, wealthy Chinese native. With her mother's coaching, she gradually gave herself to him physically, extracting money for as long as possible.

At fifteen, Duras was a bright but disruptive student. Her mother sent her to boarding school in Marseilles in a last ditch effort to get her on a social track that with their reputation was no longer possible in Indochina. Eventually her mother and brothers joined her, but it was a grueling life of genteel poverty and keeping up appearances. Duras was again encouraged to sell herself for the family's expenses. She still endured savage beatings from her brother who stole her money for gambling and opium. Not surprisingly, she received terrible grades, but even then she was noted for her gifted writing.

In 1933, her education was complete and degree in hand, she headed for Paris where she studied law and had many affairs, the most passionate one ending when her lover discovered he was gay. In 1938, she met Robert Antelme. They fell in love but their happiness was threatened by the approach of war. They married—one of the witnesses was Duras' lover. She was soon pregnant but food was scarce and medical care primitive or nonexistent. After a hellish labor, the child was stillborn and Duras was devastated.

It was a dangerous time to be in love, and a frustrating time to be an aspiring writer. It was hard enough to get essentials like food; finding enough paper to publish a book was almost impossible. This did not stop Duras from writing and she published her first novel, *Les Impudents*, in 1942. She also worked under the Vichy government in the Organization of Books. Under its eye any book published in France had to be pro-German and in line with German interests. To some, this made Duras' job tantamount to collaboration with the Nazis.

After she and Antelme met Francois Mitterand, who became their roommate, she quit her job and they both joined the Resistance. This gave Duras the opportunity to play a variety of roles. As earth mother, she cooked meals for her circle and gave them a home to go to; as sex goddess she took lover after lover; as avenging angel she supervised the brutal torture of a suspected informer.

She was also a woman in love. Dionys Mascolo was a young, handsome and passionate member of her circle, and her feelings for him were equal parts obsession and abandon. This did not stop her from taking lovers. She felt that if she was not in love with them, then she wasn't cheating on Mascolo.

In her role as Double Agent things started to get complicated. She gave herself the assignment of courting Charles Delval, a man who claimed to be an agent of the Gestapo who could offer her information. As his lover, she was playing a game both dangerous and morally ambiguous. Delval's wife was being interrogated by Mascolo on behalf of the Resistance when she became pregnant with Mascolo's child. Soon after, so did Duras, who was still married to Antelme. This all accomplished little except to muddy the local intelligence waters.

In 1944, the war became more than making do and café intellectual intrigue. Antelme was arrested by the Gestapo and disappeared. He spent many months in Buchenwald and was believed dead, until he was found at the liberation of the Bergen-Belsen camp, more dead than alive. He was too weak to lift his head, too weak to eat, and Duras nursed him with devotion.

Her care for Antelme was painful and real, but so was her sense of self-drama. In her memoir *La Douleur* she writes:

> The throbbing in my head is still there. I must stop it.
> His death is in me, beating in my head...In the street
> I am like a sleepwalker...Just before he died he must
> have spoken my name.

The memoir shocked Antelme and other friends. Her account exposes Antelme's incredible pain, humiliation and vulnerability, and many felt that she exploited these in order to tell a story that is still somehow shamelessly all about her.

After the war, Paris was the center of European life, and at the center of Paris were the Left Bank intellectuals, and in their center, Marguerite Duras. The largely male group suited her. "Women do tend to be boring still, and a lot of them haven't the nerve to step out of line," she wrote later. She preferred joining men in long nights of drinking and talking, arguing politics and philosophy, having brief, intense love affairs to the accompaniment of Edith Piaf and smoky jazz. Even in this *laissez faire* environment, Duras hid the fact that she was often drunk or getting there. "Alcoholism is scandalous in a woman," she wrote. "And a female alcoholic is rare, a serious matter. It's a slur on the divine in our nature."

Although they divorced in 1947, Robert Antelme remained her best friend. His second wife would be one of her few women friends. It was for Mascolo that she ate out her heart, weeping, ranting, pleading. There is no doubt that he loved her and their son, Jean, who was born in 1947, but he was not interested in monogamy. In 1956 they finally separated sexually although in typical Duras fashion, they lived in the same house for ten more years.

In 1950 her third novel was published to mixed critical reviews and tepid sales, but Duras was determined. She proclaimed herself a genius, bullied her editors for more money and attention, and continued to write. When her novel *The Sea Wall* was made into a successful movie in 1957, there was revived interest in her earlier writings. After all those years, she had arrived. Arriving with her, however, was an enormous attachment to brandy, wine, and whiskey. They were part of the territory of her life, her ideas and thoughts, and now, her writing.

Her short novel *Moderato Cantabile*, published in 1958, was one of her first works to explore the psyche of an alcoholic heroine. It is the story of a society woman who spends her afternoons drinking wine in a working class café. One day she leaves the café to host her rich husband's dinner party where she continues to drink. The descriptions of Anne's oblivion amid the gowns and jewels, the chilled salmon and the pressed duck, are exquisitely subtle and painful:

A man, facing a woman, looks at her as though he does not recognize her. Her breasts are again half exposed. She hastily adjusts her dress. A drooping flower lies between them. There are still flashes of lucidity in her wildly protruding eyes, enough for her to succeed in helping herself to some of the salmon when it comes her turn.

And when her husband prompts her:

> "Anne didn't hear what you said."
> She puts her fork down, looks around, tries to grasp the thread of conversation, fails.
> "That's true," she says.
> They ask again.

In 1957, Duras met and fell in love with Gerard Jarlot. She wrote:

> We'd met at a party one evening at Christmas. I'd gone there on my own to find a lover. If I make him out to be so irresistible it's because he was a born lover, a born lover of women. At a glance he could see them, make out the very essence of their desire.

This born lover of women was also a writer, and married with three children. This did nothing to hamper the intense relationship between Jarlot and Duras. They became traveling companions, writing partners, lovers, and drinking buddies; they fought, wept and raged in front of a backdrop of squalor, booze and violent sex that involved severe beatings. Duras no longer tried, or even wanted to try, to conceal her alcoholism.

Her life with Jarlot changed her life and writing. It made her see her creative journey differently. During this period she wrote two more novels and the script for *Hiroshima Mon Amour*. Directed by Alain Renais, the movie became a new-wave sensation and international hit.

She bought a country house and garden called Neauphle-le-Chateau, and here she continued her prolific writing. Her new novels continued to explore the terrain of women who drink and are aware that they are being watched and judged, but who never consider giving it up. They are women obsessed with love and desire, and they drink to fill up a need that is insatiable.

The novel *10:30 on a Summer Night* gives some insight into Duras's own love of drinking. In the story, Maria is traveling with her husband, child, and friend through the Spanish countryside. After waking from a nap, her first thoughts are:

> If [she] were to get up, if she were to go to the dining room she could ask for a drink. She thought of the first sip of manzanilla in her mouth and the peace in her body that would follow.

All she finds, however, is brandy.

> Maria took the brandy bottle and drank. A long, enormous gulp. It burned so much that she had to close her eyes with pleasure.

But soon,

> She was trying not to breathe too deeply so as not to vomit. The last gulp of brandy at daybreak, probably, coming up in her throat like a sob that you have to keep holding in.

Like her character, Duras was drinking to unconsciousness in cafés. She chose for years to be blind to Jarlot's hopeless infidelity, to say nothing of his wife. They wrote scripts together and she coached him in his writing. As Jarlot's writing became more confident, their love became even more complicated. Jealousy, sexual and professional, started poking out of their affair in different ways.

She sought help for her escalating alcoholism and went into a detox program. Seeing things more clearly gave her the strength to break with Jarlot, which she did around 1963, with fierce hatred and resentment. Two years later she was still sober and known as a woman of letters. Her literary style became more daring, attempting to deconstruct desire and writing to their essence. But she was unhappy. At the end of the affair with Jarlot she was fifty-one years old and living alone, her thoughts were too much with her. She was sober, but she didn't like it. "Nor is there any consolation for stopping drinking," she wrote. "Since I've stopped, I feel for the alcoholic I once was." When she began a new novel about an alcoholic, she began to drink again to get into the character's skin, sometimes writing in an alcoholic stream of consciousness to catch the words of intoxication. The book, *The Vice-Consul*, was published in 1966 and was grouped into a new genre, the *nouveau roman*. Duras is now considered one of the foremost practitioners of the school, although she hated being classified and disdained the connection.

She began to spit up blood and was diagnosed with cirrhosis. Again she quit drinking, this time cold turkey, and stayed largely sober for ten years. In 1975 she started drinking again and this time when she spit up blood, she just drank through it. This did not stop Duras—she now referred to herself in the third person—from falling more in love with herself and with her vision of herself as the living center of the literary world.

In order to gain control over filmed versions of her works, she became a director. At Neauphle she gathered a filmmaking team that lived with her in a sort of commune. Actress and legend Jeanne Moreau starred in four of her films. (In 2003, Moreau would portray Duras in *Cet-Amour La*.) She gave Gerard Depardieu his first screen role. Her son shot stills of the works and former lover Dionys Mascolo was a sometime actor. Some movies were conventional, such as 1975's *Song of India*, which remains an art-house standard. More often they were *avant garde*, attempts to bend the rules of storytelling and see if you could make them break. It could sometimes be fascinating, but more often this cinematic anarchy was ridiculous and unwatchable: static shots, an entire movie with no images, extreme close-ups that made recognition impossible, filming upside down. Duras promoted herself and her movies as politically dangerous and refused to discuss either with the press except in terms of their political impact.

Her behavior became more and more erratic, even as she gathered considerable critical attention. The success of *Song of India*, and the fact that her early novels were being reprinted gave her financial and critical vindication, which pushed her self-absorption into megalomania.

Her filmmaking, however, was eventually derailed by her drunken confusion.

In *Marguerite Duras: A Life*, Laure Adler's excellent biography, a co-worker reports that during the editing of one film:

> [Duras would] arrive in the morning and then leave immediately for the bistro and knock back three or four glasses of white wine at the bar. Then she'd give the boss empty Evian bottles so that he could fill them with white wine. At the bistro, when her film editor ad friend Genevieve Dufour begged her to eat something, she wiped each potato chip with her handkerchief. She couldn't eat fat. Her body could tolerate only alcohol.

She now spent hour after hour alone and drunk, buying and drinking cheap wine by the crate.

> I've spent whole summers at Neauphle alone except for drink...That is how alcohol took on its full significance. It lends resonance to loneliness, and ends up making you prefer it to everything else.

She began writing letters to an imaginary lover, pouring out her heart. Being the arch creator that she was, beautiful letters started coming to her from an unknown, but very real, man. She refused to meet him. "I get letters that make me fall in love with the people who wrote them. But of course one can't reply." For five years the letters came daily, and at last she relented. "I did reply to Yann."

The young student was Yann Andrea Steiner. "And then one day he phoned and asked if he could come. It was summer. Just listening to the sound of his voice I knew it was madness. But I told him to come."

Yann was twenty-nine, thin, pale and handsome. He was also gay, which made the sixty-three-year-old Duras jealous. As with all her previous great loves, she was obsessed with him and obsessed with being in love. She chose all his clothes, ordered for him in restaurants, and put words in his mouth. She tried to invent him. Yann quickly became her caretaker and passionate friend. "He's here, guarding me against death. That's what he's doing, though he tries to ignore it." He also made a prodigious drinking partner. Duras continued to write and drink, bottle after bottle of cheap wine, non-stop. In 1982, she was in detox again and this time it was accompanied by bizarre and terrifying hallucinations. When she was released from the hospital she continued to see things that weren't there.

She ate rarely now, and would vomit up the first two glasses of each day's wine.

> Instead of drinking coffee when I woke up, during the last few months I started straight away on whisky or wine. I'd vomit the wine I'd just drunk, and start drinking some more right away. Usually the vomiting stopped after the second try, and I'd be glad.

In 1983 she wrote her last great success, *The Lover*. The erotic novel became an international bestseller, won the prestigious *Prix Goncourt*, was translated into forty languages, and made into a popular movie. She also wrote books for Yann and books about Yann. He typed her manuscripts now since she could no longer make her own hands do it. Together they drank up to eight liters of wine a day.

In 1988 Duras fell into a coma that lasted nine months. When she came to, Yann was by her side and sure enough she rose like a phoenix and began creating. "One day, if I live to be very old, I'll stop writing. And no doubt it will seem to me unreal, impossible, absurd." She was already very old by other people's standards, but she definitely wasn't going to quit writing. She was working at another book when death finally came in 1996. She was eighty-two.

SOURCES

Kingsley Amis

Amis, Kingsley. *On Drink*. Harcourt Inc., 1973.

———. *Lucky Jim*. Penguin Books, 1993.

Amis, Martin. *Experience: A Memoir*. Talk Miramax Books, 2000.

Jacobs, Eric. *Kingsley Amis: A Biography*. Hodder & Stoughton, 2000.

Fussell, Paul. *The Anti-Egoist: Kingsley Amis Man of Letters*. Oxford University Press, 1994.

John Berryman

Berryman, John. *Recovery*. Farrar, Straus and Giroux, 1973.

———. *Collected Poems, 1937-1971*. Farrar, Staus and Giroux, 1989.

Haffenden, John. *The Life of John Berryman*. ARK Paperbacks, 1983.

Lowell, Robert. "For John Berryman." *The New York Review of Books*, June 23, 1977.

Mariani, Paul. *Dream Song: The Life of John Berryman*, William Morrow & Company, Inc., 1990.

John Cheever

Cheever, John. *The Letters of John Cheever*. Cape, 1989.

———. *The Journals of John Cheever*. Alfred A. Knopf, 1991.

Cheever, Susan. *Home Before Dark*. Washington Square Press, 1986.

———. *Note Found in a Bottle*. Washington Square Press, 2000.

Donaldson, Scott. *John Cheever: A Biography*. Delta Books, 1988.

James Dickey

Dickey, Christopher. *The Summer of Deliverance: A Memoir of Father and Son*. Simon & Schuster, 1998.

Dickey, James. *Self-Interviews*. Doubleday, 1970.

———. *The Whole Motion: The Collected Poems, 1945-1992*. Wesleyan University Press, 1992.

Hart, Henry. *The World as a Lie*. Picador USA, 2000.

Marguerite Duras

Adler, Laure. *Marguerite Duras: A Life*. Victor Gollancz/Orion Books, 1994.

Duras, Marguerite. *Four Novels: The Square/Moderato Cantabile /10:30 on a Summer Night /The Afternoon of Mr. Andesmas*. Grove/Atlantic 1990.

———. *Practicalities*. Grove Press, 1992.

———. *The War: A Memoir*. New Press, 1994.

A DRINKING COMPANION

F. Scott Fitzgerald
Bruccoli, Matthew J. *Some Sort of Epic Grandeur*. Harcourt, 1981.
Buttitta, Tony. *After the Good, Gay Times*. Viking Press, 1974.
Fitzgerald, F. Scott. *This Side of Paradise*. Scribner, 1998.
Fitzgerald, F. Scott & Edmund Wilson. *The Crack Up*. New Directions
    Publishing Corporation, 1993.
Turnbull, Andrew. *Scott Fitzgerald*. Grove Press, 2001.

Dashiell Hammett
Johnson, Diane. *Dashiell Hammett: A Life*. Ballantine Books, 1987.
Hellman, Lillian. *Pentimento*. Back Bay Books, 2000.
Mellen, Joan. *Hellman and Hammett: The Legendary Passion of Lillian
    Hellman and Dashiell Hammett*. Harper Collins, 1996.

Jack London
London, Jack. *John Barleycorn*. Modern Library, 2001.
Perry, John. *Jack London, an American Myth*. Nelson Hall, 1981.
Sinclair, Andrew. *Jack: A Biography of Jack London*. Weidenfeld and Nicolson,
    1978.

Robert Lowell
Hamilton, Ian. *Robert Lowell: A Biography*. Vintage Books, 1983
Heymann, David. *American Aristocracy: The Lives & Times of James Russell,
    Amy & Robert Lowell*. Dodd, Mead & Company, 1980.
Schoenberger, Nancy. *Dangerous Muse: The Life of Lady Caroline Blackwood*.
    Da Capo Press, 1992.

Malcolm Lowry
Bowker, Gordon. *Pursued by Furies: A Life of Malcolm Lowry*. St. Martin's
    Press, 1997.
Day, Douglas. *Malcolm Lowry: A Biography*. Oxford University Press, 1973.
Gabrial, Jan. *Inside the Volcano: My Life with Malcolm Lowry*. St. Martin's
    Press, 2000.
Lowry, Malcolm. *Under the Volcano*. Perennial Classics, 2000.

Carson McCullers
McCullers, Carson. *Illumination and Night Glare: The Unfinished
    Autobiography of Carson McCullers*. University of Wisconsin Press,
    1992.
Carr, Virgina Spencer. *The Lonely Hunter: A Biography of Carson McCullers*.
    University of Georgia Press, 2003.
Savigneau, Josyane. *Carson McCullers: A Life*. Houghton Mifflin, 2001.

SOURCES

Jean Rhys

Angier, Carole. *Jean Rhys: Life and Work*. Little, Brown and Company, 1990.

Athill, Diana. *Stet: An Editor's Life*. Grove Press, 2002.

Rhys, Jean. *Smile Please: An Unfinished Biography*. Harper & Row Publishers, 1979.

——. *The Letters of Jean Rhys*. Viking, 1984.

——. *Jean Rhys: The Compete Novels*. W. W. Norton & Company, 1985.

Anne Sexton

Sexton, Linda Gray. *Searching for Mercy Street*. Little, Brown and Company, 1994.

Middlebrook, Diana Wood. *Anne Sexton: A Biography*. Vintage Books USA, 1992.

Sexton, Anne. *The Complete Poems: Anne Sexton*. Mariner Books, 1999.

Trinidad, David. "Searching for Anne's Grave." *Boston Review*, 2002.

Jean Stafford

Cavett, Dick. "A Dash of Bitters." *Vanity Fair*, September 1983.

Goodman, Charlotte Margolis. *Jean Stafford: The Savage Heart*. University of Texas Press, 1990.

Hulbert, Ann. *The Interior Castle: The Art and Life of Jean Stafford*. Alfred A. Knopf, 1992.

Laskin, David. *Partisans: Marriage, Politics, and Betrayal Among the New York Intellectuals*. Simon & Schuster, 2000.

Roberts, David. *Jean Stafford: A Biography*. Little, Brown and Company, 1988.

Tennessee Williams

Devlin, Albert J. *Conversations with Tennessee Williams*. University Press of Mississippi, 1986.

Isherwood, Christopher. *Diaries*. Harper Collins, 1996.

Leverich, Lyle. *Tom, the Unknown Tennessee Williams*. W.W. Norton & Co., 1997.

Spoto, Donald. *The Kindness of Strangers: The Life of Tennessee Williams*. Da Capo Press, 1997.

Williams, Tennessee. Tennessee Williams: Memoirs. Doubleday & Company, 1972.

Windham, Donald. *Lost Friendships: A Memoir of Truman Capote, Tennessee Williams, and Others*. William Morrow and Company, 1983.

PHOTO CREDITS

Page 11, Group photo taken at the Yaddo artists' community, 1943. Includes: Carson McCullers and Jean Stafford. Courtesy of The Corporation of Yaddo.

Page 19, John Berryman. Courtesy of the National Book Foundation.

Page 39, Jean Stafford. Courtesy of the University of Colorado at Boulder.

Page 57, John Cheever. Courtesy of the National Book Foundation.

Page 77, Jean Rhys. Courtesy of the University of Tulsa.

Page 97, Anne Sexton. Courtesy of the Harry Ransom Humanities Research Center, The University of Texas at Austin.

Page 117, Malcolm Lowry. Courtesy of the University of British Columbia Library, Special Collections, Negative no. 1614/107.

Page 145, F. Scott Fitzgerald.

Page 163, Jack London. Courtesy of the Bancroft Library, University of California, Berkeley.

Page 185, Robert Lowell with Jean Stafford [bMS Am 1905 (2859)]. Courtesy of the Houghton Library, Harvard University.

Page 201, James Dickey by Joyce Pair.

Page 219, Carson McCullers by Carl van Vechten. Courtesy of the Library of Congress American Memory Project.

Page 235, Tennessee Williams. Courtesy of the Billy Rose Theatre Collection, The New York Library for the Performing Arts, Astor, Lenox and Tilden Foundations.

Page 261, Dashiell Hammett by Ric Botelho. Courtesy of Yellow Tulip Press.

Page 277, Kingsley Amis. Courtesy of South West Wales Publication Ltd.

Page 295, Marguerite Duras by Jean-Paul Dupuis, Paris.